Jenny

Thanks for your support!

Jane

EYES ON HAVANA

*Memoir of an American Spy
Betrayed by the CIA*

VERNE LYON
with PHILIP ZWERLING

McFarland & Company, Inc., Publishers
Jefferson, North Carolina

ISBN (print) 978-1-4766-7090-4
ISBN (ebook) 978-1-4766-3079-3

LIBRARY OF CONGRESS CATALOGUING DATA ARE AVAILABLE

BRITISH LIBRARY CATALOGUING DATA ARE AVAILABLE

Front cover images of Havana © 2018 tunart/iStock;
inset Verne Lyon at the portico of the White House

Manufactured in the United States of America

*McFarland & Company, Inc., Publishers
Box 611, Jefferson, North Carolina 28640
www.mcfarlandpub.com*

Dedicated to the memories
of my mother Alice and my sister Sharon,
who are angels on my shoulder.
May their eternal voyage be less burdensome.
—Verne Lyon

Table of Contents

Introduction   1

1—Descent into Hell   5
2—American as Apple Pie   14
3—I Spy   25
4—The Frame-Up   41
5—Back with the Company   50
6—Down on the Farm   55
7—Undercover   66
8—Our Man in Havana   76
9—Red Square   84
10—A Double Life   99
11—Dirty Tricks   115
12—Going Dark   123
13—Trapped   132
14—No Way Out   142
15—Flight   153
16—Framed   160
17—In Hell   167
18—Doing Time   178
19—Survival   189
20—Rebirth   204

Index   217

Introduction

Fifty-two years. Where have they gone? So much happened so quickly. That's how long ago this story really began. Only after trying to piece together all that happened to me during those years have I realized the scope and complexity of what I finally present here for the first time. Not only does this book detail how I arrived at this stage of my life and the ups and downs ... and downs again of all I dealt with during those five decades, but it also presents the reader with a unique perspective on how and why it all happened. It explains how things went from bad to worse and pitted three United States government agencies against each other and against me in games of cat and mouse around the globe.

When I first sat down to write, it seemed impossible to explain my situation in a reasonable narrative format, let alone marshal the facts, dates, names, places, events, and results stemming from that ill-considered decision made by a Midwestern college boy at the height of the Vietnam War. Those old enough to recall when TV brought the weekly deaths of thousands in the jungles of Indochina into our living rooms with each evening newscast remember the turmoil this nation went through, which split the country right down the middle. Every male college student in the country lived in fear of the draft: fear for his own future, his career, his life, and the fate of his friends. The Cold War threatened to turn hot at any moment and the U.S. saw enemies everywhere, from Cuba to Central America to the "falling dominos" in Asia to a divided Germany and a rising Soviet Union and Red China.

I was born, raised, and educated in Iowa, America's heartland. I dreamed of going to the moon, or at least helping my country get there. This dream set me on course to become a pilot, an aerospace engineer, and, hopefully, an astronaut. Politics and world events seemed far away from my life, but the government manipulated my skills and ambitions to completely alter the course of my life and the lives of others. Certainly I share the blame for the seemingly small change in direction my senior year at Iowa State and the self-serving decision I made back then. I tried to dodge a bullet in a rice paddy halfway around

1

the world in a war I didn't understand. Other students took other options, of course, but they never faced the choice my government offered me.

Many have written about the proverbial forks in the road that we all encounter in our life's journey. The decision to go left or right, to choose this path or that, and the ultimate consequences of those choices take many forms. At a young age and under duress I made a fateful decision, the consequences of which grew and mutated and changed my life in unimaginable ways.

My purpose is not to write a general exposé of the CIA. Others have done that in many books over the past few decades. Nor do I seek to identify or harm anyone living or dead; I see no purpose in that. I use the real names only of those who through their own actions or due diligence are already identifiable.

My signature oil painting. I made several copies and gave them to family and friends. It depicts me emerging from a very dark period of my life but full of energy and confrontational, ready to face whatever comes my way.

Rather, I want to explain, to the best of my ability and within the constraints of this book, the transformation of a young patriotic engineer with, some said, great promise into the second class citizen I am today: a convicted felon, who has survived fear, prosecution, and the utter collapse of my dreams, and yet survived and, I hope, flourished.

Friends and family have warned me not to write this book for fear of new reprisals. I don't have a death wish, but after having been accused of the things I detail here, I thought the time had come to tell my side of the story. Bits and pieces have come to light over the past 40 years as I have written numerous articles, given countless speeches on college campuses, been quoted in many publications, and answered intimate questions put to me by family and friends who broke protocol to ask. The government has long held to its version of these events, assuming that nobody will question its veracity. To those who fall into that myopic category, I can only hope that you find comfort there. Those who have an open mind and understand that a government agency, founded on deception, secrecy, illegal and immoral actions, and disregard for national and international law, and directed by highly paid people who know how to deceive, lie, manipulate, and hide their misdeeds from the public, might sacrifice an American citizen like me to its own "greater good," may learn and understand what happened to me and why. I leave it to the reader to decide.

I want to thank Professor Phil Zwerling for helping me write this book, because without his help it might read like an engineering instruction manual. I also want to thank my wife, Mayo, and my daughter, Valeria, for their many years of support and encouragement, as well as past colleagues at ARDIS and ANSA who have always encouraged me to share my story with you, the American people.

1. Descent into Hell

The commotion and clatter woke me out of a restless sleep and I sat upright in my bunk with a start, shakily unsure of my location. "They're pulling the chain," yelled someone to my right. Chain? What chain? I tried to clear my head and stared first at the steel bars in front of me and then down at the thin mattress beneath me. I had awakened to a nightmare. Jail. From my left, close by, someone, a prisoner, no, another prisoner, another prisoner like me, shouted: "It's the feds." Past events returned to my half-sleeping consciousness: my two-day trial, the jury's brief deliberations and the judge's stern sentence. "Seventeen years," I heard him say, "You shall be remanded to a Federal Penitentiary for 17 years." My freedom, my youth, my wife, my son all disappeared with those words. The scene haunts me as if it happened yesterday.

The swirling, gurgling sounds of toilets flushing away contraband mixed with hurried last minute shouted instructions between prisoners soared toward a crescendo as the three guards marched down the corridor and opened the steel door between the tier of cells and mine. The deputy in charge stuck his head up to the bars, stared in my direction and bellowed above the animalistic din: "Lyon, get your shit together!" "You have five minutes," he added, almost as an afterthought.

It didn't take that long. I didn't have much anymore. A few letters, a file of legal papers, and a half dozen photographs of my wife, child and parents, comprised the sum total of my "shit." That was all that remained of a Midwestern college graduate and a once-promising career as an aerospace engineer. I already wore the bright orange jumpsuit and ugly brown plastic sandals issued the day before. I got my "shit" together in less than a minute.

The guard returned at a trot and from the far end of the long row of cells he unlocked the control box that allowed him to choose which of the individual cells to open. My cell door, constructed of reinforced steel bars, slid open with the raspy crunch of metal on metal. "Let's go, Lyon," he shouted.

Clutching my few possessions, I walked the length of the tier nodding goodbye to those of short acquaintance who remained behind. "Hey spy man, don't take no shit from those fuckers, ya hear!" and, "Stay cool, man," shouted those who had traveled this path before me. "Good bye, 'boom boom,'" yelled the rapist down the hall, alluding to the bomb-making charges against me. We walked past "Cold Cuts," who, they told me, gutted his mother-in-law, chopped off her arms and legs and stowed her in the family freezer. Now he started the chant: "CIA, CIA, CIA," as others joined in down the length of cells. To the cadence of the "USA, USA" heard at hockey matches, they called out the initials of the Central Intelligence Agency, my former employer, more in anger than in awe.

I stepped out of the cell into the hallway while the guard slammed the door shut behind me. He prodded me to a holding cell near the front of the jail and locked me inside. Pushing through the bars some civilian clothing left behind by former prisoners. he told me to get dressed and left. I discarded the jumpsuit and sandals and put on the too big shirt and too small trousers worn by previous miscreants. I gagged at the musty smell, a mixture, it seemed to me, of fear, sweat, and inevitable resignation.

Minutes later, the guard returned accompanied by two fat Federal marshals sloppily dressed in ill-fitting suits and loosely knotted ties. One of them carried a manila envelope bearing my name in his right hand, lazily wiping the remains of breakfast off his face with it. Looked like scrambled eggs and tomato. While the other marshal signed a prisoner Transfer of Custody form, the one carrying the envelope put it down, roughly hooked leg cuffs around my ankles, and swiftly ran a chain around my waist that passed through a set of handcuffs he locked tightly on my wrists. Restrained like this I could not lift my hands above my waist. He pushed me forward, forcing me to take small mincing steps, like a ballerina or a manacled dancing bear. He thrust a cardboard box into my hands, opened it to show me that it contained my few remaining personal items and then closed and sealed it with tape. Suddenly I saw my life in a box and my body in chains.

They led me out into the sally port of the jail to their waiting car, a newer model Crown Vic. While one retrieved their personal handguns from a locked storage container, the other opened the trunk of the car and directed me to place the box I carried inside. He then opened one of the car's rear doors and ordered me in. After some struggling with the restraints, I managed to wriggle in without falling on my face and twisted around to sit up in the back seat. One marshal, the fatter of the two, slammed the car door behind me and both took their places up front, settling their wide butts into the welcoming vinyl. They made a show, undoubtedly for my benefit, of examining their chrome-plated .357 Magnums. Already trussed like a pig on his way to the slaughterhouse, I hardly thought their large caliber weapons necessary.

"Fatso" honked the car's horn to signal the jail staff to open the sally port gate, and the darkish sedan glided out into the summer sunshine. The trip from Illinois to Kansas would take four to five hours. So began a descent into hell I could hardly have imagined just months before.

We drove west towards St. Louis, a city I knew well, too well, crossed the Mississippi and turned north to catch Interstate 70, which would take us west. The traffic lightened as we left the city, and the marshals exchanged meaningless small talk. I gathered they considered themselves both overworked and underpaid. They acted as if I didn't exist. In a sense, I suppose they had that right. My life had ended, and the fearful monotony of the car ride directed me back to all the wrong decisions that had led me to this nightmare.

"Fatso" steered the car off the highway just outside Kansas City and pulled into a fast food joint. To this day I can't remember which. The marshals told me that I could order anything I wanted as long as it didn't cost more than two bucks. For that I got the standard burger, fries and Coke but don't recall eating any of it, while they ate like hungry and sloppy wolves. My mind sputtered through my past, the kidnapping, trial and imprisonment, and unspooled into an unimaginable future of 17 years in prison.

I hadn't said a word in the last four hours and the marshals hadn't addressed me since leaving the St. Louis jail, but now they started to pepper me with both questions and advice.

They asked if I needed to use the restroom and, before I could answer, told me that if so, one of them would have to accompany me just to make sure that I didn't have any "rabbit blood," as the thinner fat marshal put it. If I ran, they assured me, deadly force would be justified. I recalled those .357 Magnums and imagined the holes the bullets would drill in my skull and the way they would explode in my brain.

They told me that the Marshals Service usually transported federal prisoners by bus. They explained that the service maintained a fleet of specially equipped buses that ran on fairly regular schedules between selected jails and federal prisons and camps. Only in special cases would they transport individual prisoners like me. Their superiors considered me an escape risk and therefore made me their very own special case. I didn't feel all that special.

As they relaxed after eating, the two regaled me with stories of their normal runs with several dozen prisoners cuffed, shackled, and seated in the caged center section of the bus. Armed guards would occupy smaller caged sections located fore and aft. The driver carried a gun too. The windows, covered with bars and screens, allowed prisoners to see outside, but those driving by could not see in. The outside of the bus bore a nondescript gray and white paint scheme. Numbers and the letters BOP painted on the roof of the bus indicated

My wanted poster. Funny, they claimed I had suicidal tendencies. How am I still alive? Just proves an old adage: don't believe everything you read (courtesy Dennis Desenberg).

the Bureau of Prisons, facilitating surveillance and tracking by planes if prisoners actually ever succeeded in commandeering a bus. They packed food and water onboard to avoid stops, and in the rear of the center cage sat a toilet of sorts, mounted in full view of the rear shotgun-toting marshal. They assured me that Uncle Sam, my former and their current employer, was treating us very well today to a "restaurant" meal instead of the usual bus fare of sandwiches of baloney on white bread, a piece of fruit, and little schoolkid-size milk cartons.

However, they wanted me to know we were all missing some special fun on the buses because sometimes girlfriends or wives of federal prisoners waiting to be transported would hang out at the local jails waiting for a bus to load up.

Then they would follow the bus onto the highway, drive alongside and begin a striptease for the benefit of their departing men, flashing their breasts as a parting memento. Fate would decide whether their boyfriend or husband ever saw the show or not, as those in the car didn't know on which side of the bus he sat. At any rate, everyone else onboard also enjoyed the spectacle. Although the marshals assured me they despised this practice, they couldn't prevent it, or so they said. Often the bus driver would attempt to maneuver the bus into traffic in efforts to disrupt the show and lose the pursuing car. From all their talk I got the idea they enjoyed the erotic farewell demonstration.

No such luck for me. It seemed that nobody noticed the seemingly sedate suburban sedan with the three of us inside. And no one turned up to see me off or to bare their breasts. I was doing most of the stripping these days in jail and in prison.

We finished eating on that note. They stuffed me awkwardly into the back seat once again and we pulled back out onto the highway and headed for the flat plains of Kansas. With no trees, hills or other variations of topography to distract them as they crossed the Kansas state line, and having seemingly exhausted their own dialogue on both crime and sex, the marshals turned their attention to me for their entertainment. They told me that even though they hadn't yet deposited me in a Leavenworth cell, my history had preceded me by several weeks because prisoners avidly read and followed crime stories and trials in newspapers and magazines. This intense interest allowed them to compare their personal conviction circumstances with the most recent ones, as well as allowing them to contemplate how they might receive those about to make their way into the system. New "fish" like me.

My well publicized trial, the original airport bombing and the many contradictory rulings by my trial judge, combined with the prominent role of the CIA and national security interests in determining my fate, they warned me, had already caused many a prisoner to personally decide how to treat me if, in fact, I became a guest in their penitentiary. The two marshals also wanted me to know that they also would be keeping an eye on me in the St. Louis office, not so much out of a concern for my welfare but because they had taken bets on how long I would survive on the "inside." I would always be considered a federal agent gone bad and consequently distrusted and disliked by others, whether their own crimes included rape, murder or drug running. At least those criminals loved their country. The consensus in the St. Louis Marshals' Office, they said, figured I'd be dead in less than a year. The taut knot in my stomach drew even tighter.

Maybe they held the longer odds, because they then offered me all kinds of advice: "Watch your back and remember your survival skills," remarked the driver. "Stay away from the sissies, don't gamble or do drugs and do your own time," added the second. I don't know how many times they had offered this same advice to others, but I took it to heart. After all, I was entering prison for the first time; they knew the score and they had a bet to win.

We approached the federal penitentiary of Leavenworth from the east. A little beyond the military fort, also called Leavenworth, and a bit farther west on Metropolitan Avenue, the prison suddenly loomed into sight on my right. Its sheer size and massive stone construction dominated the surrounding area like an Egyptian pyramid rising from the desert.

The penitentiary sits well back from Metropolitan Avenue, the two separated by wide manicured lawns. The entry drive is an elongated "U" with the building entrance located at the bottom of the "U." Directly across from the main entry rises a guard tower that offers a full view of the entire area. My two companions proved compendiums of trivia on the maximum security prison, telling me it had housed Nazi spies; famous gangsters like "Bugsy" Moran and "Machine Gun" Kelly; James Earl Ray, before he killed Martin Luther King, Jr.; Robert Stroud, later known as "The Birdman of Alcatraz," who raised over 300 birds while at Leavenworth and killed a guard there; and political prisoners like American Communist Party chief Gus Hall, convicted under the Smith Act, as well as several Puerto Rican Nationalists convicted of shooting up the House of Representatives. I did not share their excitement at entering such hallowed grounds.

Opened in 1903, and thus the oldest federal pen in the country, with walls rising 40 feet high and sunk another 40 feet underground, extending almost a mile to enclose 23 acres and 2,000 prisoners, Leavenworth was alternately referred to as "The Big House," for its huge bulk and impressive central dome, or as "The Hot House," for its less impressive lack of air conditioning in the searing Kansas summer heat.

My marshals—I thought of them as "mine" by now—drove up to a metal intercom and pushed the call button. This prompted a response by the guard in the tower, who wanted to know their business. "Fatso" informed him that they had a federal prisoner, namely me, to deliver. The tower guard told them where to park and to check their guns at the base of the tower.

As we exited the car, I managed a quick glance at my future home. The massive, stark façade caught my eyes and would not let them go. The central structure stood out like a four story stone box supporting a huge silver-colored dome on top. Two massive cell wings, each seven stories high, stretched to the east and west from this central structure. One could almost see inside through the large rectangular barred windows that soared above us, or at least my imagination could. The whole structure sat on top of what looked like a manmade mound of dirt. Flowers, being tended by a couple of men dressed in army kakis, bordered the "U" shaped entry and exit road. The two workers stared at me. I avoided their gaze. What would my parents have said to see their son locked up with these miscreants? How low could one fall?

"Take this fucking box," said the "bad haircut" marshal after he removed it from the truck of the car, "and follow us." I tried to keep up with them as they started to climb the steps that led to the front doors. The leg cuffs and chains impaired my ability to lift my feet and I nearly tripped. I decided to count the number of steps it takes to actually reach hell. The stone steps stretched out before me. I guessed they measured some 60 to 70 feet wide and I counted 43 of them. After reaching the top, the marshals hustled me out of the sunlight, through a set of heavy oak doors and into the darkness of the prison. It took a while for my eyes to grow accustomed to the sunless interior. We passed another set of doors and found our path blocked by sliding steel bars. To our left, behind a glass window, a couple of guards stood in front of a huge keyboard. They exchanged greetings with the two marshals, like longtime friends bringing a gift to the party, with me as the offering. One of the guards pushed a button and the barred gate slowly slid open. We stepped beneath the rotunda and into the very belly of the beast.

I will never forget that first impression of a cavernous circular area with 16 marble columns rising from the polished floor towards a covered dome some 150 feet high. I could see a second floor above me. The rotunda held no furniture except for a desk located in the exact center. A guard sat behind the desk, dressed in a blue shirt and gray pants. He rose and crossed the rotunda to receive us. I noticed that his footsteps echoed and re-echoed through the vast empty room. I thought of Cerberus, the watch dog of hell, at the river Styx, his three heads representing the past, present and future. I still didn't quite understand my past; my present seemed beyond my control; and I could not predict my future within these stone walls.

Beyond the desk, several doors led to other areas of this medieval dungeon. To my left a glassed-in area contained what looked like a radio station with receivers, switches, and so on. A man, a prisoner no doubt, sat inside wearing a headset. He stopped turning the dials and looked at me. To my right I could see a library full of easily recognizable law books. Several prisoners sitting there turned their attention from the books before them towards me. My skin began to crawl and I started to feel nauseous. In my shame and degradation I did not crave this kind of attention, least of all from this kind of people.

The guard instructed us to follow him across the rotunda towards a long hallway that I assumed reached back into the bowels of the prison. After crossing the portico, we made a right turn and headed down a set of steel spiral stairs towards the basement. Reaching the bottom, we made several turns until we reached a door that bore the sign "Receiving and Discharge" on the wall above it. I knew which one applied to me. Another guard appeared from the gloomy depths, produced a huge bronze key, unlocked the steel-barred door and motioned for us to enter. Instead of waiting for me to pass through the door, the marshals, once so chummy but now with an audience, assumed a tougher stance and simultaneously both pushed and dragged me through the opening.

They handed the manila envelope with my name affixed to the prison guard and, after examining the papers he had extracted from inside, he signed a couple of forms and returned them to the marshals.

I was standing there, still carrying the cardboard box containing my "shit," when the guard told me to place the box on the nearby table. I did as instructed and then the marshals produced keys to unlock and release me from the cuffs and chains that I had worn for the entire trip. Once I was free of the restraints, they ordered me to strip and place my clothes on a separate table. Again I complied without a word.

"Show me your hands, palms open," ordered the guard. I complied. What choice did I have?

"Raise your arms," followed. Again, I did as told.

"Run your fingers through your hair, then open your mouth," came next.

"Do you wear dentures?" the guard asked. I replied in the negative.

"Lift your feet, show me your soles with toes spread."

"Lift your balls and shake them," followed. I did as ordered.

"Bend over and spread 'em," the guard commanded next. I complied yet again and suffered the humiliation of having the guard stick his gloved finger deep into my rectum. After what seemed an eternity, the guard satisfied himself that I carried no weapons, drugs, or other contraband on or within my body. I could have told him that if he had just asked.

I stood there naked on the bare concrete floor, feeling insignificant and completely alone. My body trembled from the combination of fear and cold. The guard then instructed me to take a shower in the open stall located just a few feet away. While I showered, the guard disappeared for a few minutes and then reappeared carrying a set of prison garb consisting of white cotton socks, white boxer briefs, a white t-shirt, and army green pants with matching shirt. He also carried a small paper sack that contained a toothbrush, a black pocket comb, a tin of tooth powder, a breakdown razor, a solid stick of lather soap, a brush to agitate it with, and a couple of razor blades. He gave me a set of plastic sandals to wear, saying, "You'll get shoes later." Without any word of warning he then dusted me with some sort of white powder before allowing me to dress, delousing me, I suspected.

As I dressed, the guard separated my few personal belongings into different stacks on the table in front of him. "You can keep this and this," he said, "but not these." My legal papers and some personal letters could stay with me, everything else went. My own civilian clothing and other personal property had been sent home while I resided in the county jail. After placing the clothing I had worn during the trip on the table, the guard asked me if I wanted to keep it. My expression answered his question, so he threw the items into a canvas bag. He then took down a clipboard and, after consulting the forms it contained, turned to me and proclaimed, "89,649-132, that's your new identity. Memorize it."

I had a number now and that number was me. My name and all that it stood for, all that I had studied and learned and all the degrees and honors I had earned counted for nothing and meant nothing here. The U.S. government had tagged me with a number just as it did to everything else it owned. With that simple stroke, it took from me the last vestige of my identity and humanity. I had lost my freedom, my friends and family, my career, my respect, and now my name. What remained in this world, I wondered. I retained only the faintest hope that my appeal in the courts would succeed. Beyond that I had only my life. Prison had reduced me to the very primordial basic goal of life itself: to survive, if possible.

The two marshals were finished with me now, and without any parting comments they exited the locked receiving cells and disappeared up the stairwell, back to their car, the road, and their homes where I could not follow. The guard motioned me to follow him through a maze of doors, first left then right, that finally took us to the basement of "A" cell house. The sign above the door said "A&O." "It means Assessment and Orientation," the guard said as he rang a buzzer to summon someone to open the door. "Go right in." Yes, "Welcome to Hell," my new home.

2. American as Apple Pie

I started out as a good kid. Really, I did. I was born in 1943, the second of four, three boys and a girl, in Davenport, Iowa, in the American heartland of cornfields, apple pie, and patriotism celebrated on the 4th of July and every other day of the year as well. Thousands of miles away the Russians stopped the Nazi invasion in the killing fields at Stalingrad. The Thousand Year Reich collapsed in fire and blood two years later, and American boys soon left off being soldiers and came home to their families, not yet realizing that another war, a Cold War, colder than Stalingrad's frozen winter, lay ahead and that it would someday conscript me into service on foreign soil.

My dad, who did war work at the Rock Island Arsenal, where they turned out howitzers and tanks, died when I was four and just before my mother gave birth to my youngest brother, in a senseless car crash he might have survived if they had had seat belts back then. Mom moved us from big town Davenport, on the border with Illinois in the Quad Cities area, to rural Boone, Iowa, smack dab in the center of the state, closer to some family and friends, and got work as an office administrator and bookkeeper. We didn't have much growing up, and although we usually had food on the table, there wasn't room for extras.

I was a good kid, although I felt different from my friends, growing up without a dad. In grade school my teachers enrolled me in some advanced classes. They thought I showed promise, that I could succeed. None of them looked into the future and ever imagined seeing me behind prison bars.

At age nine or so, when I could ride a bike, I scraped together my life savings of $2 amassed from collecting empty Coke bottles thrown in the weeds at the side of the road and returned to the corner grocery for two cents each. I sweated through the summer mowing lawns behind a balky push mower and borrowed $3 more from my sister to buy what passed for a bicycle in name only, with a frame, two wheels, a seat without padding, handlebars, and a chain but no fenders. Its faded red paint nicely accented the growing patches of rust now speckling the frame, but I loved it. Suddenly I could pedal free of my immediate neighborhood and explore a larger world. Looking back, I realize now

14

how greatly freedom—freedom from the limits of my home and my block, and later freedom from the earth's very gravitational pull—figured in everything I did growing up. How ironic that later I would work industriously and secretly to limit the freedom of others and then lose my own freedom.

Owning that old bike also meant that I learned how to make repairs on the cheap. This necessity launched my desire to understand all things mechanical and electrical. I dismantled everything around the house and out in the garage that didn't work and set to repairing it. Sometimes I failed, but many times I succeeded and found to my amazement that spare parts remained to build new things with. My two younger brothers watched in awe as I wielded screwdriver and hammer sitting in the driveway surrounded by two or three dozen loose parts that had once formed a single machine.

I started building model airplanes, the fighter jets that came in colorful boxes with fifty or sixty plastic parts to glue together. I pasted on

Christmas at our home in Boone, Iowa, when I was either six or seven years old. I am wearing my new toy six-shooter with accompanying belt and holster. Like all boys that age, I was going to be a cowboy!

the decals and hung them from the ceiling of my room and thought about flying them: the Catalina flying boat, the Sikorsky helicopter or the B-29 Superfortress bomber. Or I took them outside and ran around the backyard pretending to sit at the controls, cutting through the clouds and dodging anti-aircraft fire. Then I discovered models I could actually fly on a control line, and even later radio-controlled models that flew free of wires. I bought gasoline engines for these beauties and flew them hard and fast. They crashed fairly often and I put them together again until one too many crashes rendered them inoperable. I joined a local club that met out at the airport, where we found plenty of room to fly our models.

One day at the airport an adult offered me a ride in his plane. Scared out of my wits, but attracted to the adventure and the thrill, I said yes. I don't remember much of that first flight except the result: I got hooked on aviation for life. I was going to be a pilot. How I could ever pay to make that ambition a reality? My teenage brain harbored no plan, just a dream.

I moved on to junior high school and my life kept changing. I made new friends and at some point discovered girls. They seemed creatures from another planet, and the few girlfriends I found didn't last long. We didn't have the word then, but "nerd" would have fit me like a glove. Anything mechanical drew my interest; anything on four wheels or two wings drew me in.

I also took a paper route during those years to make a little extra money. Back then parents let their kids wander the neighborhood and no one worried about kidnappings or molestations. I rode miles each day to deliver the *Boone News-Republican*, flinging papers onto lawns from my bike.

When a friend of mine received a Go Kart for his birthday, it made me insanely jealous. I couldn't afford to buy one, but I could try to piece one together by copying the design of my friend's. I made some modifications, of course, and I asked another friend to weld the frame parts together for me. I purchased a two-cycle chainsaw engine, a couple of sprockets and a chain. Adding an old gas tank from a defunct lawnmower, I had a car. To start the thing, I ran alongside and gave it a push. Once it started I jumped on board and took off. It would reach speeds of nearly 50 mph. I enjoyed zipping around town on the thing, until early one Sunday morning I decided to take it for a spin outside the city and I ran afoul of the law for the first time. I headed north out of town and opened it up. As I reached top speed I went through a "T" intersection where I had the right of way, but off to my right I saw an Iowa State Highway patrol car coming toward me from about ¼ of a mile away. I raced up over a small hill and swerved into the yard of a farmhouse, where I quickly steered behind a small shed. I turned off the engine and waited while my heart beat about 100 mph. Within a minute or so, the highway patrol car whizzed by with the lights and siren on. I waited a few minutes, restarted the motor and prepared to leave. Just as I did, the patrol car pulled into the farmer's driveway. He had turned off the lights and siren and returned silently to block my exit.

I recognized the patrolman: Orville Beaman from my home town. We sort of knew each other, but that didn't stop him from writing me a bunch of tickets for things like failure to have a driver's license, failure to have proper lighting, failure to have a license plate, failure to have a windshield, failure to have a brake light, and a bunch more. When I appeared before the magistrate some weeks later, I paid a $50 fine, a small fortune at the time. I would only lose my respect for the law and the police many years later.

When I entered high school I got my driver's license with no problems from that incident some two years before. I drove to my classes with a purpose and took all of the college prep courses offered at Boone High School. Most fit my nerdiness to a "T:" science and math. I loved chemistry, physics, mechanical drafting, and trig. And I began experimenting with flight once again. My A.P. Chemistry teacher, Ben Burns, and I came up with a plan to launch a weather balloon filled with hydrogen with a small cage housing a hamster slung beneath. We filled the balloon up on the school roof with hydrogen we made from chemicals mixed up in a glass jar. Having filled the balloon half way, we let it go into a cloudless windless sky. The balloon rose rapidly and I could see it expanding in size as the air pressure decreased. It was almost out of sight when it burst and the cage and hamster came plunging to earth. They landed about three blocks away and we rushed to the site to recover the wreckage. Inside the mangled metal cage lay my poor furry little friend, who we laid to rest in an unmarked grave behind the garage. This small but simple experiment, failure that it appeared, ignited a flame inside me. I resolved then and there to build bigger and better things and make them fly. And survive.

In those days we watched "Forbidden Planet" and "The Day the Earth Stood Still" at the movie house in town and "Flash Gordon" and "Space Patrol" on the TV. Then Sputnik spun through the fall sky in 1957, its faint lights flashing from high above among the stars. Girls wanted Barbie and Ken, but we boys wanted rockets, aliens, and blasting into space.

I got together with a couple of like minded students and we decided to build rockets. We read everything we could on how to build them from scratch out of wood and aluminum, how to make the nozzles, and, most importantly, how to make the propellants we needed. In those days we could easily get most of what we wanted at the local pharmacy. We bought chemicals like flowers of sulfur, potassium permanganate, potassium perchlorate, potassium nitrate, and other exotics. We also experimented with zinc dust and sulfur soaked in alcohol. This powerful fuel burned with a hot yellow-white flame that produced thick clouds of dense white smoke. We built crude launching pads out of wood and made our own fuses to light the rockets that ranged from six to 18 inches tall and about one inch in diameter. Some blasted off spectacularly, while others blew up on the launch pad. We kept at it, always building bigger and more sophisticated models.

At one point my brothers and I worked together to build our largest rocket to date, about four feet tall and a couple of inches in diameter. We built a special compartment into the top nose cone section, where we placed a little parachute, a small explosive charge and a baby chicken. The Russians blasted dogs into space and the U.S. used chimps. The three of us could only find a fluffy little yellow chick. We set the explosive charge to detonate a few seconds after the

At the Boone, Iowa, airport at age 16. I'm standing next to a fabric-covered airplane that I took flying lessons in. I think it was a Stinson, but I'm not sure. It had the bare minimum amount of equipment and was for VFR (visual flight rules) only.

rocket's fuel charge ran out and designed the charge to blow the hinged compartment door open and expel the small package containing the parachute and baby chick. We watched in horror as the charge failed to ignite as the rocket reached its apex, turned earthward and plummeted towards the ground. It smashed into the earth about a block from the launching site. We ran to the damaged rocket and found the compartment door open and the baby chicken fallen out. This time our animal astronaut lived but appeared to have a broken neck. We took it home and my youngest brother raised it. The chick grew into a large white leghorn rooster, never quite right in the head, that feared no dog or cat in the neighborhood and ruled the roost around our home. It liked to perch in a small tree near where we parked our cars, in a branch about eight feet off the ground. One day while my mother walked from her car to the back door, passing the rooster in the tree, she heard a fluttering of wings and turned just in time to see the chicken flying towards her. She dropped the groceries and fled to the back door, barely escaping the wrath of space chicken.

On the west edge of Boone sat a couple of abandoned shale piles left over from the old coal mining days. We selected one and built a crude but effective bunker of wood and brick. We added a launch pad and wires that ran from the bunker to the pad about 40 feet away. We would use the battery out of my car to provide current to the igniters that we had learned to make from resistance wires recycled from old toasters. I had moved away from most other fuel combinations and started to use only zinc dust and sulfur for my rockets after a little accident on the enclosed back porch of our home. My brothers and I had cooked up a mixture of potassium nitrate and sugar to turn it into a paste that we could then pour into the rocket casing. While we were discussing the procedure, the fuel caught fire, and in the blink of an eye the entire mixture of several pounds of fuel raged into a fire. The reddish flame reached upward, torching the ceiling before spreading out from there. In just a few seconds the flames consumed the fuel, but the thick black cloud of smoke filled the back porch and billowed out into the sky. By some miracle, none of the neighbors noticed. Once we cleared the smoke out, opening windows and waving towels, we examined the aftereffects of the conflagration. The flames had scorched some pots and blackened some potted plants, but had only done real damage to Mother's electric frying pan. It now showed deep spots and holes where the fuel had actually melted the aluminum. We caught hell for that.

Sometimes we launched several rockets in a single day and some locals would drive out to the site to watch our firings. At one point, a fellow student and I attended an Amateur Rocketeer's convention in Indianapolis, Indiana. About 100 students from all across the U.S. attended. Amateur rocketry was on the rise as interest in the space race took hold. I remember the day, October 4th, 1957, when the Soviet Union launched Sputnik into orbit. I was shocked just like the rest of the world. How could the U.S. be so far behind? I believe that day I decided exactly what I wanted for my future. I was going to design rockets and go to the Moon. I committed myself to the race for space and an American victory.

With that goal in mind I settled into high school, taking electronics, advanced physics and advanced math courses to get me into the nearest engineering college only 15 miles to the east, in Ames. Iowa State University offered degrees in aerospace engineering and ranked third in the nation in this discipline behind the California and the Massachusetts Institutes of Technology.

This is the Boone High School slide rule class in 1960. I am in the back row, third from the left. My friend Jerry Converse is in the back row, first on the left. He died in the 1967 Israeli attack on the spy ship USS *Liberty*.

Officially renamed Iowa State University of Science and Technology in 1959, in the midst of the space race, ISU seemed poised on the cutting edge of space exploration and technological innovation. Competing for admission with students across the state and the country, I studied every book I could get my hands on regarding space and flight while I finished high school. My chemistry, physics and electronics teachers encouraged me to apply to ISU and predicted a bright future for me. Then on my birthday, April 12, 1961, when I turned 18, I became even more convinced of my calling. The Soviet Union launched Yuri Gagarin into space as the first man to orbit the earth. The U.S. now really lagged behind in the space race, and I wanted to help my country not only catch up, but take the lead.

I didn't have the money for tuition at ISU and neither did my family. I worked at several jobs during my high school years and saved as much as I could. Some of my high school buddies also enrolled at Iowa State in careers ranging from electrical engineering to architecture to aerospace engineering. Jerry Converse, who I now suspect of having brought me to the attention of the CIA in the first place and who later paid a high price of his own to the Agency, had enrolled in electrical engineering and wanted to drive his VW bus to campus and form a car pool. He charged a reasonable rate and several of us rode back and forth with him each weekday between Boone and Ames.

No one owned personal computers in those days or even imagined such a luxury, so we used the next best thing at the time, slide rules. I had two: one a full sized, two sided, 22 scale model, the other a smaller model that fit in my shirt pocket. I probably sported a pocket protector too: the full nerd gear. Most engineering students carried both, as well as a leather suitcase that would hold multiple notebooks, textbooks, pens, and all the other sorts of items we needed each day. We learned that if your slide rule said that 2×2 equaled 4.002, then that was what it was. I eventually learned to use all 22 scales with great proficiency.

The only computer that existed on campus sat like a hulking marvel of the future in the Electrical Engineering building, but to use it you faced a multi-step process. First you learned to program your problem. This deliberate step-by-step approach required that you type out special punched cards, in order, and arrange them in a tray. Then you took the tray of cards to the computer lab and turned it over to specially trained computer operators. They would feed your cards into a tape machine that would produce a roll of paper tape about one inch wide with holes punched in it. They spooled this roll of tape onto a reader and fed it into the computer. If you had messed up somewhere in the process, the computer would halt processing the roll of tape and play "Jingle Bells" so everyone would know you had screwed up. The operator would then throw away the roll of punched paper and give you back your metal tray of cards. You needed to find your own mistake and correct it. This process took a lot of time and raised my anxiety over public failure. If, on the other hand, your program loaded into the computer, you could expect some sort of results, although you did not always get what you expected. I spent many an hour in that small metal Quonset hut typing and re-typing those punched cards.

I also spent many hours hidden away in the silence of the library stacks. I used a desk high up in a small corner that almost nobody else occupied. I had all the resources at my disposal, as well as time to think. Even though I had gotten into ISU, I saw that the competition within the Engineering College still raged fiercely, as many of the students stood among the best and brightest from their respective high schools as well as from around and outside the country. They forced me to keep studying hard just to keep up.

In those Cold War years, which threatened to turn hot in places like Berlin, Vietnam, and Cuba, the government required all young men to enroll in one of the three major military Reserve Officer Training Corps (ROTC) programs to stay in school and avoid the draft. I chose the Air Force ROTC due to my deep interest in aviation. During the next few years, I learned to march in formation, spit polish my shoes, and keep my uniform in top notch condition. I also took numerous aptitude tests to see just where I would fit in their programs. With my own good health, my flying experience, and my aerospace studies I felt myself moving ahead in my career path, certain to become a pilot candidate upon graduation. Off campus the country sank ever deeper into the quagmire of Vietnam, and I saw some of my fellow students, not enrolled in "essential technical studies," get drafted in spite of their student deferments and shipped off to Southeast Asia. The body count in the jungles climbed higher and higher each month and we saw anti-war demonstrations on campus, even in Iowa. At first I kept my distance from politics, didn't much read the newspapers, and put my head in my books.

Over the next few years I studied things like chemistry and qualitative analysis, economics, physics and more physics, electronics and magnetism, engineering mechanics, aerodynamics, aerospace engineering, differential equations, applied mathematics, metallurgy, AC and DC circuits, mechanics of materials, structures, missile and space theory, thermodynamics, electronic instruments, more applied math, dynamic stability and control, stress analysis, flight controls, high speed aerodynamics, reaction propulsion, design and analysis, mechanical vibrations, viscous aerodynamics, nuclear energy, advanced aero problems, orbits, space theory, and on and on. This really was rocket science, leaving me no time for a social life or anything but homework and study. I could hardly breathe between classes and studying. Sometimes on the weekends, hometown friends would invite me to a local bar for a beer or two just so I could unwind. They would complain that even at the bar with a drink in my hand, I would be working out a problem on a cocktail napkin.

I remember that the freshman class in aerospace engineering started out with almost 30 students. As the years wore on, that number dwindled as many changed majors, dropped out, transferred schools or got drafted. Those of us who stayed in the program hunkered down and formed a close knit group of committed science wonks. In our senior year, recruiters descended on campus offering great starting salaries, prolonged draft deferments, and promises that they had an "in" with draft board officials and could guarantee defense industry exemptions. Our small group of Aero E students who had survived the program could pick what part of the country we wanted to live in, the starting salary we desired, and the company we wanted to work for. All the big names came calling: McDonnell Aircraft, Boeing, Northrop Grumman, Rocket Dyne, Pratt & Whitney, Cessna, NASA, Redstone Arsenal, and more. They all offered interview trips so we could look them over. For a small town Iowa boy this sounded great. I accepted interview trips to several companies that I really didn't have an interest in, just so I could have the travel experience, feel appreciated, and see parts of the country I had never visited before. Many of the trips were made on old DC-6's with four propeller-driven engines. After these trips, we students would put our heads together after class and compare notes on the offers as well as the pros and cons of each employer. The whole world opened up to us and the future looked bright.

I even met Elizabeth, a girl I liked, and we quickly moved from friends to lovers. I'd never been lucky with girls before, but something went right this time. Liz stood five foot four and had blonde hair, green eyes and a slender, well shaped frame. As an engineer I approved of the design and I liked her mind as well. I tried to spend as much time with her as I could, but school still came first and she would take me to task for that. One of my younger brothers joined the Air Force and I worried about him surviving Vietnam. He did, and later went on to get his MBA. My youngest brother got mixed up with a group of people more interested in drugs and partying than anything else. I broke away from classes one afternoon to sit him down for some tough love. He straightened out and enrolled in a junior college in our home town. He later got his Bachelor's and Master's in psychology in Missouri.

To keep up with school expenses, I worked at a number of odd jobs during the summers. One summer I worked on the maintenance staff at Iowa State, mowing the greens at the campus golf course and helping rewire the old football stadium press boxes alongside professional electricians from AT&T. I also worked in a manufacturing facility in my home town for a couple of summers. The company made chest-style freezers and coolers and I helped wire the units. All in all, I learned a lot about how engineering design and manufacturing work together to produce a viable product. Another summer I worked as a draftsman for the Mid-States Steel Company, located on the east side of Boone. The company provided structural steel components for buildings, especially for the Iowa Department of Transportation, which built maintenance sheds throughout the state. My drafting skills improved greatly and the company often sent me out to construction sites to oversee placement of the steel beams we had designed. Once again I experienced engineering, manufacturing and construction going hand in hand to get the job done and gained practical experience.

On weekend nights I tended bar at the local Golf and Country Club in Boone. I worked back-up to the regular bartender. He showed me how to mix most cocktails and, as the clients became more inebriated, how to cut back on the amount of hard liquor in the drinks. I also learned to keep a secret when local businessmen showed up to drink with ladies not their wives. This discretion produced great tips. The bar windows rose just a few feet off the ground at the 19th hole. As we prepared to shut down the bar at the end of the shift, our friends would show up outside the windows and we would pass partially filled bottles of booze to them. This insured us all something to drink later on. I knew it was stealing, but everyone did it, and to get along with fellow employees I went with the flow. The hourly wage didn't amount to much at any of these jobs, so I couldn't save a whole lot of money. I put away every cent I could for the next year's college expenses. To save money I still lived at home and my mother never complained. At the end of my junior year, I remember thinking that all my hard work had paid off. I had positioned myself in a good spot: the job interviews were pouring in, I got to travel, and I had a girl and just enough money to pay for school. My future looked bright until the Central Intelligence Agency paid me a visit.

3. I Spy

Early September of 1965 found me back on campus at Iowa State going through class registration for my senior year. The process seemed like barely organized chaos, but after completing the paperwork in Beardshear Hall I exited out the back door and headed for the small one-story brick building hidden in the shadow of Marston Hall, the hub of most engineering activities on campus. This small building housed the offices and classroom of the Aerospace Engineering Department in the College of Engineering. The department, though relatively small and limited in resources, possessed a reputation as one of the five best such departments in North American academia. By most measures, other students regarded us with awe due to the rigorous class work and difficult subject matter. They also easily identified us by the two slide rules we carried everywhere, along with our bulging briefcases full of thick math, science, and engineering textbooks.

As I entered the building, some of the staff and several of my fellow students greeted me. I paid a quick visit to the famous "tally board" prominently displayed at the front of the classroom. It listed each senior's name, number of job offers received, and the names of the companies issuing the offers. I noticed that after my name the number 31 appeared and I swelled with pride to say the least. After the exchange of pleasantries, talk turned to missing classmates and future plans. Several of my peers had dropped out of school, been drafted, enlisted in one or another branch of the armed services, changed their major, or transferred to another school. The widening war in Vietnam, however, impacted every aspect of our lives. We each feared a letter from our local draft board informing us of our classification and telling us to report for a physical examination and, perhaps, military duty. The local draft boards followed the academic progress of each student from their districts and knew very quickly of any changes in status. Anyone could be drafted at the discretion of the board, so we all played the lottery and the waiting game. Those of us in the College of Engineering had a slight advantage because the boards knew that many engineering disciplines qualified as "defense related" and almost guaranteed a draft deferment.

25

Here I am in 1965, as a student at Iowa State University, with a group of aerospace engineering students who belonged to a professional engineering fraternity called the American Institute of Aeronautics and Astronautics (AIAA). I am in the back row, second from the left. This photograph shows only 23 of us remaining from a starting freshman class of 34. The attrition rate was high.

My fellow aero-e students understood the importance of making the right employment choice. We didn't see ourselves as unpatriotic, but after years of study, living at near-poverty levels and generally having no social life, we felt we deserved better than humping a rifle through a rice paddy halfway around the world fighting a war we didn't understand. While we had to take ROTC our first two years at ISU, many of us did not continue on the track toward an officer's commission. My two years in the Air Force ROTC program taught me to march to orders, maintain a dress uniform in spotless condition, and prepare myself to fly Phantom F-4 fighters over Hanoi. While I loved to fly, doing it in a small Cessna was just fine by me.

That semester, I had just settled into the familiar routine of rising early and going to class when I received a letter from Brown Engineering in Huntsville, Alabama, asking for a follow-up interview. I had flown to Huntsville previously to talk with this company that built ground support equipment for NASA. I had gone for the free trip to the city that housed the Redstone Arsenal, primarily to see where Dr. Werner Von Braun had developed America's rocket programs after World War II and secondarily out of curiosity about the whole hiring process. When I got home I sent the company a nice letter turning down their offer. I saw myself as a propulsion engineer with little interest in structural engineering. Their request for a follow-up interview surprised me and again

Although I had little time for social life while at the university, I did occasionally attend parties on and off campus. Here I am with a young lady I dated during those years, whose name I don't recall. I think this photograph was taken before I joined the Agency.

raised my interest, so I accepted and agreed to meet with their representatives a couple of weeks later in one of the private rooms in the Memorial Union building on campus.

When the day arrived, I went to the meeting not knowing quite what to expect. I anticipated a better employment offer with a higher starting salary, even though I knew I probably wouldn't accept. The door stood open, and when I entered two men greeted me. They reminded me of Mutt and Jeff, one tall and the other much shorter. The taller one introduced himself as William Harris and the younger one claimed to be Gus, just Gus. After saying hello, the shorter one closed the door and Mr. Harris asked me if I had decided where I'd work after graduation. I said I didn't know yet, so he began to tell me that Brown Engineering Company had taken a second look at my credentials after receiving my letter declining their original offer and had put together a new offer suited to my qualifications. Harris said something like: "This offer is so unique that before we present it, and regardless of whether you accept it or not, I have to ask you to sign a document stating that you will never disclose the nature of this offer to anyone without prior approval." This certainly took me aback. What did he have in mind? For a moment I fantasized that maybe they wanted to make me president of the company or something like that. I mean, what could it be? I hesitated. Then I figured, "What the hell, there's only one way to find out what's going on," and signed. The short guy, Gus, silent to this point, pulled out a notary seal and signed, dated, and stamped the document right then and there. Harris also signed.

I sat back in silence waiting for the big reveal, never imagining what would come next. Harris explained that they didn't really represent Brown Engineering, but rather a branch of the U.S. government. He told me they had selected me from a very small group of people to approach in this manner. I remember he apologized for the subterfuge. He informed me that without my knowledge or consent, they had already investigated my background, "checked me out," he said, and so could make me a special offer.

Harris went on to paint a scenario of the current political situation in the U.S. He said that as protests against the nation's involvement in Vietnam had increased, the government had come to believe that outside influences were promoting these protests; that they were not home grown. He explained that the government had other agencies and methods looking into these allegations, but that it needed additional independent confirmation.

He then told me that he and Gus worked for the Central Intelligence Agency (CIA), an independent intelligence branch of the federal government, and that the President had tasked the CIA to develop its own set of eyes and ears on major college and university campuses across the country to gather intelligence and respond to the increasing number of antiwar protests and the associated violence. The CIA thought the best intelligence could come from students and professors on campus who could identify agents, foreign or domestic, who might be stirring things up. "The CIA would be grateful, Verne," Harris said, "if you'd help us out here at Iowa." He offered a small monthly stipend and an absolute guaranteed draft deferment for students helping the CIA, as well as future employment.

He warned me, however, that if I accepted the offer, I could not share that fact with anybody, family included. If I did, I could face prosecution and fines. In fact, even if I declined to help them, I could face the same consequences for even disclosing our meeting. The secrecy documents I had already signed took care of that.

I sat in stunned silence, trying to grasp the situation. Unreal, I thought. Did I just enter a dreamland? Or a trap? I didn't know what to say. Maybe they had chosen the wrong guy? I held no political commitments. I never much thought about the war other than wanting to avoid dying there. I had set my heart on becoming an aerospace engineer and maybe an astronaut. I knew nothing about intelligence operations and I didn't have a clue about how to spy or get the type of information they sought. Finally I asked, "Why me?"

After exchanging looks with his partner, Harris responded by talking about my past. He knew a lot about me. He recounted that while a sophomore in high school I had cofounded the Boone Rocket Society and impressed many of my teachers, that I had taken the tough science and math courses in preparation for entering engineering college, that I had taken flying lessons. He told me that my name had reached them through independent but reliable sources, but refused to say who. He went on to say that they'd already done a thorough background investigation on me without my knowledge. They'd interviewed friends, teachers, family, and others using various covers so as not to reveal their true intentions. I assumed they'd conducted these interviews with agents pretending to represent various aerospace firms wanting to know a little bit about my background. I knew that most of the positions I wanted required a minimum security clearance just to start out, and since most friends and my family knew what field I was studying, they would assume everything was on the up and up. Following this investigation the CIA made the decision to contact me and make this offer. Harris said it reflected my country's confidence and interest in me. He suggested I could also see it as a way to serve my country without stopping a bullet in a rice paddy halfway around the world. They wouldn't just take me in, though. First, I'd need to complete a formal entry application process with more interviews, tests, and evaluations that, if passed, would allow the government to begin my training and employment on campus during my senior year.

I thought it over quickly. Too quickly, I realized only later. It seemed a win-win. I could decline future involvement after graduation and I would have a guaranteed draft deferment, a monthly cash stipend, a secret life, and still serve my country. In a patriotic moment filled with pride and a little too much ego, I signed the documents.

We shook hands all around and I signed a few other procedural documents. They told me they would contact me within a short period of time with instructions on how and when I should come to Washington, D.C., for processing. I could expect to spend several days there, so I would have to plan accordingly.

Gus asked if I had any other questions, and I asked if university officials knew of their work on campus. They said yes but admonished me to keep this to myself. Apparently some officials at Iowa State not only knew of the CIA recruiting on campus but actually suggested names of select students to approach. Nobody mentioned that the work I had just signed up for was illegal at worst and immoral at best.

Since I would work in secret, they would pay me in cash with no record keeping. No one could know about our arrangement. I didn't question the legality of it all then. How could I? If the government asked you to do it, it must be legal, no? Years later I learned that then–University President William Robert Parks and the Dean of Male Students, Millard Kratovil, knew about the CIA and FBI recruitment on the ISU campus. They kept it hush-hush and only a handful of university officials knew. I can only assume that the CIA had convinced them that the process was entirely legal and a serious national security secret as well.

Some years later it dawned on me that a high school and university friend might have put my name in the basket. Jerry Converse went through the same college-prep courses in high school with me, joined our car pool during the first three years of study at ISU, and enrolled in electrical engineering. He had dropped out of school and gone into the Navy without really providing anyone a real reason for doing so. He ended up in Naval Intelligence and then died while assigned to the naval spy ship USS *Liberty* in 1967 when the Israeli Air Force bombed and strafed the ship during the Six-Day War. I recall a phone call I received from him months before that incident, when he told me that he was doing "interesting stuff" and that he had dropped my name to some people, supposedly as a reference. No one ever contacted me about Jerry, so today I can only assume that the people he referred to were recruiters of some sort. I'll never know for sure.

As I left the Memorial Union that day I stopped on the lowest step for an awkward moment, thinking that I had just entered an alternate reality. I had led a sheltered life in central Iowa, had never involved myself in politics, had never traveled beyond the borders of the country, and had always looked at the happenings in Washington, D.C., and other world capitals as occurring in another dimension unconnected to me. The world had come to roost at my door, demanding some heavy decisions from a naive and inexperienced 22 year old. I pushed these thoughts out of mind. I was working for the government now and duty called.

I took advantage of a previously arranged engineering-related interview trip to add on the visit to D.C. I notified the CIA contact person assigned to me and gave him the dates. He instructed me to check into the downtown YMCA under the name "Gary Bryant" and await further instructions.

I got to the YMCA the day before my appointments and immediately flubbed my cover by using my real name to sign in, having forgotten the admonition to use the alias. The next morning I waited for the phone to ring, but time went by and nothing happened. I went out to get something to eat, did a little sight-seeing, and returned to the "Y" about noon. As I started up the staircase, a man approached out of the shadows and asked, "Are you Verne?" "Yes," I replied. He asked me to step outside. He bought me a cup of coffee at one the stands that dotted downtown. Then we walked toward a bus stop about a block away, and while walking he told me that I had caused some anxiety for the Agency because I didn't use my alias, but that could be understood as just having the jitters. I felt differently. I had just blown my first simple test! I thought that my week in D.C. wouldn't last long indeed with that type of blunder.

We waited at the stop for a few minutes and then boarded a small blue bus that carried no identification, clearly not a public bus. My guide showed his identification and vouched for me. We got off at a nondescript building, went up several floors and entered an office with no number on the door. I sat in the waiting room as my guide spoke to the receptionist. He then told me that I would spend the rest of the day there, handed me a schedule with times and places typed in, and told me to use the little blue Agency bus for transport for the next several days. He told me to show the schedule to the driver, who would deliver me to the indicated destination at the proper time. I also needed to show the card at each building to enter, and I had to make sure to surrender the card when I left town. With that he wished me luck and left. I waited briefly and then a receptionist ushered me into the adjoining room, where three men sat behind separate desks. They asked me to sit down and the process started.

I don't think they offered their names, but they mentioned something about the positions they held within the Agency. One of them specifically said that he served in the Office of Security. Another said he worked with the Directorate of Operations and the Domestic Contact Service. They said they wanted to briefly review my background and ask a few questions about my motives for accepting their offer. They knew I had worked my way through college, that I had no known debts, no wife, and no relatives working for foreign governments. They had copies of my driving record and any police reports that bore my name. They knew the names of most of the girls I dated, my high school grades, and much more. They told me things about myself I had completely forgotten. I sat there on the edge of the chair, nervous and in awe.

They went on to discuss some of the overall goals of the program I would join. The Agency wanted "resources" on selected campuses to provide reliable information regarding antiwar organizations and their plans of action. They wanted these disciplined, reliable "resources," me and other student spies, to fit in, fly below the radar, and build their antiwar credentials from scratch. They said nothing about continuing Agency work beyond graduation.

They did all the talking, and the whole event seemed more like a history lesson and lecture than an interview. Other employees photographed and fingerprinted me before I left the building and instructed me get my temporary ID at my first stop the following day. Then they reminded me to catch the bus at the proper time and place the next morning. The driver, they said, knew exactly where to take me each day.

Over the next several days the bus took me to different locations and I visited with psychiatrists and medical doctors, underwent several personality tests, and, finally, took a lie detector test. This exam would be the final step in the procedure, and after that I could go home. Only after thorough review of the week's events and results would they tell me if I had passed. The lie detector administrator said very little. He called the process "vetting" and explained that if the CIA hired me I'd repeat the test on a yearly basis just like all the other employees. Then he connected me to the machine, placing a flexible hose around my chest to measure my breathing and electrodes on my chest to measure heartbeat and skin response. He explained that he would stand out of sight but within voice range. I remember him saying that I shouldn't be surprised at any of the questions because they needed to cover a lot of ground with very directed questions.

He instructed me to answer simply "yes" or "no," nothing else. He then asked several "test" questions designed to establish a baseline of my reactions. Then he began probing, asking personal and almost insulting questions. He asked about my sexuality, whether I had ever stolen anything, whether I told lies often, whether I did drugs, whether I knew anybody from a foreign country, whether I had ever traveled outside the U.S., whether I had told anybody about this trip to Washington, D.C., and so on. The questioning went on for what seemed like hours but really was about 40 minutes. He doubled back and asked some questions a second time. He then disconnected me from the machine and escorted me back to a waiting room. A secretary arranged to reimburse me for my expenses and told me they would contact me within a few days, after reminding me again not to tell anyone about this experience.

As I left D.C. for home I sure didn't feel like a spy. Not knowing the results of all the questions and probing done over the previous days left me feeling like a failure. Why couldn't they tell me if I had made the grade or not? If I passed, what would they expect of me? If I failed, would they cut my tongue out? I felt like a fish out of water in D.C. and thought that this whole experience would end in naught except for a lifelong obligation to silence that would follow me to the grave. I had gained nothing and been stripped naked in front of strangers who now held my future in their hands. How stupid of me. Unlike a nightmare, this experience wouldn't allow me to wake up and continue a normal life. I cursed myself for having involved myself in this morass, and as I flew back to Iowa I found myself secretly hoping I had failed.

I returned to classes and threw myself into my studies, special projects, and thinking about plans for after graduation. Given my background in rocketry, my instructors permitted me to design, build and launch the first liquid fuel rocket developed at Iowa State as a special project. I designed it, my professors approved it, and the university's machine shop fabricated the parts. We assembled the whole contraption in the back room of the aero lab right next to the wind tunnel we used for experiments. It had a basic design: a glass-lined oxidizer tank filled with red fuming nitric acid (RFNA) and a fuel tank to hold Aniline. Nitrogen gas, under pressure in a third container, pushed the two fuels out of their respective storage tanks into the combustion chamber. As I assembled the rocket, all my fellow students and professors would come by and stare in amazement and wish me luck. We tested the final design with tanks full of water on a Saturday afternoon, and when I pushed the launch button everyone in the immediate area got a good soaking, including me. It took hours to clean up the mess. We fired the actual rocket later that spring, but after rising only a few feet from the launch pad, it developed a blockage in one of the feed lines and the launch failed.

Although I hadn't completely forgotten about the pending call from the Agency, it drifted to the back of my mind as I settled into my daily routine of classes, lectures, and study. I also tried to find time to spend with a girl I had developed a relationship with back home. We would talk about what we might do after I graduated, but with this new possible commitment to the government that I couldn't even tell her about, things just got more complicated and stressful. The Agency hadn't even accepted me yet and it already loomed over my personal life and future plans. I felt adrift and uncomfortable, to say the least.

After what seemed like an eternity, Harris called. He sounded upbeat and wanted to meet the next day. He didn't say if I was in or out, so as I approached the meeting room, I didn't know how to prepare myself for either eventuality. As soon as he saw me he jumped to his feet, extended his hand and said "Welcome aboard!" I sputtered, not knowing what to say. I didn't know if this was what I really wanted to hear. He may have sensed my ambivalence. "Don't worry," he said, "we've got your back. What can go wrong?" In hindsight, I realize, the answer was "everything."

Over lunch, deep in my own thoughts, I listened to him explain how the program would work, what they expected of me, how to prepare my reports, how they would contact me each month, how they would pay me and how to make contact if required. He gave me a contact number in St. Louis. The answerer would always say something like: "This is the office." I would then use my code name of Gary Bryant to identify myself, hang up, and await a return call. Harris expressed a lot of interest in my recent rocket experiments and always asked in-depth questions about my classes and my knowledge of rockets whenever we talked.

For my first assignment he asked me to identify all student groups on campus that expressed any political ideas at variance with stated government positions on domestic and international issues. The CIA would contact me monthly with new assignments and expect me to turn in regular reports. Harris told me to "blend" into the protest environment to allay any suspicions. I asked him if the Agency had contacted my draft board about the guaranteed draft deferment they had promised, and he assured me that, though they hadn't done that yet, I shouldn't worry; if I heard from the board I just needed call the contact in St. Louis and they would take care of things. I didn't pursue the subject any further.

Armed with my first mission, I began the long and tortuous path into the world of smoke and mirrors. I was a secret agent! I felt important, exalted onto a level of trust and confidence only those who lived and worked in the *sanctum sanctorum* of the government could relate to. I stood on the front lines, doing my part in the struggle against foreign infiltration of our society and way of life. I wanted to shout out to the world these new feelings of service and importance, but I could not. My euphoria lasted for weeks.

As instructed, I began to monitor selected student groups with activist agendas, as well as selected students, assistant professors, tenured professors, and foreign students who voiced opinions over the U.S. involvement in Vietnam. I transformed myself into a political activist although I had never taken a stand before, didn't really know the issues, and had not previously mingled with these folks. I didn't know them and they didn't know me. I also dealt with the mental whiplash of attending a meeting of campus Democrats one night and then a meeting with the Republicans the following night.

Sometimes people asked me why I attended their meetings. I offered a convincing answer: I was trying to determine which groups offered ideas that matched mine before I committed. Without actually joining, I volunteered with many student organizations, including the Young Democrats, the Young Republicans, the fledgling Students for a Democratic Society (SDS), Ban the Bra, and more. I'd volunteer to staff their offices and booths at weird or late hours when no one else came around, and then I'd copy membership lists, donor lists, activities planned and past, everything I could get my hands on. The CIA impressed upon me their interest in names and identities of the "travelers" list, not ISU students but folks who traveled from campus to campus organizing antiwar protests and demonstrations. This group seemed well funded, and the

Director of the FBI, J. Edgar Hoover, believed they were serving as witting or unwitting agents of the Soviet Union who wanted to manipulate the antiwar movement. Hoover had not convinced Lyndon Johnson, and LBJ, to develop his own independent intelligence, authorized the CIA to undertake the largest covert and illegal operation ever to spy on the citizens of the U.S. The Charter of the CIA allowed it to operate outside the U.S. only. The FBI covered domestic intel and the two Agencies often fought a turf war. They didn't trust each other or share information. As I saw with my handlers, the CIA considered FBI agents nothing better than Keystone Cops. Let them chase car thieves and petty crooks, they told me; the CIA looked for bigger fish to fry.

I soon learned that many of the groups under suspicion actually attracted few members. Most of their work revolved around getting a statement published in the university newspaper, the *Iowa State Daily*, known for its anti-establishment positions on most subjects. Many of the student groups could count on fewer than 10 core members and perhaps an equal number of on-lookers when they held rallies on campus. Additionally, the groups I looked into maintained only tenuous connections to larger national movements that bore the same names and ideas. A couple of the groups actually achieved charter status with the national affiliates, but I don't recall which ones. I do remember that some of the information I secretly collected on these groups indicated that they had received some funding and literature from larger national groups, but I don't recall the level of outside support as amounting to much.

The campus cops always showed up at these public gatherings, but to the best of my memory they did not take photographs. However, I did notice a couple of individuals who would show up, stand on the fringe of the group and take pictures. At first I thought they worked with the campus newspaper, but later I learned that only one of them did. The other worked freelance, and I determined to find out who he worked for. Later the program I worked for received the official code name MHCHAOS; it was launched by CIA Director Richard Helms and overseen by Richard Ober. I found out I wasn't operating alone on campus; the FBI had developed its own sets of eyes and ears on most major university campuses to monitor the same student and faculty members and groups that I spied on. I believe that the person I almost always saw taking pictures at local events worked for the FBI. Did he know about me and my purposes? Did he submit photos of me to his handlers? I doubt it, but cannot be 100 percent sure.

A couple of blocks from the Memorial Union stood a two-story wood frame structure called "International House." Some foreign students resided there and had offices for their activities. One of my fellow students from the Middle East lived there, so it didn't attract attention if I showed up and took part in meetings and discussions. I noted that they all planned on returning to their home countries to practice skills learned in the U.S. Few, if any, desired to stay in the States after graduation. Most came from wealthy and politically connected families and seemed to have positions already secured in their home nations. While most held views about our involvement in Indochina, those opinions ranged all over the map. They concerned themselves more with grade point averages and graduation than anything else. At any rate, I saw them as foreigners and didn't really concern myself with how my reports would affect them down the line. I never expected to see any of them again, so what the hell!

I wrote all of my reports out in longhand and turned them over each month to the contact the CIA sent to collect them. At the same time he paid me my $300 monthly stipend in a plain white envelope filled with cash. These exchanges usually took place on the first Monday morning of each month at the "Hub," a coffee and donut shack on the north side of Beardshear Hall. The contact, about my age and dressed like a student, would stand just outside the door holding a red knapsack. I would approach and ask if he wanted to see the campus newspaper. When he said, "Yes," I would hand him a copy of a newspaper wrapped around an envelope containing my reports. In the same exchange he would slip me the envelope with the cash. We might exchange some meaningless small talk and he would ask if I needed anything. He would relay my reports and any needs to my case officer for action. The meetings never lasted more than a few minutes and looked normal for a campus setting.

My assignments varied; some seemed downright strange and others time consuming. Soon the amount of time I needed to spend on gathering information on a particular person or group began affecting my studies, so I began to fudge my reports in spots where I felt I could get away with it and making things up where there were no witnesses. After a few months of this, I concluded that the CIA must be testing me and that the information I provided didn't serve the national interest in any important way.

Since I didn't have access to student academic records or files, I collected bits and pieces of information whenever and wherever I could. Sometimes I gathered information in casual conversations with the target in the classroom or at a rally. I would also use any mutual contacts that I and the target might have. I recorded personal history, like and dislikes, family size, hometown, course of studies, plans after graduation, views on the university and its staff members, and, of course, political views and feelings towards the war in Vietnam. I carefully formed my inquiries so as not to sound like an interrogation. For the most part, I found the subjects entirely forthcoming and not paranoid about discussing these issues with another student.

I considered myself a good spy, even a friendly spy. My contact would give me a name of a student or a professor or a teaching assistant, and I would try to develop a relationship with the person, elicit views on Vietnam, and later copy these down and deliver them to my contact. Just your friendly spy on campus. I also initiated files on students without the CIA's knowledge. One pretty young lady caught my eye. I tried to date her, and when she refused I initiated a file on her, thinking it might benefit me down the line.

I worked harder to gather information on teaching assistants and professors. How does one get information about their affiliations, beliefs, and activities? One could always ask students enrolled in their classes, but that information only dealt with class subject matter, the way they taught and if they were tough graders. Did they grade on strict percentage or on a curve? Could one earn extra credits? Did they frequent the local watering holes on campus or in town, and did they like to party? One could also "monitor" one of their classes if one had the time by attending class without getting credit; this allowed one to meet the instructor and sort of break the ice. I chose this route in several instances and found I could then approach the instructors when I saw them in the bookstore, in a restaurant, or on the street. On several occasions while attending a campus political event or rally, I would recognize some of the teachers and professors at the outer fringe of the group listening to the speakers. If they stayed around, I could assume and later write up that they had an interest and go from there. Sometimes they would make a comment in class about their disgust or agreement with a military decision made by commanders in Vietnam or by politicians in Washington. I wrote that down, too.

At times, professors asked their students what they thought about current issues and invited class discussion. Then the professor would express an opinion, both personal and from an academic point of view, that students would remember. I tried to painstakingly piece all of this together into some sort of comprehensive report. It took a lot of time and often my personal views would creep into the reports. My case officer took me to task about this a few times. I could only wonder who else worked for the CIA identifying these academics as targets, because 90 percent of the time my case officer gave me the specific names of people to collect intelligence on. The other 10 percent of the time I initiated a file if I learned about a professor's actions or views through independent sources. I never knew if the CIA employed other students on the ISU campus. They never asked me to recruit anyone else, and I believed I labored alone.

A feeling that I worked hard but had little to show for it permeated my subsequent attitude toward the CIA. I decided to pursue my engineering profession upon graduation and tell the CIA "thanks but no thanks" for its offer to go into the Agency equivalent of the Officer Candidate School (OCS) and become an employee in one of its several divisions. The CIA wouldn't guarantee me a spot in the Deputy Directorate of Operations (DDO) or an overseas assignment, and I would need to take language classes and intern a bit with the State Department under a special relationship deal between the two agencies.

I wanted to join the moon race instead, so I made the decision to continue with the program until just prior to graduation before turning down their offer of full-time employment. That way I could keep collecting the much needed monthly cash and extend the guaranteed draft deferment. Several fellow students went to work for McDonnell Aircraft in St. Louis and received their promised deferments. McDonnell designed and manufactured the various versions of the latest fighter aircraft, the Phantom F-4, in St. Louis and I calculated that as long as the war in Indochina raged, they would be offering deferments. I just needed time to plan exactly how I would announce my resignation to the Agency.

I also harbored concerns about my pending application for the security clearance needed for my type of engineering work. I apparently had a clearance now through the CIA, but I couldn't tell any prospective employers about it. If I chose to take a government position with NASA, for example, I couldn't tell them I already worked for the federal government. The more I thought about the challenges that I would have to face, the more intimidated I felt. I didn't know if I had made the right choice.

I wrestled with all this on a daily basis as graduation drew closer. I also noticed that it affected my relationship with my girlfriend. I wasn't spending the time that I should with her and I couldn't share with her the secret work I did. We were growing apart and I felt I bore that responsibility as well. The lies of omission, not sharing my full life story with her, my family, or my friends, and having to constantly compartmentalize what seemed like two different lives, kept me tightly wound and on guard. Even the most innocuous remark, a reference to a campus demonstration I had attended or a popular professor I kept tabs on or the cash always filling my wallet, sent me into amateurish and unnecessary attempts to dissemble. Little by little my lying grew more fluid and more facile, and that ease of deception scared me too.

As the end of the school year approached, I put my activities for the Agency on the back burner. I accepted an offer from McDonnell Aircraft in St. Louis over a great offer from United Aircraft/Pratt & Whitney in Florida because it kept me closer to home and might offer me a better chance of saving my relationship with my girlfriend. When the day came to finally inform Harris, I nervously blurted out my decision. He listened politely and then asked a few questions. He thanked me for the time and energy I'd given to the Agency and

Here I am in August 1966 after the graduation ceremony at Iowa State University with Elizabeth, my girlfriend at the time. The fountain on the north side of the Memorial Union is in the background. I would leave for my new position at McDonnell Aircraft in St. Louis, Missouri, a few days later.

told me they held my work in high esteem. He said I could always contact him if I changed my mind. If I needed a recommendation, the Agency could provide one under the name of a "cover" firm in place for those who had done acceptable work. He told me that the Agency would contact me from time to time just to check on how I was doing and ask if I wanted to work for it again.

Hearing these offers, I returned one of my own. I told Harris that if the Agency needed my help on a specific item, it could count on me and my patriotism. That cheered him up and we shook hands and went our separate ways. I felt free: a great weight had been lifted from my shoulders! The separation went smoothly with no apparent animosity on the Agency's part. I thought I had done the proper thing by offering to help if needed, but I couldn't imagine the CIA ever contacting me again. Why would they want someone who had walked away from them?

4. The Frame-Up

The people who bet on me back in 1966 won big. Graduation day dawned bright and sunny in Ames, a perfect summer day on campus as hundreds of us pulled on our gowns, slicked back our hair and slipped on our mortar boards at jaunty angles. Four years of hard work paid off as I crossed the reviewing stand, shook hands with the university president, and received my diploma in Aerospace Engineering. My mom and siblings sat in the stands surrounded by other Iowa Cyclone families. Everyone smiled. I felt ten feet tall.

Later that summer I loaded everything I needed into the old Ford I'd driven since high-school and set off. A new life away from campus promised a new start and a chance to leave the CIA behind. In a northern suburb of St. Louis I found a place to rent that seemed reasonably priced and close to my new employer. Several production line employees at McDonnell also lived there in a boardinghouse type of situation. The owner would prepare an evening meal and we all sat down together each night with lots of conversation about work. The friendliness of the others made my transition to the big city a lot easier.

Then one day, out of the blue, the CIA made contact. The Agency's resident officer in St. Louis, Louis Werner II, an investment banker and graduate of Princeton, came from a wealthy and prestigious St. Louis family. He called to introduce himself and tell me that the Agency remembered me. "Keep in mind, Verne," he assured me, "if you ever want to talk, we could meet anytime, day or night."

I tried to evade his approach. I muttered something like, "Thanks. I'm sure we'll meet. Just give me some time to get established in my new job."

"Well, Verne, give me your address and we'll be in touch." I gave it to him. But later I wondered why he wanted it and how he knew my telephone number, as it wasn't listed in my name. It didn't seem significant at the time, so I put it in the back of my mind in order to concentrate on my new career.

The MAC assigned me to a design team located in Building 211 on the east side of Lambert Field with most of its offices and production facilities. I worked on two projects at the same time: components for the cockpit of the General Dynamics F-111 swing-wing fighter-bomber, and also the two-man Gemini spacecraft. The work challenged me and I slowly got to know my fellow workers on both projects. I had previously worked for some small central Iowa manufacturing facilities during the summers, so the change to working within the system of a large aerospace company, even as a small cog, boggled my mind. And now I was working on prototype jets and manned spacecraft! Once again I dreamed of becoming an astronaut.

On the home front, I would try to travel back to central Iowa as often as possible to keep up on projects that my younger brother and I kept on the drawing table and to see my girlfriend Liz, now my fiancée. My brother and I decided to experiment with a larger homebuilt multi-stage solid fuel rocket that we would launch the next year, and I planned to purchase some vital components for it in St. Louis. Liz and I kept holding on, but I developed serious doubts the relationship would work out. One weekend Liz and my mom flew into St. Louis to make wedding plans and we looked at a couple of apartments, but we also disagreed about timing and other things. She didn't think she saw enough of me and said I seemed consumed by my work. She and my mother returned home after several days without any real planning accomplished. Not long after that, a letter arrived from Liz. When I sat down and opened the envelope, the engagement ring I had bought her fell out. She wrote that she couldn't go any further with me. It hit me hard, as I felt she had come to that conclusion way too abruptly, but I didn't see anything I could do about it. I called her a few times trying to talk to her on the phone, but she wouldn't budge. She was moving to Kansas City with a couple of girlfriends but never gave me her address or phone number. I remember hoping that, perhaps when I had settled in and established my life in St. Louis, we could work things out, but that never happened.

The breakup upset me, so I threw myself into my work to keep busy. I purchased some of the things my brother and I needed for our rocket. Most importantly I found some low-grade dynamite that we could cut to size to separate the various stages of the rocket during its flight. I locked it into a metal box with a few electrical squibs and tucked it under the bed in my room, planning to take it home at a later date.

Being an engineer made me popular at the boardinghouse. One resident's radio kept shorting out, so I made a continuity tester to find the problem. I also helped a couple of others with minor automobile problems like solenoids and starters. The various residents now formed a community that included me. So when Christmas rolled around, with the breakup still on my mind and making it seem more and more depressing to travel back to Iowa for the holidays,

I decided to just stay put. Coworkers threw holiday parties and scheduled get-togethers. They knew I planned to stay in town. A fellow engineer, Langefeld, who had joined the local Playboy Club downtown, invited me to join him and a couple others from the office for food and drinks one evening. It took a good 30–45 minutes to drive from where I lived to the club through thick holiday traffic, but I found it worth the drive when I received a Bunny welcome: "I'm Suzie and I'll be your Bunny tonight," said the longest legged beauty this Iowa boy had ever seen. From her strapless corset teddy, bunny ears, collar and cuffs, to her cotton-tailed derriere, Suzie put me in mind of no rabbit I'd seen before.

I'll always remember the details of that gathering the week before Christmas because of what followed. The drinks and conversation flowed and I felt surrounded by friends. My coworkers and I talked about work, personal lives, and future goals. The club unfortunately enforced a strict "look but don't touch" policy, and when night turned into morning and a coworker named Barney asked me to drop him at his car parked back out at our office, I agreed since I drove past MAC on my way home. To get to the office we needed to drive past the Lambert–St. Louis airport on the west side of the city, and as we did, I noticed a lot of activity there. Lights flashed from police cars, fire engines and ambulances all around the airport. I remember that Barney and I speculated about a medical emergency or even a plane crash. I drove around to the east side of the airport, where we found my friend's car. I dropped him off and drove home, giving no more thought to the scene at the airport.

The next day the newspaper headlines blared the news about a small blast at the airport the night before. A porter had found four sticks of dynamite under a chair and raised the alarm. They evacuated over 500 people before the bomb went off and blew apart a bench and a window in the terminal. The papers reported no injuries, no motive and no suspects. I knew that antiwar demonstrations had occurred in St. Louis, just as in cities across the country, and that earlier some one or some group had set off an incendiary attack on the St. Louis building where the Army kept its medical and draft records.

Students at local colleges and universities protested the draft and the ever-escalating war in Vietnam that now saw 200,000 U.S. troops there. In the local papers I learned that a man had called in a threat a few days earlier warning of an impending attack at the airport, but he didn't mention specifics. Now I understood all the commotion we had seen as we drove past the night before.

Sometime during the weekend, I went to the apartment of our office secretary, Martha van Diver, who had offered to help me wrap Christmas presents. I couldn't wrap gifts worth a damn and so I couldn't refuse her offer of help. When we finished wrapping the presents, she suggested that we drive to the airport to see for ourselves what had happened. We drove my car, but when we got into the parking lot we couldn't go any further due to barricades, so we abandoned the plan. She asked for a ride to work on Monday and I told her I would pick her up.

Early Monday morning, the 20th of December, I got a call from Martha saying she would drive herself as she needed to run errands after work. I thanked her for the call and went to the office. Around noon a MAC security officer, accompanied by a couple of other men, approached my desk. They introduced themselves and asked me if I could accompany them to a supervisor's office nearby. Ken Cook, the office manager, looked at us as we walked by and just shrugged his shoulders, indicating he didn't know what was happening. Once in the office, one of the visiting officers asked to see my car. I said, "OK. But what's this about?" "Just show us your car," he said.

I walked them down the stairs to my car and opened it for them. In the trunk they saw the .22 caliber rifle that I had forgotten to put away after a hunting trip on my last visit home, but they showed no interest in it. They searched the trunk and then the car's interior. I couldn't imagine what they were looking for, but whatever it was, they didn't seem to have found it.

The older guy, who seemed in charge, then asked to see my apartment. Again I agreed and again I asked, "What are you guys looking for?" but got no answer. We stood in the lot for a few more minutes in silence as my agitation grew. Then one of the guys who had stayed behind in the office came up and reported that they had searched of my office and desk and found nothing. What was going on?

They put me in the back of an unmarked car and we headed for my apartment. As we approached the building I noticed many cars, including a couple of police vehicles, parked in the driveway as well as the street. People had come out and stood in the street watching our arrival as if they expected us.

Two men got a grip on me and forced me up the stairs to my living quarters, where several police officers were already peeking in drawers and examining everything in sight. One of them turned to me and asked, "Have you bought dynamite?"

"Yes," I answered.

"And fuses?" he asked.

"Yes," I explained, "my brother and I use the dynamite and fuses for rockets."

"Where is it?" I pointed under the bed and one of the men fished out the metal box and placed it on my desk. The older man opened it and removed the sticks of dynamite one by one. He counted only seven. I knew that I had purchased ten. Where were the other three? Who could have taken them? The plainclothes officers talked among themselves and on their hand-held radios, and suddenly one turned to me and said, "You're under arrest."

"For what?"

"Setting off a bomb at the airport two days ago."

"That's nuts. I'm an engineer. I make rockets, not bombs."

"Hold your hands out," he said as he clicked handcuffs onto my wrists.

I tried to explain again. I told them I had been with friends at the Playboy Club downtown. They'd made a terrible mistake. I hadn't done anything and I could prove it. It would all get cleared up and then I could forget this ever happened. Maybe my friends and I would gather at the Playboy Club again in a week and have a good laugh about all this. Maybe I'd see Bunny Suzie again and tell her all about this.

Maybe, but in the meantime they kept the handcuffs on, put me back in the car and drove me downtown to the county jail. When we arrived, a few reporters with notebooks tried to shout questions at me as photographers' flashbulbs exploded in my face. The cops placed me in a holding cell alone.

I couldn't think of what to do next. What would my family and friends think of this? What would my employer think—and do? What would become of my career? How could I resolve this? They allowed me one phone call, so I called home, got hold of my brother and, with a brief explanation of the situation, asked for help. Then I sat down on the steel bunk feeling frightened and alone.

A few days later, an attorney from my home town showed up, instructed me to say nothing, and said that he would try to find local attorneys in St. Louis to help me out. He told me that everyone back home couldn't believe what happened. I assured him that I felt the same.

Days passed. Days of mounting anxiety and fear. Nights of distant shouting and screams, of clanging metal doors and rattling metal bars. After what seemed like an eternity, two local attorneys came to see me. The lead attorney, a Mr. Spaulding, tried to determine how much money I could raise to defend myself. When I answered that I might have a few hundred dollars to my name, they exchanged looks and then told me their services didn't come cheap and that in addition to their representation they would need to hire an independent investigator, which would only add to the costs.

I told them to talk to my coworkers. We had all spent that night together. I couldn't have bombed the airport without everyone from MAC knowing all about it. They conceded my alibi but wanted to know about the missing dynamite. I didn't know: could someone in the apartment house have stolen it? They assured me that the cops couldn't find either witnesses to place me at the airport or any other evidence: no fingerprints, no parking lot receipts, nothing at all, just the missing sticks of dynamite. That reassured me for a few days, but then I got hauled in front of Federal District Judge John K. Regan. The federal prosecutor told the court my crime was damaging property used in interstate commerce, a federal offense punishable by up to 20 years in prison. My lawyers entered a plea of not guilty and argued, on the basis of my college education, security clearance, and good job, for a low bail. Not swayed, the judge set bail at $500,000, an amount I could never hope to raise. Christmas, arriving three days later, found me pacing my cell as the days and nights slowly passed.

Just after Christmas the two local attorneys reappeared with an odd question, asking me if I knew Nicholas Katzenbach, the U.S. Attorney General. I'd heard of him, of course, but certainly didn't know him. They told me that Katzenbach, or someone acting in his name, had contacted the U.S. Commissioner in St. Louis and wanted to know why I hadn't already been released on my personal recognizance. This floored me. Then they told me that the State of Missouri had decided not to seek any state charges and had turned the case over to the federal government. They said they'd never seen anything like it before.

Then they asked me again about money and how I would pay them. I still couldn't offer a good answer to that question.

My youngest brother, his fiancée, my mother, a couple of lawyers from Boone, Iowa, who knew me, and a Methodist minister, a personal friend of one of my cousins, came to visit. They sat in the prison visiting room as stunned as I was by the accusations. We could hardly talk through a heavy metal screen in the noisy, crowded room. I knew my family didn't have money for bail, but at least I could still see them and hear the news from home. They still supported me. My mother cried throughout. It broke my heart.

A few days later and without explanation, Judge Regan called me back into court and reduced my bond from $500,000 to $500. Nobody knew why and nobody on my side wanted to ask.

Free again, I traded my jail clothes for those I was wearing when the agents first arrested me, went back to the boardinghouse and packed up the rest of my stuff, checking for the box of dynamite under the bed and finding it gone. I threw my things into my car and drove straight home to Iowa, thinking and planning what to do next without coming up with any great ideas. I hauled my stuff into my old room and took my first shower in privacy in two weeks. Mom made a pot roast and invited friends over. Things seemed normal again and I tried to relax.

In the days that followed I noticed that some old friends avoided me, while others tended to gather around me and offer what moral support they could. The Iowa papers reported on the St. Louis bombing when they picked up that the leading suspect was a native son. Everyone seemed to know about the case. Everywhere I went I sensed people watching me, judging me.

FBI WASH DC

FEDERAL BUREAU OF INVESTIGATION
U. S. DEPARTMENT OF JUSTICE
COMMUNICATIONS SECTION
DEC 23 1966
TELETYPE

FBI ST LOUIS

4:02PM URGENT 12-23-66 RCR

TO DIRECTOR

FROM ST. LOUIS (149-160)

VERNE ALLEN LYON, DAMV, OO SL

    REMYTELS, DECEMBER SEVENTEEN, EIGHTEEN, AND TWENTYTWO
LAST.

    USC WILLIAM R. O'TOOLE ,SLMO, ADVISED THIS DATE HE
RECEIVED A CALL FROM AN UNKNOWN INDIVIDUAL WHO STATED HE WAS
NICHOLAS KATZENBACH, DEPUTY SECRETARY OF STATE, AND GAVE A
TELEPHONE NUMBER OF TWO ZERO TWO - EIGHT SIX ONE - TWO NINE
THREE FOUR ,AND STATED HE RECEIVED WORD FROM PRESIDENT JOHNSON
TO THE EFFECT COULDN'T UNDERSTAND WHY SUBJECT VERNE ALLEN LYON
COULD NOT BE RELEASED ON OWN RECOGNIZANCE. COMMISSIONER
O'TOOLE ADVISED THIS UNKNOWN CALLER'S VOICE SOUNDED AS IF IT
WAS A NEGRO CALLING.   EX-104   REC 30
    IT IS REQUESTED THAT BUREAU CONTACT KATZENBACH, DEPUTY
SECRETARY OF STATE, TO DETERMINE AUTHENTICITY OF THIS CALL.

P

END

MR. ROSEN
FBI WASH DC

MR. DELOACH FOR THE DIRECTOR

P

This FBI cable should have raised a great deal of concern. It states that someone purporting to represent Nicolas Katzenbach (then U.S. Attorney General) had inquired as to why I was arrested for the incident at the St. Louis airport. Apparently it was sent either the day of my arrest or the very next day. I never received any explanation for this cable.

MAC let me go 90 days after my arrest, citing suspension of my security clearance and the fact that the situation probably wouldn't get resolved for some time. That pissed me off. I had worked hard and done a great job for them. Nobody from MAC had visited me, and the company sent a letter to my home firing me.

One evening I sat and assessed all my worldly possessions to calculate my net worth. It didn't amount to much. The attorneys in St. Louis kept calling, asking for more money and again suggesting hiring a private investigator if I could raise the dough. How could I even begin to prepare a defense without knowing who would represent me? I heard from my fellow workers at McDonnell, and they each told me they would verify the fact that we spent that night at the Playboy Club together and that nothing seemed out of place. With those assurances I started to think that the case against me would fall apart if not for the missing dynamite. What had happened to it? Did someone living in the same building take it? Did the federal agents take it? If so, why would they do that to me? I could not understand any of what was happening, and I don't remember sleeping for weeks on end.

Six months later I received a summons to return to the court in St. Louis for a hearing. I drove down alone, parked my car in a public garage, and started walking towards the federal courthouse a couple of blocks away. I had arrived early, and when I approached the courthouse I saw one of the federal agents who had arrested me talking to another man who looked awfully familiar. As I drew closer I saw Harris, my CIA recruiter from Iowa State. I hadn't seen him in over a year, but I had no doubts about it. Harris, my old CIA handler in Ames … in St. Louis … at my trial. As I drew closer they noticed me and quickly walked away in opposite directions. I stood dumbfounded in place, unable to move. What was going on here?

I entered the courthouse and found my two attorneys. Once again they asked for money and said that they were going to tell the judge that they wanted to withdraw from the case due to my lack of "resources." I mentioned to them what I had witnessed on the courthouse steps and gave them a very brief story about my CIA affiliation on campus. They just looked at one another in silence. Did they even believe my story?

The judge entered and called everyone to order. My attorneys asked to be relieved. The judge granted their request and asked if I owed them any outstanding monies. They replied in the negative. The judge then told me that he would assign a public defender at a later date. I asked him how much later, as now I had nobody to confer with or to prepare my defense. He stated that I would have ample time to do all of that, and added that the prosecutor also wanted more time to assess some new issues that had arisen. New issues? Without elaborating he adjourned the hearing. I left the courtroom and St. Louis even more puzzled than before. Once again I returned home to more uncertainty.

Back in Iowa I scratched for work and got jobs here and there to try and support myself and make some money for my upcoming trial and defense. I had time to think, and my mind ran wild at times. I thought about seeing Harris in St. Louis, about the earlier contact from Werner on behalf of the CIA, and my coworkers' keen interest in my life. A former "friend" named Besso had disappeared from MAC not long after my arrest, and again and again I returned to those three missing sticks of dynamite. Who had taken them, and why?

When I refused the offer to join the CIA upon graduation, I thought the Agency and I had parted amicably. I told them that if I could offer any assistance they could count on me, but I didn't really mean it. I wanted to get away from them, the spying, dissembling, and secrecy. What if they knew the only way to get me working for them again involved setting me up so I had no one else to turn to, no place to run, no other job? Their offer to stay in touch also seemed like just a formality at the time, but maybe it meant much more. Perhaps it signified a promise ... or a threat? I spent sleepless nights reviewing different scenarios, suspicious of anyone and everyone. My bright future of a challenging and remunerative career, a loving wife and an eventual family of my own went up in a cloud of smoke with an airport bomb. Paranoia crept in. I doubted everything I thought I'd known and everyone I'd trusted. I doubted my sanity, if indeed such ideas proved more paranoid than real. Then, one day, the phone rang and I learned what had really happened.

5. Back with the Company

I picked up the ringing phone that weekend at home and found myself talking to Harris for the first time in several months. He began by telling me how sorry he felt about what had happened in St. Louis. I asked if he'd read about the bombing and he said he had. "It's all a mistake," he assured me. I told him I had had nothing to do with it. "I already know that," he said, "and the Agency can help clear up the whole situation and make it go away. What I need you to do now is just come to Washington again and talk things over. We'll work it out."

His call both frightened me and gave me hope. Why did the CIA take notice of my predicament? Could they have been behind all the trouble I was in and, more importantly, could they get me out?

So I went back to Washington and checked in again at the same downtown YMCA and called the number Harris had given me. He came by about an hour later and picked me up. We drove to a large building on the east side of the city and joined four other men in suits who were already waiting for us. Highly nervous about everything that had happened, I spoke immediately as we entered the conference room. I quickly laid out the facts of my predicament, which Harris, at least, already seemed to know. Then I asked what was happening. One of the men, whom I did not know, told me again that mistakes had been made and that they were working to make it all go away. He told me they were all on my side.

"Listen," he said, "while we're working to make it all go away why don't you come back to work for us. Think about it. You've lost your security clearance. You've lost your job. You're not getting married anytime soon."

How did they know about Liz and the broken engagement? I thought to myself.

"…so if you do some work for Uncle Sam you get paid, you get a security clearance, and you get your life back."

I could think of few other options. "Okay," I answered. "What do I do?"

One of the shorter guys, silent until now, moved to the head of the conference table and unrolled a paper scroll. I recognized a map of Cuba. He told me the Deputy Directorate of Operations (DDO) had formed a plan to send an "asset" into Cuba for a period of two to three years to gather information. After that time period, the "asset," meaning me, would return home. And in this time period the incident in St. Louis would have been resolved and forgotten.

This seemed ridiculous on its face. "Why," I asked, "would you think of sending me to Cuba? I don't know any Cubans. I've never been there. I don't even speak Spanish."

And then they tied it all together, describing how the Cubans had invested a lot of resources into cloud seeding to produce rain for their crops. My background in flying and rocketry fit their needs.

The airport bombing was the bow on the package: my arrest on what some would call domestic terrorism made me look like a political dissident, even a revolutionary.

They also reminded me that, even if I beat the charges in St. Louis at trial, I might never get a high level security clearance again. That would preclude me from ever working in the aerospace industry, as nobody would want to hire an engineer who couldn't get a clearance. The room fell silent as they let this information sink in.

They offered me a way out. They said they knew I had nothing to do with the airport bombing, but how could they know? They guaranteed that if I undertook this mission for my country I would get a security clearance from the United States government.

What choice did I have? Without their help, without money, without an attorney and a defense team to support me, the outcome of any trial in St. Louis looked like a losing bet. They told me to take my time and think the offer over, and they reminded me that I could never repeat to anyone a word they had uttered.

Following handshakes all around they dismissed me and a driver took me back to the YMCA, gave me a few dollars to pay for the room and a couple of meals, and bade me goodnight. Needless to say, I did not sleep. I re-ran everything over and over in my mind. What had happened in St. Louis? Who had really bombed the airport? What did they mean by a "mistake"? What options did I have? I stayed up all night putting the pieces together.

When Mr. Werner had contacted me in St. Louis, it underscored the seriousness of the CIA in keeping tabs on me. Perhaps they had planned that whole operation from the beginning to insert an asset into Cuba. The cloud seeding background fit my own. They chose me without my knowledge or agreement. I already had a year of experience working secretly for the CIA domestically, so they knew what they could expect. But how to get the Cubans to welcome an American into Cuba? To accomplish this, the CIA created a "legend," the fictitious, but documented and believable, life story of a dissident. By staging the incident at the St. Louis airport, the CIA had created the newspaper stories, the photographs, the arrest and court records to allow them to offer me to the Cubans as someone with the *bone fides* they might want to invite to their island, a dissident bomb thrower with the rocketry skills they desperately needed.

I called Harris the next morning and accepted their offer. What choice did I really have? Besides, the plan seemed crazy on its face. Surely the Cubans would never fall for it? And if I played along and nothing materialized, the CIA couldn't blame the failure on me, and I figured they'd still get me off the hook back in St. Louis.

So we went back to the office complex on the east side and they hooked me up to the polygraph once more, to be "vetted" again before resuming the discussion of the previous day. Back in the conference room with Harris and the little guy from the previous day, "Shorty" rolled out the map of Cuba again and they briefed me in more detail.

The Agency, they told me, suspected that the Castro government had not returned all offensive Soviet missiles at the end of the Cuban Missile Crisis in 1962. They thought that Castro had hidden a few of the smaller and shorter range rockets in some limestone caves located in the province west of Havana called *Pinar del Rio*, out of sight of U.S. spy planes like the U-2.

Castro had grown ever bolder in his efforts to taunt the U.S. and export his brand of revolution not only to the South American nations of Bolivia, Peru and Colombia, but also to the rest of the world, including places like the Congo and Angola. Back in '62 President Kennedy had signed an agreement with the Soviet Union stating that the U.S. would not launch another invasion of Cuba if the Soviets withdrew their missiles from Cuba. So, "Shorty" said, without worrying about a new invasion, Castro had turned to the task of eliminating all internal opposition on the island, leaving the CIA with few ears and eyes on the ground. The Cubans had identified and imprisoned most of them, and those that remained lay low, fearful of being caught. With the closing of the U.S. Embassy, CIA case officers didn't have a diplomatic base from which to operate. Anyone going into Cuba for the U.S. would have to operate as a "NOC" (no official cover). The CIA couldn't just drop an asset into Cuba, but what if the Cubans invited an asset in? My documented history as an amateur rocketeer, combined with my degree as an aerospace engineer from Iowa State, established my engineering credentials. The bombing and my arrest in St. Louis made me look like an antiwar, anti-establishment renegade. They could embroider my back story by sending me to Canada as a possible draft dodger, have me approach the Cubans with a request for asylum, and see if the Cubans took the bait.

That made me the bait: exposed and alone.

"Shorty" saw the beauty in it: " You don't speak Spanish, and the Cubans would never suspect any foreign intelligence agency would send in an intelligence officer who couldn't read, write, or speak the native language. They'll see you as a useful but politically naive dissident."

I asked what I would have to do and what I would get paid. They told me I would check out visiting foreigners from Soviet Bloc countries, from North America, and from South America: visiting scientists, engineers, technicians, and military people who would turn up in Havana, in major hotels where other foreigners, like me, would naturally meet and mingle.

"Of course," he warned me, "you'll be on your own." A lot of Cubans made contact with the CIA, but the Agency didn't know who sincerely wanted to help them and who worked undercover for Cuban security. If I made contact with and tried to recruit a plant, the plant would expose me. They instructed me to use my own judgment and vet each person personally and individually. Whom could I trust? "No one," "Shorty" admonished me.

And if I got caught? The Russian KGB had trained the Cubans. When the Cubans suspected someone of being a spy, they delayed an arrest and monitored the suspect's comings and goings as long as they could to identify whom the person contacted, with what frequency, what information was being sought or passed, how it was communicated to the outside, and what the ultimate goal of the operation might be. Harris added: "Well, they probably won't kill you, so be glad of that. You'd probably get picked up, given the third degree and then either swapped for a Cuban 'asset' in our custody or just tossed out of the country. Of course, they'd probably kill any Cubans you'd been in contact with."

For all of this they offered to start me at a GS10 or GS11 level. With hazardous duty pay, I could make around $9,000 a year, about what I had made at MAC without risking my life.

Later on, other officers briefed me on ongoing projects in Cuba that made mine look benign. Air Force Brigadier General Edward Lansdale at the Special Operating Group in the White House and CIA Case Officer Bill Harvey had run Operation Mongoose since 1961 following the fiasco at the Bay of Pigs. With President Kennedy's approval, Mongoose attempted various exotic assassination attempts on Castro using exploding cigars, a poison syringe hidden inside a fountain pen, and even exploding sea shells positioned where Castro scuba dived. They sabotaged ports, power plants and factories, all in hopes of sparking an internal revolt and bringing down the regime. The CIA even brought in Mafiosi, displaced from their formerly lucrative gambling, drug, and prostitution businesses in Havana, to "hit" Castro as they would any other gangland rival. Harris warned me to stay away from this project.

The U.S. government also created Operation 40 with Cuban exiles and dissidents to assassinate loyal Cuban military officers and diplomats and to sabotage the infrastructure on the island to induce dissatisfaction with the government and, hopefully, spark civil war. Harris told me to stay away from the Cuban exile groups as well.

So who remained for support? No one. I would truly be operating on my own.

And yet the laundry list of what the CIA wanted went on and on: monitoring the economy at the street level, gauging the confidence of the populace in the Castro government, determining the availability of basic food products in the local markets, estimating the level of transportation and/or the lack thereof, getting a take on the number of Soviet military personnel on the island and where they were stationed. This seemed a lot to expect from an amateur like me working alone.

We discussed how I was to be paid, why I shouldn't be seen as having a lot of cash (dead giveaway), how I was to communicate with my family (infrequent phone calls, letters, and telegrams), when to expect supportive contact in Cuba, and other matters. We also touched on what I should do if identified and apprehended by Cuban counterintelligence: play dumb, deny everything and ask for diplomatic help from the Swiss. I kept thinking to myself that the whole thing was so preposterous it would never work. I remained extremely skeptical and scared, but saw no other viable option.

If the CIA had set me up for the St. Louis bombing, if they had planned all of this for years, they never admitted it to me, but I believed it more every day. How could I work for people who had done this to me, who had ruined my life? Simply, I saw no other option. How could I risk my life in a harebrained scheme? At this point I had little else left to lose.

6. Down on the Farm

As instructed, I traveled southeast of D.C. and reported to the guardhouse at Camp Peary for the four- to six-month training session in tradecraft required of all future CIA officers. I rode from Washington to the camp in a bus with 12 other individuals, all males, just like every other recruit I saw on base, who I assumed all shared the same assignment. In orientation in D.C. they had told us that, although we might exchange small talk, we should refrain from giving out any real personal information to anyone we met on the bus or in the camp, an example of the CIA's tightly compartmentalized mentality and structure. Camp Peary sits near Williamsburg, Virginia, just south of the U.S. Navy Weapons Training Center. Though located on a military base operated by the Army, it has areas dedicated to the Defense Intelligence Agency (DIA) and the CIA and yet falls under the auspices of the Department of Defense (DOD). Its more than 9,000 acres contain everything from swamps to fake international borders with guard towers and electric fences, roaming guard patrols, an airport, and all of the training equipment found at other military training bases around the U.S. The CIA calls it "The Farm."

At the gatehouse the bus driver handed an envelope to the gate keeper, and after a few minutes they waved him through to the JOT (Junior Officers Training) area where we all went into an amphitheater called "the pit" where two individuals welcomed us and explained some of the camp rules: as a "secret" paramilitary base Camp Peary served a multitude of functions, and although our training would take place at many different spots inside the base, they warned us to remain in the JOT area as much as possible. They would issue us military fatigues with accompanying numbers that would begin with the letter X and assign each of us a cryptonym and a pseudonym which we should always use. They said only the person in charge of our training saw the files containing our real names and identities.

They also said that our class work and field training would take a lot of time, but we'd have some free time on weekends when we could go into town or back to D.C. if we had transportation. They warned us to always check back in before any deadline. If asked by anyone, they instructed us to respond that we served in the Defense Department undergoing special training and nothing more. If outside the Camp we found ourselves in a tight spot, we should call a phone number we would memorize and someone would handle the situation.

Then they issued our clothing and the standard military items like toothbrushes, underwear, and boots. Once we were outfitted, they directed us to a wooden barracks that appeared left over from World War II, though inside it proved more comfy than it looked: beds instead of cots and its own washroom, toilets and showers. We then assembled and they led us to the mess hall for dinner. They informed us we would eat all of our meals together unless our individual training schedules interfered. At any given moment, they said, different units and people trained at the camp and ate as a group as well; they discouraged any interaction.

We each had a supervisor of sorts to oversee our training, change the schedule and classes as needed, and write up our progress reports. They would set individual schedules for each of us, but about 70 percent of our instruction would take place as a group. They assigned each of us separately: some to the Deputy Directorate of Operations (DDO), others to the Deputy Directorate of Intelligence (DDI) and still others to the Deputy Directorate of Support (DDS). They divided each of these three major groups into yet smaller categories. For example, I served in the DDO designated as a NOC (No Official Cover). Others in the DDO would serve in U.S. embassies and/or consulates overseas, where they would operate undercover as supposed low level State Department employees.

Foreign nationals trained on one part of the base, supposedly unaware that they had landed in the U.S. Because of that they warned us to be very careful not to leave anything lying around that might identify our actual location. The foreign training area had no contact with the other areas to help maintain the subterfuge.

My supervisor assigned me the pseudonym of José Felipe Salamon for use later in Cuba. In addition, and apparently to confuse any Cuban counterintelligence operations, he gave me the additional moniker of AMLOVE. The Cubans, if ever alerted to my actions, would be looking for an agent instead of an officer. U.S. citizens who work for the CIA serve as case officers. They call foreigners working for the CIA agents, even if they don't know they are actually working for the Agency. Such agents might accept assignments for monetary gain (the CIA trusted them the least), or come from those who believe their country and government would be better off allied with the U.S. (more trusted), or support agents who might provide logistics, transportation, and so on. The CIA also categorized some as prospective agents: people already working for foreign intelligence, counter intelligence, or security services. The CIA always looked for individuals in foreign governments who might develop into assets somewhere down the road. These included diplomats, journalists, union leaders, political leaders, military, and just about anyone else who could wield some power or influence within their own country. The CIA identified, approved for contact, and later vetted these types prior to putting them on the payroll. It took time and a variety of techniques to persuade them to work for the U.S. Most frequently the CIA offered these people money or promises of special privileges such as expedited visa applications for coming to the U.S., or they might use a "false flag." Under this plan, they might tell the prospective agent that an American company needed certain information or access not normally available through public knowledge in order to make financial decisions. Of course, the company offered to pay for such information. Only after a sometimes lengthy apprenticeship would they tell the agent for whom he or she was actually supplying information. They could never predict the reaction to this revelation, but normally, after a person had accepted money for quite some time, he or she had a hard time saying no, having become used to having money and knowing that the Agency held the receipts to the payoffs as potentially incriminating evidence if the person's government found out. The CIA always questioned these agents' loyalty to the process, however.

Another technique they employed from time to time I found particularly underhanded and disgusting. A recruitment team would approach foreign officials and invite them to work as agents, offering money, access to the U.S. Embassy, and visa waivers. If they refused to betray their own countries, the team would inform them that their supervisor already worked for the CIA, and if they refused to accept the offer they could lose their position and power. Sometimes the recruiters told the truth, but many times they did not; the person receiving the pitch didn't know for sure. If they did recruit people this way, they could never really trust them, and everything they provided had to be verified by other sources. While they used this verification process with all agents, only those coerced into cooperation always remained under suspicion.

We divided our time at The Farm between classroom lectures and field demonstrations. Our instructors came from the ranks of current CIA case officers whose cover might have been blown, making re-deployment impossible, or they may have just wanted to come "out of the cold," so to speak. In addition to teaching, the CIA allowed them to publish their histories. If they chose to write their stories, they published the book in a single edition and made it available only to other CIA people at headquarters at Langley, Virginia. The public never got to read it.

In orientation, the instructors explained how the CIA was divided up into its different divisions and subdivisions or compartments. Again, an officer working in one subdivision might never know of activities taking place in another subdivision. They divided all work at the CIA this way in order to protect operations and people in case an enemy apprehended an officer who then revealed information. We all strictly adhered to a "need to know" basis at all times.

I served in the DDO, headed by a deputy director advised by the Office of Current Intelligence and the Office of Security. They oversaw three basic subdivisions: Foreign Intelligence (FI), Psychological and Paramilitary (PP), and Counter Intelligence (CI). These three basic divisions divided the world into operational areas: Africa (AF); Soviet Union (SR); Eastern Europe (EE); Near East (NE); Far East (FE); Western Europe (WE); International (IO); Records (RD); and the Western Hemisphere (WH). All of these subdivisions and divisions worked in coordination with the Deputy Directorate of Plans (DDP), the DDI and the DDS.

My own assignment in the subdivision of the WH fielded operations into areas like Central America and the Caribbean; the Northern Cone of South America; and the Southern Cone of South America. The Cuban Desk stood alone, and that's where they sent me.

The Cuban Desk operated out of offices in Florida, Langley, and Mexico. After the Cuban Missile Crisis of October 1962, when President Kennedy agreed not to invade Cuba and to remove U.S. missiles from Turkey in exchange for the removal of Soviet ICBMs from the island, the U.S. limited its operations to monitoring Cuban activities around the globe, carrying out sabotage on the island or wherever it could strike, and clandestine infiltration of former Cuban nationals onto the island to carry out disruptive covert actions. We also looked to recruit Cuban nationals in areas of responsibility. Disgruntled Cubans were not hard to find, and several Cuban expatriate groups actively worked to send teams into Cuba for sabotage and surveillance. These groups included ALPHA 66, the Democratic Revolutionary Front (FRD), the Cuban Revolutionary Council (CRC), and a host of others that came and went or that the CIA invented for limited periods of time.

In our training in the classroom we learned how to open and re-seal letters surreptitiously, often using steam. The trainers also showed us how to write secret messages with the old technique of using citric acid and paper. The invisible words only appeared when heated. We learned how to burn a piece of paper to the point that no one could reassemble or read it. We did this by folding the sheet of paper like an accordion, standing it on edge and lighting the top. It burns down to the base and leaves nothing but ash.

Another class dealt with maps: how to interpret them, how to orient them, how to calculate distances and elevations, and how to identify obstacles and understand just about everything else a detailed map can tell you if you know where and how to look. These extremely detailed maps were the best I ever saw as far as quality and detail.

In the field we trained on several weapons, including machine guns, 30 caliber, if I remember rightly, a heavy and impractical weapon for someone like me and my mission. I also trained with three different hand guns: a High Standard .22 caliber semiautomatic pistol, nice and lightweight, very accurate, feeling just right in the hand; the old military standard issue Colt 1911 .45 caliber semiautomatic handgun, heavier, with a lot of kick to it because of the weight, and so not as accurate; and a Walther PP9 handgun, small, lightweight, easy to aim and fire, my favorite. We also practiced with long guns, rifles of different calibers, but again I didn't see any real purpose for these for my future use.

One of the trainees who arrived with me at the beginning looked Hispanic, but I hadn't any experience with the different Latin American nationalities yet so I never did find out what country he came from. They held religious services at the camp and some of the trainees came from different religious backgrounds, but over the years I found that the CIA liked to choose Catholics, Mormons, and others who believed and practiced set procedures and rarely questioned higher church authorities. The CIA probably believed that they would make good followers and not question authority. My own Methodist tradition, though I embraced it only tepidly, made me a little more skeptical.

In the classroom and in the field we learned how to build and use explosives, making them from readily available chemicals and household products. We jury-rigged detonators from things as simple as a book of matches and a cigarette or a little glycerin laced with potassium permanganate. We experimented with different concoctions that allowed enough time for one to start them working and still have time to make good one's escape. They taught us where to place explosives in a structure to produce the desired result. For example, to open a locked door you place a small charge at the weakest part where the knob and lock sit. This was a lot easier than trying to destroy the hinges, which required at least three times the effort.

We learned how to effectively destroy an automobile, a small truck and a bus, demonstrating how an expert with a small amount of explosive material could truly do a lot of damage. I couldn't see myself running around Cuba with bags of chemicals or explosives, but I have to admit it was entertaining to watch. They showed us how to destroy small structures like foot bridges, where to place the charge and the amount of explosive needed. They assured us that if we needed assistance, a special ops team would do it and that we didn't have to do everything on our own. I always assumed they only employed explosives when they could avoid civilian casualties, but I came to suspect that many times that didn't matter and that they could use these methods and so-called "collateral damage" to enhance the civilian population's level of disgust and distrust of their own government. It also occurred to me how easily the CIA could have managed that little bombing in St. Louis and then placed the blame on someone else: me.

In classes, which usually began around 8:00 a.m., we learned the difference between covert operations and covert actions, though the two definitions overlapped. In a covert operation the U.S. might influence a foreign election or the choice of a cabinet minister, or place a newspaper report aimed at influencing the decision of a foreign government. The U.S. would then publicly deny any involvement in the operation. A covert action, on the other hand, could mean the direct involvement of a U.S. operative to carry out a covert operation, with the goal of masking his identity as well as U.S. involvement. Hence the term "plausible deniability": the target might suspect U.S. involvement, but could not prove it.

The trainees in the program had access to a great library and language labs. I took the Spanish language course prepared by the State Department to train the foreign service officers assigned to embassies and consulates in Latin America. I would spend hours in the lab at night and on weekends, as I really had nothing else to do. After I actually got to Cuba I wished I'd spent even more time absorbing the language, but my lack of expertise probably helped with my cover, as the Cuban counterintelligence people would find it hard to believe that the U.S. would insert an intelligence officer into their country without a high level of proficiency in Spanish.

We also received instruction in the importance of communications and how to establish them even under hostile and difficult conditions. The whole purpose of having an intelligence officer or team operating in a foreign country is to ferret out the targeted government's secrets and get them back to the analysts at CIA headquarters. A U.S. diplomatic post, like an embassy or consulate in the targeted country, made the task of communicating with Langley easier, sending and receiving encrypted message by secure systems as well as by travel and by diplomatic pouch. International law permits each represented nation to send and receive diplomatic pouches undisturbed by the host country's security services. This process actually allows for "support devices" like weapons, radios, tape recorders, and other items to be brought into a country without inspection. On the other hand, if one were operating in a country like Cuba, where the U.S. did not maintain a diplomatic mission, things grew difficult. Sometimes a friendly nation would allow limited access to its diplomatic pouch

Here I am at the portico of the White House, photographed by a fellow CIA recruit during one of our training trips to Washington, D.C. I don't recall who we met with while in the White House, but often these training trips included meetings with high level officials at different locations in the city. I always thought that these events were done more to impress us than for any other real significance.

to people like me, but that required that they know me, if not what I was doing—a dicey situation at best.

For someone like me, training as a NOC in a hard target (no diplomatic representation), special conditions prevailed. To establish a method of communicating with one's supervisors in a different country or back in the U.S required the use of a special tape recorder that could be recorded at normal speeds but played back at very high speeds. Additionally, one needed a transmitter to send the message. But first one would encode or encrypt the message to ensure that if somehow the message got picked up by the host country, it couldn't be decoded. And one needed to maintain transmission times and frequencies, a difficult task for a NOC trying to avoid the predictable routine of driving to a remote location to operate the transmitter. One also had to hide all this equipment from the prying eyes and ears of counterintelligence agents. Having such equipment found in one's residence, for example, guaranteed arrest and expulsion, if not worse.

In cases like this one looked to a "friendly nation" to provide some assistance in communications. Its representatives could make their diplomatic pouch or their secure communications systems available. In the best scenario, the CIA already had an agent on the friendly nation's payroll or the nation had instructed one of its own intelligence officers to cooperate with the CIA.

High risks loomed in whichever scenario was employed. To communicate clandestinely with foreign nationals who supplied information proved challenging. One needed to identify places where one could hide and retrieve messages, and these needed to be fairly public places like parks, transit stations, and restaurants where one's presence could be explained to any suspicious authorities. One also needed a system to let an agent know one had left a message. One could mark a permanent structure with tape that the contact could remove after retrieval, but even that might appear suspicious. One needed to develop a prearranged but varied schedule that an agent knew and could meet. It took a lot of thought to make the process as safe and efficient as possible.

We learned to insert a prearranged code phrase, a phrase in a popular book for example, that if used at the beginning of a message tipped off the reader back at Agency HQ that our cover was blown. Along with the classes on communication, we learned some basic photography skills concerning lighting, focal length, film speed, and so on. In Cuba one couldn't get Kodak color 400 film, and the best I could find would be a low speed black and white roll. I would have no way to develop or print photos, so I would need to get any exposed rolls of film out of Cuba for processing elsewhere. It would arouse suspicion if I entered the country with a good camera, so I would have to find one after I arrived in Cuba.

Our field exercises tested our classroom instruction. In one exercise several of us went into D.C. on a mission to retrieve messages left for us by another team of trainees. We had to retrieve the message without being detected. Our team worked together to scope out possible surveillance teams and avoid them. In D.C., we hustled on and off the Metro and retraced our path and then entered and exited a shopping mall with several entrances to throw off anyone following us. The team split up and just one of us retrieved the message while the rest of us deflected any surveillance. It played like a game of cat and mouse, but we took it seriously because our lives could depend on it at some point.

Back in the classroom we learned that if a need arose to disburse money, every request required approval prior to disbursement and we had to do everything in our power to get a signed receipt. If the recipient couldn't sign for fear of leaving incriminating evidence, then we required them to make a "mark" attributable to that agent. They told us that, in the past, some case officers had invented "agents" who required payment and then pocketed the money for these nonexistent agents. In Cuba I would have no access to large amounts of cash and any payments to an agent would come from an account in another country that the agent could access if allowed to travel off the island. If not, I could promise a payout to family members living outside the country. If an agent suddenly flashed extra cash it would immediately draw suspicion. They told me I could access some cash in small amounts and I'd have to sign for it at the Swiss Embassy whenever I created a pretext to visit.

In the field we underwent some basic military training that included formations, marching with field packs, carrying weapons, climbing ropes, covering rough terrain, push-ups, pull-ups, and all of the regular physical chores one associates with military duty. We heard that at the more remote areas of the camp, they also trained teams for infiltration into foreign countries either by swift rubber boats launched from mother ships or by parachute. These folks learned how to navigate through swamps, protect themselves from mosquitoes and snakes, and get around fences, watch towers, and military patrols.

I did undergo an endurance test of sorts. They dropped me in a wilderness area of the camp equipped with only my military fatigues, some water purification tablets and a small pocket knife. They gave me 72 hours to arrive undetected at a predetermined spot in the camp. If I didn't make it they'd dispatch search teams to find me. I studied some maps in advance so I had a fairly good idea of the size of the area and what physical conditions lay in each direction. The area appeared heavily wooded, with several swamps. I needed to keep as dry and as warm as possible. They took me out in a Jeep at night with the windows of my compartment blacked out. I could feel us driving in circles, with some areas of the road extremely rough. I remember that we crossed two metal grates in quick succession about 30 minutes before they took me out of the Jeep and led me into a clearing. They told me to wait for 30 minutes before removing the hood that I wore. I could only estimate the passing of 30 minutes, because they had removed my watch before releasing me. Once I took off the hood, I stood in complete darkness. The clouds covered the sky and I couldn't see any stars or the moon. It was completely disorienting. I guessed that the time was around 2 a.m., and since I couldn't see a thing, I decided to wait until daylight before moving. I needed to determine which way was north so that I could at least orient myself. I knew that traveling northeast would ultimately take me to a river. If I headed southeast, I would be going down the peninsula and it might take days to reach the end. The same would be true traveling to the north-northwest. Once I determined which way was north, I could head southwest, which I knew would take me towards the James River and a road.

The sun rose and I quickly determined where north lay and set my direction for the southwest. I did climb a tree to see if I could spot any identifiable landmarks, but that proved a waste of time. I could see, about a half mile away in the direction I wanted to travel, a small clearing of some sort, and I knew that if I reached it I would be traveling straight, more or less. My mouth felt dry. I assumed anxiety caused this more than real thirst, but I determined to drink my fill of water if I could find a suitable source.

I reached the clearing, so I knew I had held the course, but I sought another vantage point to determine if I could continue in a straight line. It had rained the day before, so puddles of water stood in depressions along my path. I wanted to drink but couldn't trust the cleanliness of the rainwater. I needed a container of some sort, but I had only the boots on my feet. I took one off, crushed up a purification tablet, filled the boot with water and added the crushed powder. I stirred it with a small stick, held my nose and drank. It tasted terrible but it quenched my thirst. I determined my path as best I could and continued. I passed the entire day this way, going short distances, trying to ignore the growing hunger pains in my stomach and my ever-increasing thirst. As night began to fall, I picked a spot in the notch of an old tree that seemed comfortable and hopefully out of reach of any snakes. I used my T-shirt as a mosquito net and tried to rest as best I could.

When dawn broke the next day, I figured I had used up about 30 hours of my allotted 72, so plenty of time remained. I woke up both hungry and thirsty and I needed to find water. It hadn't rained again, so no standing water. I doubted I would find anything to eat, and that thought made me even hungrier. Once again I determined my direction and set off at a steady pace. The ground remained rough and wooded with no signs of civilization anywhere. Around midday I got my first piece of luck. I spotted an empty ammunition canister sitting upright with the hinged flap open. The army green paint on the outside looked nearly new, so someone had left or lost it there recently. I looked inside and saw a couple of inches of water in the bottom, presumably from rain. I saw nothing floating around and no rust, so I decided to take a chance and just drink it without using a purification tablet. I drank about half of the warm but refreshing water and closed the lid. This could really come in handy as a container.

Another stroke of luck followed later that afternoon. I came across a rough dirt path and a metal grate. I followed the path and found a second grate not far from the first, most likely the two grates we had passed over on our way to the drop-off point. I headed in the direction I assumed we had come. My pace picked up as I didn't have to maneuver my way through tough stands of trees and brush. Elation seemed to stem my ever increasing hunger, but the steamy atmosphere increased my thirst. I drank the remainder of the water in the ammo container, rested for a few minutes and resumed my pace.

As the sun started to set I saw my objective not far away, a guard post on the northern edge of the base. I had instructions to present myself to any guard post I came across. On reaching the shack, I showed the guard my identification. He told me to sit down, and as I did he offered me a candy bar and a drink from his canteen. Both the candy and the water hit the spot. He made a phone call and in a few minutes a Jeep pulled up. We determined that it had taken me about 44 hours of my allotted time to return to the camp. While I basked a little in the glory of having made it back with time to spare, I knew luck had played its part. Looking back on the experience, I have no idea why I needed to undergo this type of training, as I would never be part of an infiltration group or ever have cause to use wilderness survival skills. Maybe it just made me a little tougher for the challenges I did face.

As my time at The Farm drew to a close, I noticed that, of the dozen or so people who had arrived with me, several no longer appeared in either classroom or field training events. The instructors offered no explanations and none of the other trainees seemed to have any additional information. We each did our own thing and couldn't afford curiosity about others. We couldn't disclose to each other where they had assigned us or what we might be doing. I assume only a few of us actually knew our future assignments. The majority received this basic "spycraft" training as a requirement for later assignment at a legitimate diplomatic post somewhere. Wherever such an assignment took them, they would have access to the post's communications equipment to send RYBAT cables, the CIA cryptonym for secret and sensitive communications, back to headquarters; cables so sensitive that even the State Department's ambassador or counsel could not read them. At a consulate or embassy my classmates would have the protection of diplomatic immunity if detected and arrested by the host country's counterintelligence services, and after being declared *persona non grata*, they would simply be shipped home. Once they were identified, their clandestine service at an overseas post would end, more or less honorably. I could expect no such niceties in Cuba.

I found my fellow trainees a patriotic group, at least on the surface, and during a couple of trips to the city to party, any mention of future work reflected this sentiment. Nobody ever drank themselves into a stupor or lost control. I think we all knew the stakes and understood the dangers. We also assumed that the CIA had undercover ops observing trainees at the major watering holes. We had come too far to blow it this close to successfully completing our course.

When my training came to an end after about four months, I packed my bags while everyone else completed a field exercise and left on a bus back to D.C. with no goodbyes. I didn't know if I would ever run across any of my classmates again, but I had more than that on my mind.

7. Undercover

My handlers told to me report to a safe house in Toronto and present myself as a draft dodger on the lam. A lot of young Americans had headed to Canada to avoid service in Vietnam, so I could blend into that crowd and not attract unwanted attention. Once there I planned to present my "legend" to the Cubans and await their reaction. On my way north my handlers instructed me to go the Cuban Mission to the United Nations in New York to make my initial contact.

As I rode the train to New York, I continually mulled over the highlights of this seemingly hare-brained plan they had concocted to make me attractive to the Cubans. Everything hinged on the Cubans needing my skills and their acceptance of this carefully crafted legend. I have to say that I never expected the scheme to succeed.

I left Grand Central Station in lower Manhattan for our safe house located on 76th Street on the Upper West Side. As I walked up the steps to the front door, I noticed that right across the street thieves were stripping a car in broad daylight. People walked by without showing any surprise at all. I could see immediately that I was a long way from Iowa ... and I didn't think I would like New York. Two other guys, also passing through, who had resided in the safe house for a while, lost no time in orienting me to the ins and outs of operations in the city. Following our orders, we scoped out the Cuban Mission to the United Nations and even shadowed Rogelio Rodriguez, a Cuban diplomat. He also served as the resident DCI (Cuban Intelligence Directorate) officer in the U.S. at the time.

We spent several days trying to arrange an appointment for me with Mr. Rodriguez without luck. My name didn't ring a bell with him and we couldn't advertise my reasons for wanting the meeting over the phone. Finally, persistence paid off and he agreed to meet. I gathered my collection of newspaper clippings and supporting documents and presented myself at the mission. He made me wait for over an hour before a secretary ushered me into a bare-bones office where I sat for another 15 minutes before Rodriguez entered with another secretary.

We exchanged greetings and I blurted out my rehearsed speech: I knew about Cuba's intentions to increase its agricultural production by seeding clouds to increase rainfall during the dry season. I laid out my relevant background in amateur rocketry and my education as an aerospace engineer. I also presented myself as an antiwar activist who wanted to use his talents in peaceful endeavors.

Rodriguez asked several questions about my politics and motives, and even asked if someone had sent me. I assured him that I had come of my own volition and referred him once again to the newspaper articles about the bombing in St. Louis. The secretary had taken copious notes, and when we finished the interview, Rodriguez told me to contact her in a few days. I took her name and phone number, thanking them both as an official escorted me out. I walked out into the sunshine and noticed that I was dripping wet with sweat. I wiped my brow with a red handkerchief to signal our watchers located across the street that I had met with Rodriguez and we could hope for future contact. Then I headed to a bar for a drink.

I waited a few days before contacting the Cuban Mission again. This time Rodriguez saw me almost at once and gave me a brief statement to read. It said that the U.N. Mission couldn't deal with my situation and that I should go to Canada and make myself known to the Cuban diplomats at their consulate in Toronto. Rodriguez assured me that he would notify them in advance of my coming. He needed to know if I would do this, and I assured him that I would move to Toronto as soon as I could but that it might take a few weeks. He also told me he would consult with Havana about possibilities because he believed that the Revolution could use me. I thanked him profusely and left.

Back at the safe house we all agreed that the Cubans had made a smart move. They didn't want to jeopardize their mission or people in New York on hostile U.S. soil, and it made more sense to approach them in Canada, which still maintained diplomatic relations with Cuba and offered a site with less tension in the air. We celebrated the fact that the Cubans seemed interested, and I began making plans for travel to Toronto. We'd notify our people there that I was coming and they'd find a spot for me. We'd set up operational funds easily enough through the Bank of Montreal and a numbered account. I packed my bags and headed for Ontario. I'd never visited Canada before, so I looked forward, rather naively, to this new experience.

In late 1968, using a passport bearing the identity of Gary Bryant from Kansas City, Missouri, I drove a rental car across the bridge that separates Lakes Erie and Ontario at Niagara Falls and followed the 401 north and then east to the sprawling metropolis of Toronto. I parked the car in the parking lot of the Hotel Royal York downtown, left the keys under the front seat, and took the bus and subway to the suburb of Rosedale and our safe house. My superiors had told me that the Royal Canadian Mounted Police and its intelligence division didn't know about this safe house, although they had recently stumbled on the one near the intersection of Eglinton and Yonge Streets in midtown.

The stately three-story building, my new temporary home, was located on a quiet tree-lined street with plenty of off street parking and stood just far enough from neighboring buildings to insure a good degree of privacy. The basement housed an office and the kitchen, while the bedrooms, including mine overlooking the backyard parking lot, took up the upper floor. The building looked like most of the others in the vicinity, a neighborhood of private homes and converted apartments. Plenty of traffic came and went, so our routines didn't raise suspicions.

The residents briefed me on the house rules and showed me where to lock up my sidearm, where the burn box was, and how to use the secure communication line. They gave me a map of the city's subway system and an emergency local phone number, and told to me explore for a week and familiarize myself with the layout and selected locations.

The city fascinated me. On this, my first-ever visit to Canada, I found little difference between the Canadians and my fellow countrymen except for the "Eh" and the long "oout" sounds. I took the bus and subway to their turnaround points, located the Cuban Consulate on the 3rd floor of an old building west of Yonge Street, explored the college campus in the same area, and generally got to know the city. Once I settled in, I prepared to implement my mission.

The plan seemed simple. I would present myself to the Cubans using my real ID, mention the referral from Rogelio Rodriguez in New York, and take copies of newspaper articles regarding the incident in St. Louis. I'd tell them that I felt safe for the time being but that I didn't expect I could maintain my situation in Canada for long. By keeping to these items, timelines, names, and events I hoped to keep my story straight. One Tuesday morning I climbed the stairs to the Cuban Consulate. The outer door stood open, so I entered a sparsely furnished and empty waiting room. A Cuban flag hung from the wall above a large framed photograph of Fidel Castro and several slogans in Spanish which I struggled to translate.

I could hear a heated conversation in Spanish in an adjoining room, so I sat down and waited. After a few minutes, a young girl left the inner office. She almost jumped out of her skin when she saw me, and then hurriedly ran back to the inner office and returned with a man by the name of Hernández, maybe 30 years old, who spoke only broken English.

I showed him a piece of paper bearing my name and references, all the while spouting a completely different introduction to foil any counterintelligence surveillance systems that might be in place in the office. He motioned me to the inner office and closed the door. He told me that he had been expecting me for the past several weeks and wanted me to know that the Revolution had great interest in contracting me to work in Cuba but that they still needed to work out the details. He asked me to stay in touch with him, in person, every other week or so, until instructions arrived from Havana. I told him that I would do that but that I didn't have much time, since I had entered the country illegally and I would have to find employment to make ends meet, which would increase the chances of being identified and caught by the RCMP. I gave him the paperwork and left the office feeling that too much remained up in the air. Maybe something would get worked out, but who knew how long it would take?

Later that evening I communicated the situation to my supervisor in Langley, and within a day received a "well done" and the OK to seek employment using my alias. I found a position in a clothing store on north Yonge Street. It catered to big and tall men and was under the ownership of a retired Canadian wrestler named George Richards. I used my cover story of being a draft dodger in need of a new life in Canada and they hired me almost immediately. I started work right away and learned a lot about the retail clothing business. I found it easy to work with my Canadian coworkers, characters all, who accepted me, the "Yank," without further explanations on my part.

I spent the next several weeks working in the clothing store, accepting invitations from fellow workers, getting to know some of the local girls, and always maintaining contact with the Cubans. They never offered any definitive word, and this worried me. I maintained secure but limited communications with my family back in the States, but the news depressed me. The Feds had labeled me a fugitive and were searching for me high and low, keeping my mother and younger brother under surveillance. My other brother, serving in the Air Force, believed all the official propaganda and wanted no contact with me lest it affect his military career.

On more than one occasion I expressed my growing depression to my supervisor in Langley, but he repeatedly told me that this served my situation well vis-à-vis the Cubans, whom they had detected checking out my legend and background. They were interested but moving cautiously, just as we might expect. This information, combined with a pep talk, always sustained me until the next bout of anxiety and depression descended. My supervisor also told me that the Canadian RCMP Intelligence division had shared information with the CIA about increased cable traffic between the Toronto Consulate and Havana, perhaps about my case.

While I was waiting for a response from the Cubans, the CIA assigned me to the task of a departing member of the team in the safe house: to apply for and obtain at least two legitimate Canadian passports. This might sound strange, because the CIA has a special arrangement with Canada, England and Australia in which they can request a number of legitimate passports from each of these countries to use on selected missions, anything from a one-time insertion to gather information to a mission to make a contact in a "hard target," a country where the U.S. does not have diplomatic representation, or a mission requiring covert action.

To comply, I would search records of institutions that housed the mentally retarded or physically handicapped. Many of these facilities needed volunteers to visit with their residents or help with other chores. No one ran background checks on the volunteers, and if one appeared to be clean cut, one was accepted. As a volunteer I would identify an individual who fell within the right sex and age group, act as an advocate for the person, and then extract all the information I needed: name, place of birth, and age; whether relatives or friends visited; and everything else I needed to know. Armed with that information, I could seek copies of the person's birth certificate and Social Insurance card (which works like our Social Security card), and with that I could fill out a passport application. Since the people I picked didn't have passports and probably never would, I found them easy to obtain. I just exercised caution and prudence and tried not worry too much about the ethics.

My cover employment, the clothing store, helped me apply for a Social Insurance card and I received it within a matter of days. My efforts to obtain the legitimate Canadian passports took a couple of months. To process the application by mail, I attached the photos provided by Langley, and once the passports arrived I sent them back to the office. I didn't know who used them or when or where. During this same time period, I received my own passport in my real name, good for five years. The CIA opened a numbered bank account under my *nom de guerre* of Gary Bryant at the Bank of Montreal. To retrieve funds from the account I only needed to present the correct combination of two different sets of numbers in the proper sequence. I never reported this additional income to the IRS or any other governmental agency. These laundered funds were charged to "ongoing field operational expenses" in some obscure area of the DDO at Langley.

To test out the identity-changing kit the Agency had given me, I sat down in my room in front of the mirror one evening and put on the black wig, adjusting it forward and back on my head until it seemed natural. I pasted on the matching fake mustache and horn-rimmed glasses and went out one evening to my favorite watering hole, the bar in the Hotel Savarin in downtown Toronto.

It offered a cosmopolitan atmosphere and a good opportunity to people watch. The bar staff usually recognized me and I wanted to see if my disguise would fool them. It worked! Nobody said "hello" using my name, although I thought, or imagined, that the disguise drew some unusual glances. The next time I returned to the bar without the benefit of the makeup kit, the staff once again offered greetings. Oddly, wearing the disguise made me feel more vulnerable and I thought it actually drew attention. I never used it a second time.

During one of my regular visits to the Cuban Consulate in Toronto, I finally received good news: the Cubans wanted me both for what I could do for them professionally and the publicity they could reap from my defection to Cuba. Mr. Hernández sat behind his desk talking about the weather to confuse any bugging devices while he handed me a letter from the Cuban Institute for Friendship Among Peoples (ICAP). They had arranged for a ship to take me from Montreal to Havana in mid October. The letter suggested I move to Montreal immediately and make the connections it outlined. Although I still had three months, the letter warned that sailing times could change and I needed to prepare for an earlier departure just in case.

I memorized the phone numbers, names, and addresses for contact in Montreal and returned the letter to Mr. Hernández. He then loudly announced, again for the benefit of any covert listening devices, that it looked like they could not offer me a visa to Cuba at this time.

I left the consulate with mixed feelings. It looked like the insertion plan had worked and my efforts had paid off, but this prospect of a new future frightened me. From Canada I could go home in a matter of hours with relative ease. But in Cuba, among enemies and far from support, I'd be on my own. Could I really do this? Might I screw up, get caught, face prison or a firing squad? I had no idea. I felt unprepared and scared.

However, I went ahead and planned my move to Montreal, packed my things, and arranged to meet with a DDO rep in New York State on my way to Montreal. We selected the small town of Malone in upstate New York, just south of the Canadian border and quite out of the way. We met in a coffee shop with high back booths that offered some privacy. Apparently the CIA used the town and the coffee shop frequently and had cleared it as a safe spot. During the brief meeting, my contact gave me a couple of possible apartment rental sites in Montreal. I knew that the Agency maintained a safe house in the city, but we decided that now, in the best interests of security, I should limit my contact with Agency personnel to the absolute minimum. We had created a "real," though completely fake, person ready for insertion into Cuba with a carefully fabricated past put together by some of the best and brightest working for the U.S. clandestine intelligence service, combining bits and pieces of operational techniques with new security efforts to increase the number of layers of protection I would have once on target and in country.

To personify my CIA handlers individually and collectively I created the name TIO, Spanish for uncle, one of the few words I remembered from my beginning Spanish class. To me TIO represented my own Uncle Sam; in this family everyone's life depended on the other. TIO normally assigned random names to its officers and agents operating in clandestine operations worldwide. The CIA assigned a two-letter identifier to each country in which they operated, which included almost every country in the world. Those protocols related to Cuba operations predetermined that any generated code name begin with the letters AM followed by a unique identity designator. They assigned me the code name of AMLOVE. Additionally, I received an undercover name as well as the code name: José Felipe Salamon. In communications being sent back and forth between myself and TIO, we could use either name in hopes the Cubans would think they were dealing with two different entities. The legend TIO had created for me seemed complex but also straightforward in a way. Anyone checking my past could find my work history, my educational history, my activities as an amateur rocketeer, and the St. Louis event all covered by the newspaper accounts. I appeared as an aerospace engineer opposed to the growing war in Vietnam and accused of being the author of an antiwar event in St. Louis. I possessed the skills the Cubans needed as well as the activist past that the Cubans would find sympathetic when they checked it out.

The CIA would pay me through deposits to a numbered account in the Bank of Montreal which only someone presenting the proper account number could access. Additionally, we selected a one dollar bill at random and the serial number of that bill served as the identifier of last resort. I memorized several of the numbers and letters on the bill. They then removed that dollar bill from circulation and its numbers remained connected to my name forever.

We once again discussed my role as a NOC, no official cover, the most difficult and dangerous position to have because it left one almost entirely on one's own. I would be operating in a country that was still engaged in a Cold War with the U.S. and where we didn't have a consulate, embassy, or other home base to run to if needed. This meant no source of money, no communications and no real safety. I could not identify myself to any foreigner operating on behalf of the U.S., nor could I send or receive any RYBAT cables with TIO. If discovered or caught, I would have to rely on my own resources. Sure, the U.S. would evince some concern for me as a citizen, but it would flatly deny any formal connection or commitment. Standard operating procedure called for leaving me on my own, and that public independence could save my life.

TIO ran other operations in Cuba separate from my duties. The other operatives didn't know me and I didn't know them. We hoped that my inability to speak Spanish would shield me from suspicion. What intelligence agency would ever send a NOC that didn't even speak the language? My contact assured me that I had plausible denial on my side. With my confidence somewhat renewed, he drove me back across the border and I caught a bus for Montreal.

I arrived in Montreal and located the house I had selected on West Sherbrooke Street. I rented an apartment on the second floor with a good panoramic view of the street intersection out front. The elderly couple who owned the house lived on the lower floor and seemed friendly enough. They spoke more French than English and apparently thought I came from Ontario. I didn't enlighten them. I stayed away from any Agency facility, just in case either the Cuban DGI or the RCMP had me under surveillance.

I waited a few days before showing up at the Cuban Consulate. They informed me that there were no new developments, but now they knew where to find me and I suggested checking in with them every couple of weeks or so just in case. With that settled, I ventured out to familiarize myself with the city.

Needing to find something to do while I waited on the Cubans, I applied for a temporary position with an engineering firm working for both the Canadian National Railway and Pratt and Whitney, the U.S. jet engine manufacturer. The Canadian National Railway built a high speed "TurboTrain" that ran on welded tracks between Toronto and Montreal. It ran on scheduled over-night trips between the two cities, but several engineering problems had arisen due to overheating on the roof of the combined engine/passenger car and the gear shifting mechanism connecting the P&W PT6 jet turbine engine with the drive chain.

I possessed some knowledge of the PT6 engine from my experience helping the Cessna Corporation in Wichita incorporate it into the T37 side-by-side jet trainer aircraft designed for the U.S. Air Force. The company hired me on the spot and I went to work in rented offices located in a bank building above the underground train station in Montreal. When the TurboTrain pulled into the underground station, the still-hot exhaust gases made the main floor of the bank fill with steam, leading to customer complaints. I threw myself into the two projects assigned to me, one to modify the airflow over the roof of the engine car and the second to modify the high-speed gear box that refused to shift properly on the fly.

I resolved the first problem by pop-riveting a series of small vertical spoilers to the roof. These broke up the laminar airflow over the top of the cab by making it a more turbulent flow that removed heated air from the surface. The second problem required the installation of a disc-brake style set on top of the gear box that would slow the rotational speed of the flywheel in order for the ratchet and pawl mechanism to function properly. The company incorporated both ideas into the overall design and the engineering firm offered me a full-time position that I had to decline.

I informed the Cubans that out of necessity I was working, but not where. I also told them that my job required some travel and that I might be out of touch from time to time. I did this just in case they were checking on me and couldn't locate me for several days.

The weeks went by quickly, and in early October I received a postcard from the Cubans that indicated I should make contact. When I did, they gave me the name of a commercial ship, identification and a prepaid one-way ticket to La Habana. The Mambesi Shipping Line ran the freighter that would sail out of Montreal, up the Saint Lawrence Seaway and then south towards the Caribbean. It might make a stop somewhere in the Bahamas and take six to eight days to reach Cuba. The ship featured a limited number of guest rooms, and the Cubans advised me to keep to myself as much as possible during the voyage. Apparently they didn't want me and the other guests bound for Cuba to get too chummy. I later found out that some members of the Black Panthers and The Weather Underground sailed on the same ship. This worried me because Canadian and U.S. intelligence agencies surveiled both groups, and that meant they might monitor them and also identify me. Not knowing where this intelligence might wind up or who would share it caused some degree of concern. I later found out that the Black Panthers were placed in a loading container and actually lowered into the hold of the ship, and then locked into their cabins until departure. Very secretive stuff.

I donned a hooded sweatshirt and sunglasses and boarded the vessel about two hours before departure. A steward showed me to my cabin and asked me to stay there until notified I could move about the ship. Later that evening the ship began moving, and another steward informed me I could follow him to the ship's mess room to get something to eat.

I spent the next few days roaming the ship and learning where they stowed things. I would pass by the other cabins trying to get a glimpse of the other passengers, and I tried to listen for any conversations going on in the cabins but without success. Some took meals in their cabins, while the rest of us ate in the mess room. After leaving the Seaway, we entered the North Atlantic and I encountered my first real ocean experience, cresting swells and waves that tossed and rolled the ship like a fishing bobber. My first bout of seasickness overwhelmed me and I spent two days in my cabin and the bathroom sipping tea and water.

Early one clear morning, just east of Miami and west of Andros Island, one of the Bahamian islands, I saw quite a few private yachts and sailboats making their way back and forth between Florida and the Bahamas. A seaman told me we would reach Cuba that evening. As we neared Havana harbor, we passed the USS *Oxford*, a cruiser that plied the waters just beyond Cuban territory and monitored all vessels entering and leaving Havana. The U.S. embargo, imposed years before by the Eisenhower and Kennedy Administrations, prohibited any merchant marine ship, regardless of nationality, that visited any Cuban port from entering a U.S. port for several years. The sun hung low in the western sky when the pilot boat pulled alongside and off-loaded the pilot who would take control of the ship and dock it at the Sierra Maestra Terminal in the Port of Havana. I caught my first real glimpse of the capital at night and immediately noticed the overall darkness of the city, with few cars on the road and low wattage light bulbs shining from unshuttered windows. I had arrived.

After an hour two, Cubans dressed in military fatigues summoned me to the gangway. One spoke passable English and introduced himself as Captain Pedro Fernández. The other greeted me in Spanish and took my luggage and headed for a Russian military Jeep parked a few yards away. We headed west along the famous Malecón seashore drive to a house located at the intersection of Fifth Avenue and 120th Street, quite a ways west of the city. Captain Fernández told me that I would stay at this house for a couple of days before moving into a hotel downtown. A couple of soldiers were staying at the house, one a cook and the other a jack-of-all-trades, both ordered, I knew, to watch my every move.

The house contained everything I needed as well as a stock of rum and Scotch and the Cuban brand of Coca-Cola called Son. The air conditioner didn't work very well during the day, but things cooled off at night so I could sleep. The soldiers invited me to play dominoes or watch TV with them every once in a while, and I accepted. I noticed several copies of the Cuban daily newspaper *Granma* lying on a table, and began to try to understand written Spanish as I could understand little of what the two soldiers said to me. The State Department crash course in conversational Spanish that I had taken proved worthless, though I did understand through signs and words that while I waited anxiously to move into town, my hosts just wanted me to relax.

8. Our Man in Havana

The sun shone brightly, bringing with it the kind of humidity unknown in Montreal. We drove east down Fifth Avenue through Miramar, a western suburb of Havana, a beautiful avenue with the east and westbound lanes divided by a center island that featured sidewalks, benches, trees and flowers. We drove past fabulous homes and mansions with manicured lawns. The driver told me they called it *la zona congelada*, the frozen zone, since mostly foreigners, diplomats, high ranking government officials and the remainders of Cuba's wealthy class lived there. Here Cuba's upper class lawyers, doctors, engineers, politicians and other professionals had abandoned their homes as they fled Castro's tightening grip on power in the early 1960s. They left thinking they would return in a few months when the U.S. overthrew Castro's revolution as it had removed so many previous governments it didn't like.

But eight years later neither the Bay of Pigs invasion on Cuba's southern shore in April 1961, nor the missile crisis of October 1962 or repeated attempts by the CIA to bring about Castro's downfall, had borne fruit. That explained my mission in Cuba. President Kennedy had signed an agreement stating that the U.S. would not invade Cuba if the Soviets removed their missiles; one of the very few treaties that the U.S. actually lived up to. My mission: to collect information and to destabilize the Cuban government by causing sufficient domestic unrest to spark a second revolution by the Cuban people to bring Castro down. To date, none of these schemes had worked. How could I, working alone, not two years removed from college graduation and a hastily trained novice spy, succeed?

We swung into the winding drive leading to the portico of the Hotel Nacional, on a promontory overlooking the sea. Here speedboats from the Florida Keys bringing Miami revelers escaping stateside Prohibition had once docked. Fred Astaire, Mickey Mantle, Cantinflas, Marlon Brando, Frank Sinatra, Ava Gardner and even Walt Disney had joined guests as diverse as Winston Churchill, Jean-Paul Sartre, Ernest Hemingway, Errol Flynn and Rita Hayworth to party through the years under the same roof. In December of 1946, 500 U.S.

Mafiosi, including Lucky Luciano and Meyer Lansky, had descended on the hotel for a mob summit, an event immortalized in "The Godfather," and divided the spoils of Cuba's lucrative gambling, drug and prostitution rackets. The past had left its scars on the building in the bullet holes that pockmarked the façade, leftovers from a 1933 rebellion that almost killed the United States Secretary of State, Sumner Welles, there to promote President Franklin Roosevelt's Good Neighbor Policy and make a deal with future dictator Fulgencio Batista.

I checked into the ornate hotel, instructed to charge everything I needed, and received the key to room 770. Could I, alone, somehow reverse 100 years of failed U.S. policy in Cuba? The driver told me to expect contact from Captain Fernández within a day or two. With that he left me on my own. I unpacked and set out to explore my surroundings.

The main entrance faced west. I walked out the east door into a garden area where posted signs prohibited entrance. Further examination revealed two four-barrel anti-aircraft guns with their crews dug into the hillside just north and east of the hotel. Another sign prohibited the taking of photographs. The main floor contained the front desk, a souvenir stand, a post office desk,

This was taken in 1969 in the Hotel Nacional. I am sitting in the downstairs bar having a drink and a conversation with a mulatta girl. The photograph is framed and hanging in the bar even today. The bartender says it is of an Americano, the only one living in the hotel in 1969: me.

and stairways that led down to the restaurant and bar or up to the barber shop and Turkish bath. I discovered that several of the staff spoke good English and all seemed eager to serve.

I found a Western Union desk in the lobby and sent a telegram to my family back in Iowa. November had arrived and yet I hadn't contacted home for a number of months. I knew the telegram would set several events in motion. The FBI would immediately take notice of my new location, probably much to their consternation. They would pass that information on to the U.S. Marshals Service which, in turn, would wonder what the hell they were going to do now. Additionally, since the CIA monitored my communication links, they would know that I had entered Cuba alive and eager to get to work. They expected no further contact from me until I was situated at either the University of Havana or the Cuban Academy of Sciences, the two institutions which showed the greatest interest in having me join them. With the telegram on its way I stepped downstairs to watch the jeweled and feathered dancing girls at the hotel's Club Parisien.

After several days of taking ever longer walking tours of Vedado, the section of Havana around the hotel, I found a message left for me at the front desk promising to pick me up the following morning, no specific time mentioned. I already knew that time and punctuality as I had learned them in the States did not apply down here. The next morning I came down early, sat in the ornate lobby and waited.

Just before noon two men in military drab approached the front desk and asked for me. The man behind the desk pointed them to me. The tall one introduced himself as Amado Fernández and the shorter one as Eliseo Gonzales. Both worked for the Cuban Academy of Sciences. They planned to take me to meet with Captain Rafael Castro San Román, director of the Atmospheric Physics Institute of the Academy. First, however, they wanted to stop at the cafeteria for coffee, my introduction to a custom observed on all occasions in Cuba.

After our coffee break, which consisted of the thick dark sweet liquid that comprised Cuban coffee and some biscuits, we left the hotel in another Soviet-made Jeep and headed east toward the port area. We followed the Malecón to the junction of the Prado, a stately avenue running from the Havana harbor entrance to the replica of the U.S. Capitol building located several blocks away, which once served as the seat of government but now headquartered the Cuban Academy of Sciences as well as a museum located in the basement. We climbed the broad marble steps to the front doors and entered the rotunda. In front stood a large bronze statue covered in gold leaf that represented the Lady of the Republic. They showed me a glass-covered diamond (a replica) imbedded in the floor and informed me that they measured all distances in Cuba from this stone. We continued down a hallway to an impressive door that opened into a waiting room.

Soon a portly middle-aged man emerged, also dressed in crisp military fatigues, who greeted me on very good English with a smile and a firm handshake. He introduced himself as Captain San Román and ushered me into the large adjoining office. Sitting behind a massive wooden desk was a slighter built individual dressed in military garb as well. He stood up and introduced himself as Comandante Antonio Nuñez-Jiménez, President of the Academy. We all sat down and both he and Captain San Román welcomed me into the institution and outlined their plans for my work.

Apparently the Cuban Ministry of Foreign Affairs (MINREX) and the Cuban Institute for Amistad Between Peoples (ICAP) had worked together to match my skills to Cuba's needs and asked me to join either the faculty at the University of Havana or the Academy of Sciences. The Academy won out.

They placed me under a modified "foreign technician" contract for three years, renewable at the end of the term upon mutual agreement. They wanted me to work with the Atmospheric Physics Institute of the Academy, supervised by Captain San Román. They would appoint me officially as Technical Director of the Institute. I would continue to live at the Hotel Nacional with all expenses paid by the Academy. They would find me an office in the building where we were meeting and give me another office at the Institute's research station, located about 30 miles southeast of Havana near the small village of Cuatro Caminos, as well as a driver and Jeep to get me back and forth. If I encountered any difficulties I needed only to inform Lt. Amado Fernández. Additionally, I would receive a salary in Cuban pesos, with 10 percent of that in the foreign currency of my choice.

San Román told me I would work directly with Cuban employees of the Institute as well as with Soviet technicians already there. We would collaborate with the Meteorological Institute located on a hilltop across Havana Harbor. They charged me with using all the resources I could muster to help the Institute develop a cost effective, sustainable and reliable method to seed clouds to increase the rainfall over the island during the dry season. Fidel Castro himself had assigned this task to the Academy and the Institute in an effort to double crop production. They told me that Castro would personally check on this high priority project's progress at unannounced times.

I sat in shock at the offer. TIO couldn't have planned it any better. The Comandante shook my hand as San Román and I left his office, and he addressed me in English, wishing me great success and saying his door would always be open. San Román drove me back to the hotel and during the trip told me that Antonio worked as a speleologist, a person who explores caves, as well as an anthropologist, having received a doctorate from the University of Havana in the 1950s as well as another from a school in Moscow. He had also fought alongside Ernesto "Ché" Guevara during the Cuban Revolution in 1959. Obviously, he sat well placed within the hierarchy of the Cuban power circle.

When we arrived at the hotel, I invited Captain San Román to dinner and he accepted. Over some Cuba libres and wine, he told me his story. A family member, a cousin or brother, had been killed during the Revolution near the southern Cuban city of Cienfuegos, at a time when San Román was working in Miami as a route distributor for the Miami *Herald*. For a time he had also flown as a pilot for the Bacardi Rum Company. This accounted for his command of English. Currently he served as the Director of the Atmospheric Physics Institute and Director of Security for Cuban Airlines (Cubana de Aviación). He continued to fly one of the few remaining twin engine Cessnas on the island. I told him of my love of flying and he promised to take me along when he logged flight time to remain current.

He also explained how they had worked hard to develop a program to seed clouds, so that when MINREX approached him about me, he had jumped at the chance to hire me. He went on to tell me that Castro had ordered the construction of small ponds and retention basins around the island to store rainwater runoff. At each of the retention ponds, the Cubans had installed Dorman diesel engines from England and Wright-Rain pumps as well as aluminum irrigation tubing. If they could irrigate the land during the dry season, it would allow for two or more harvests of vegetables, fruits, and other plants. However, they didn't have a way of delivering the reactive agent to the freezing level of the clouds to induce the ice to turn to water droplets and return to earth as rain. They had tried a very expensive method of burning hundreds of gallons of diesel fuel in upright burners that produced an oily black cloud that rapidly rose into the sky to the clouds. The smoke contained small unburned particles of carbon that acted as building blocks for drops of water to form. Once enough droplets combined to produce a rain drop, conceivably it would rain. A French engineer had invented this apparatus, which he called the "metronome." It cost a lot of money to operate and never produced a rain cloud through a couple dozen attempts. The Frenchman had left the island and the device now sat useless.

After a while, the conversation turned more personal and San Román asked me why I came to Cuba and how someone with my background and profession could fall out of favor with my own government. He told me that most North Americans in Cuba had hijacked aircraft to Cuba claiming to be revolutionaries, though he found them, for the most part, to be criminals or mentally unbalanced. The Cubans finally sent all of them either to prison or to work farms in the countryside and allowed them into Havana once a month for a weekend if they behaved themselves. In Havana they stayed at a rundown hotel in Habana Viejo (Old Havana) where the Cubans kept them under surveillance.

I shared with him the legend TIO and I had painstakingly prepared. I told him that I had joined the antiwar protests going on across the U.S. on college and university campuses, the very protests I had spied on, and that the government had tied me to the bombing in St. Louis. I had lost my security clearance and my job, and I feared prison time for the bombing. I decided to offer my services to other nations in need of a peace-loving engineer, and Cuba seemed like a good spot. I think he'd heard this several times before, but never directly from me. He seemed satisfied and told me that I would begin work the next week. Another new adventure awaited, making me apprehensive but also elated.

The Academy of Sciences, founded centuries before by the Spanish King as the Royal Academy of Sciences, occupied the old Capitol building. In the 1920s the Cuban dictator Machado, himself overthrown by Batista in the revolt that left those bullet holes in the walls of the Nacional, had built the Capitol building, El Capitolino, modeled after the U.S. Capitol in D.C. though on a smaller scale. After the Castro Revolution it no longer served as the seat of government, and I found myself in an office once occupied by a Senator. It had a window looking out to the north, but the air conditioner had stopped working long ago. Nearby stood more offices and meeting rooms.

The basement floor contained a small museum that housed the remains of a U.S. U-2 recon aircraft that the Cubans had downed during the missile crisis in October 1962. The pilot had died in the crash and his body had remained in a Havana morgue for quite some time before being returned to the States. San Román arranged a tour of this display for me.

The Meteorological Institute sat on a hill in Regla next door to the famous Moro Castle built by the Spanish to guard the entrance to Havana Harbor. There were small ferry boats that took people back and forth across the harbor between our offices in Old Havana and Regla.

I had yet another office in a modified farm house on confiscated land about one hour southeast of Havana. We would leave Havana on the old central highway and go past the spot where Ernest Hemingway's house, Finca Vigía, stood, now a well preserved museum. Just off the main highway the Institute used a farmhouse and several outbuildings. In one of these, a large barn-type structure, I outfitted a machine shop and installed a boiler and mixing tank and a test area. The Institute assigned a select group of engineering students from the University of Havana, as well as some Cuban military people from the

While in Cuba I spent many days at the beaches and would watch storms come in from the sea. I was always impressed by the movement of palm trees and waves, and how the birds would react. I tried to capture that view in this painting I later did in prison.

Cuban Air Force, to work with me and told me I could visit nearby machine shops to find skilled machinists who could manufacture any parts I might need.

An Institute bus carried workers to and from Havana every day. Things rarely ran smoothly; sometimes the bus never showed up due to mechanical problems, and often we received no explanation and no advance warning. Getting to work became an adventure.

I outfitted an office in the main administration building at the farm and set out a plan for inseminating the clouds using a variety of methods. I knew the Cubans had no cash, so I needed to incorporate whatever we could scrounge. This presented new challenges every day. My plans included airborne balloons, reusable rockets, modified anti-aircraft shells and special aircraft. We needed to design these devices, have prototypes constructed and tested, and produce results before any mass production began. In addition, everything would necessitate widespread coordination with other sectors of the Cuban economy. I needed chemicals, raw materials, transportation, permits, access to X-ray machines—the list went on and on.

We ate a noon meal each day at the farm and a snack as well. Since most workers saw little to eat at home, they made quick work of lunch. We saw little meat but lots of rice and beans and usually a soup made of the previous day's leftovers. Because I had access to food that the workers did not, I would often bring things like coffee and bread to the farm to share. A few citrus trees on the farm provided treats like grapefruit, oranges, and avocados. We got by but struggled to make scientific progress.

9. Red Square

The year 1969 brought with it quite a few surprises and a lifting of my spirits. I saw Fidel Castro in his world, mesmerizing his audience while delivering his New Year's and Tenth Anniversary speech in the huge Plaza of the Revolution downtown. I could see why this man would cause Washington headaches in other Central and South American countries. He had a charisma that I'd never experienced before. I saw how his narrative gripped the millions in the Plaza: these people, heroic Cubans, one and all, stood up to the great capitalistic and imperialistic giant just 90 miles to the north. Like David taking on Goliath, by his leadership and their will and sacrifices Castro would prevail. Here stood my enemy at the podium, while throughout the square, shouting slogans and carrying signs, millions vowed support. The scenario for my activities seemed set. Maybe I could play at Goliath's David as well.

I had settled into my room at the Nacional, I could see my Spanish improving with each passing day, and the Cubans in the Academy of Sciences had begun to accept me more openly. Some of the Soviet advisors working with me started to invite me to their homes and parties. I cultivated these associations. However, in order to play my part well, I resolved not to limit my relations with the Cubans as many of the Russians did.

Captain Antonio Nuñez Jiménez, the President of the Academy, and Captain Rafael Castro San Román, vice president and director of the Atmospheric Physics Institute, my direct boss, had outlined our objectives and promised all of the materials and help that I needed. I developed delivery systems capable of carrying ice crystal producing nuclei to the freezing layer of the clouds that drifted over Cuba during the dry season. To do the work I received all of the documents necessary to transport and work with explosives; I was the only American since the triumph of the Revolution to have such permission. This treatment by the Cubans affected the Soviets, and they felt more secure in their relations with me. I got to know Kamile Jarulin, who was in charge of all the Soviet advisers in the Academy. He suggested I accompany him to the Soviet Embassy to meet people from their foreign affairs department. They came up with the idea that it might benefit all concerned if I visited the Academy of Sciences in the USSR where they did similar work. I consulted with the Cubans, who told me that the Cuban and Soviet Academies would pay all of my expenses. I could already see myself visiting Red Square and the Kremlin, meeting and making contacts with Soviet scientists.

The upcoming trip posed problems, however. Because I had not yet established my communication link with my CIA Chief of Station, I couldn't let TIO know about the trip until after I returned. I also worried about having to make the trip alone. To my delight, Vladimir Zaharov, a Soviet technician working with me in the Institute, would accompany me. My flight would leave Havana for Algiers, then go on to Prague, Berlin, and finally Moscow.

With Vladimir Zaharof (rear) of the Soviet Academy of Sciences. He and I were good friends and drank many a bottle of vodka together.

The Air Cubana flight passed uneventfully except for an incident during the brief stop in Algiers. We had about an hour's layover there and everyone got off the plane. I saw most of the Soviets leave the plane and run toward the terminal building. Out of curiosity I followed them inside and stood in amazement as they lined up at an old vending machine. They purchased every bottle of Coca Cola it held. They even asked an attendant there to sell them the warm bottles in storage. Apparently you could not find Coke in Moscow, and they grabbed this chance to get something from the decadent West. I watched them beaming as they carried their treasure back aboard the plane.

We landed in Moscow late in the evening, and a Soviet Academy of Sciences car and a friend of Vladimir's met us to take us to a hotel near the airport for the night. After breakfast, we transferred to a hotel near Red Square where we would stay for the next few days. The agenda consisted of several meetings with Academy officials to establish working relationships, learn about their work, and cadge necessary supplies.

I learned that they used a modified version of an anti-aircraft missile to shoot chemical reactives to the freezing level of clouds and that they might offer some of them to their counterparts in Cuba. However, the Central Committee of the Party hadn't yet decided to let the missiles go for fear of triggering a new "October Crisis." They did offer me potassium chlorate and perchlorate that I needed to manufacture my version of a rocket fuel developed at Caltech during World War II. We could heat and mix the chemicals with asphalt and oil and then pour the mixture into the rocket casing to cool and harden. I immediately ordered 300 pounds of the white powder.

I also took time for sightseeing and a visit to Red Square, where we went to Lenin's Tomb. They ushered us in ahead of a few hundred people standing in line to view the body. It didn't take long. We went up some narrow stairs, made a couple of turns and then we stood looking down at the face of Vladimir Ilyich Lenin, dead for 45 years. Guards stood at attention around his glass sarcophagus. Lenin seemed asleep, his body perfectly preserved. We could see only the flesh of his head with a light shining on him, but he looked alive. Then they rushed us out, down the stairs and back outside. The whole thing lasted but a few minutes.

The rest of the week we toured around Moscow and met with more Academy scientists and others whom I could not identify. I imagined the Soviets mixed their own intelligence officers into the group as well. At night we went out on the town, and on one particular evening as we walked near Red Square, two men came up to me and asked me if I would consider being their "third!" I entirely misunderstood the question and was preparing to take a swing at these perverts until my translator explained that they wanted to know if I would join them in purchasing a bottle of vodka in the local store. The law only allowed a party of three people to purchase a bottle, and they wanted me to be the third. Once I understood their need, I agreed. As my visit to Moscow came to an end, I made sure that I kept notes on everyone I met, who they worked for, and the kind of help they offered. Since TIO didn't even know about this Moscow trip, I resolved, once back in Cuba, to make transferring this information my number one priority. I returned to Havana on a weekend, so I spent the next couple of days encoding a telegram to send back home. I kept the text simple and innocent looking. Only the CIA would know it meant the time had come to make my first contact.

The procedure seemed straightforward. TIO instructed me to monitor the old U.S. Embassy building along the Malecón and near the site of the memorial to the battleship USS *Maine*, destroyed at anchor in 1898. The Swiss government, some of whose officials acted on our behalf, now occupied the former embassy. I waited for a red shoebox to appear in the east window on the fifth floor. If someone left it there for two days and then removed it, that signaled me to go to the embassy.

Having seen the shoebox, I made the excuse that I needed to go to the U.S. Interest Section to find out why my mail hadn't arrived from the States. That didn't seem to raise any suspicions. When I arrived at the Interest Section and showed my U.S. credentials, they ushered me into the main floor waiting area and told me to have a seat. After a few minutes, a receptionist asked me to follow her into an elevator which whisked us to the fifth floor, where I entered the spacious office of Mr. Heine, a Swiss national who welcomed me warmly. He offered me some Cuban-style coffee and told me that he had received instructions to give me an envelope containing information that I needed to read in his office. I could not take the papers out of his sight. While I don't think he knew who I really worked for or what my role in Cuba was, he must have assumed that the U.S. government and I had some sort of special relationship.

I read over the papers and tried to commit to memory every detail. They included instructions on how to begin sending information back to Langley, whom to contact in an emergency in the British and Canadian Embassies, how to notify TIO if I needed to make contact or if I noticed surveillance, and all the other things that would facilitate communications and keep me alive. It astonished me to see how very alone I stood. TIO seemed to have few other assets on the island.

After assimilating the information, I handed the package of papers back to Mr. Heine, who placed them in a safe. We talked about a number of things and how to best acclimatize myself to life in Cuba. He also told me that whenever

I felt the need to see him, or if I needed help from the Interest Section, I could count on him. With that they ushered me back to the lobby. I left the building feeling some relief, having made contact and obtained the information I needed to begin my mission. It seemed simple enough: establish myself in my position, assess my co-workers (both Cuban and foreign), feel them out on their political ideas, determine if they could become a source of useful info, determine how to approach them if necessary, look for dead drop locations, and so on. First and foremost I needed to get comfortable in my surroundings and then establish priorities.

My work in the Institute intensified. Some of the University of Havana engineering students, enthused about the project, encouraged the rapid installation of the machining equipment that I required: a metal lathe, drill presses, welder, cutting torch, wrenches, screwdrivers, everything I could get hold of. I also visited some of the local sugarcane refineries nearby. They had X-ray machines that I could use to take X-rays of fueled rocket casings to see if dangerous air bubbles remained in the dried and hardened fuel charge. Because I was making so many trips out to the farm, Antonio Nuñez-Jiménez decided I needed my own transport, as the Institute's driver and vehicles had many other things to do. He ordered San Román to take me to the underground car lot in the center of Havana. Here they stored autos and trucks confiscated from Cubans leaving the island to distribute to Cuban government and military officials who demonstrated enough clout to get one. Of all the cars available, I selected a 1960 MG hardtop with a four-cylinder engine, dual carbs, wire spoke wheels, and only two leather seats. It needed some work, so we sent it to the large VW shop in Havana for repairs.

It seemed like forever before I received the call that the car was ready. One problem: only three of the brakes worked, and they didn't have parts to repair the fourth. I accepted the car anyway. With my own transportation available 24 hours a day, I could come and go as I pleased, and while regular Cuban citizens who owned cars got only eight gallons of gasoline a month, I could go to the Academy's pump near my Havana office any day of the week and fill up without limit. The guard at the portal of the Hotel Nacional where I lived told me he would keep his eye on the car when he saw it in the lot and that he knew a kid who would wash it every day for a few pesos. He also informed me that he saw girls who noticed my coming and going from the hotel parking lot and when they could, they would leave notes on the car with their phone numbers. I began driving the car to and from the farm instead of taking the Institute's bus. The Soviet technicians noticed it at once and they began to complain to Captain San Román. I don't know how he explained the situation to them, but no one ever complained directly to me.

A British national working for a U.N. program worked on a dairy farm not far from the farm housing my lab. One day he showed up seeking to borrow a tool and noticed me. After he learned that I spoke English, we really hit it off. He and his wife lived near the public zoo in Havana and enjoyed what social life foreigners could find or create. He invited me over for dinner, and there I met the British Ambassador, a couple of Embassy employees and a couple of Swedes. I began to develop a good social relationship with these people who could provide invaluable help, information and connections.

Out of this meeting came an invitation to attend the Tuesday night movies held at the old American Club located on the Prado in old Havana. The Club, located in a multi-story building, featured a gymnasium on the top floor and a bar on the ground floor as well as a large meeting room, a restaurant, and other facilities. Every Tuesday a diplomatic flight would arrive from Nassau in the Bahamas with the diplomatic pouches for several Western embassies. It also brought a new movie reel that they would show that same night in the Club. Most Western embassy employees and their wives attended, and the conversations

At a party in my home in Havana, I (white shirt at right) am lighting the cake's candle. At far right in a dark suit coat is a Cuban guest. At center in sunglasses is a British/Irish embassy official. Behind him drinking a bottle of beer is Kamile Jarulin, the KGB officer assigned to the Cuban Academy of Sciences.

included news of all sorts of happenings on the island, a wealth of free information for me. Most all of them asked, at one time or another, what an American engineer was doing in Cuba. I just told them that the Castro government had offered me a contract and that the U.S. State Department had not blocked my accepting it. I don't know if they believed the story or not, but it seemed to end the direct inquiries. They even offered me the use of the diplomatic mail to send an occasional letter or two. Thoughtful … and useful.

I now possessed my "foreign technician's ID card," which allowed me to shop in several exclusive stores for everything from food to deodorant, clothing, boots, rum, and cigars. Cubans manufactured most of these, but they were of higher quality than similar products available in the regular Cuban stores. I also received an ID card that identified me as equal to a foreign diplomat, giving me access to three retail outlets that sold goods exclusively for foreign currencies like the U.S. dollar, the British pound sterling, and the French franc. In these outlets I found items like tape recorders, whiskey, packaged coffee, perfume, and Rolex watches, items unavailable to the average Cuban. I stocked my hotel room with all sorts of goodies that I could barter for favors. Life seemed good.

The hotel also housed several Spanish-Soviet families, working as translators in many of the Cuban offices and factories in the provinces. These Spaniards had left Spain after the Civil War in the 1930s and settled in the Soviet Union. When Cuba and the Soviet Union cozied up, the Soviets enlisted these native Spanish speakers to go to Cuba on two-year contracts as translators. They would notice me eating alone in the dining room every night and probably overheard my struggle to order dinner in Spanish, so they would come to my aid. I would befriend them later in the bar with drinks, or invite them up to have a scotch or two in my room. Since they worked in a variety of places with all kinds of people, they provided me with a wealth of information for many years.

I also noticed some Americans showing up in the hotel lobby sometimes asking for handouts like cigarettes and spare change. One day I encountered a rather disheveled young man trying to get a room. He didn't seem to have enough money to pay for it, though. I motioned him aside and asked him if he came from the States. He said yes and that he wanted to go home. I took him to the cafeteria, bought some coffee and snacks, and offered to listen. He told me he had hijacked a plane to come to Cuba. He also told me that the Cubans housed him and several more hijackers at an old run-down hotel in Old Havana called the Nueva Isla. The Cubans drove them into the countryside during the week to work in the fields. If they worked hard during the week, the Cubans gave them a few pesos and let them out of their hotel on the weekends to have whatever fun they could. He explained that the Cubans imprisoned most of the hijackers upon arrival and closely investigated them before allowing them any freedom of movement or outside contacts. The hijackers, he said, came from Mexico, Puerto Rico, and Jamaica, but the majority came from the U.S. He had already lived in Cuba for several months, hadn't found it the haven he had expected, and wanted to go home. However, he lacked travel documents and the U.S. authorities wanted him for some crimes that he had committed before fleeing the States. Now they also wanted him for hijacking. He seemed despondent to say the least, and, perhaps because of my own homesickness, my heart went out to him.

Though it certainly didn't appear on my list of objectives from the CIA, I decided to help him. I spoke to the hotel manager and told him that I would pay for a room and a couple of meals over the next 24 hours. This took some talking, but he finally agreed. I told the young man that he could probably use the phone in the room to call back to the U.S. and assure his family he hoped to come home. I also arranged to have a beer with him and then grab a bite to eat after. He agreed and went up to his room. I headed for the bar.

I knew the bartender, born in Cuba of Syrian immigrants, who had worked at the hotel for many years. He spoke good English, so I often stopped to talk with him. He talked about the "old times" when the hotel guests consisted of a few wealthy Cubans and many U.S. citizens on vacation. He made the best Cuba libres and daiquiris I've ever tasted. While we were talking we suddenly heard a loud "thud" on the roof of the bar. We rushed outside to find hotel security already on the scene taking photographs of a body sprawled on the roof. I immediately recognized the young American I'd just gotten a room for on one of the upper floors. I could only guess that he used the phone to call the States and the conversation didn't go well. I questioned my own role in this tragedy. What if we hadn't met? What if I hadn't gotten him a room? It all made me very sad.

For the next few days I could only contemplate how this young man must have felt, and I began to wonder about the other U.S. hijackers staying at that old hotel. I decided to contact a few of them and offer some assistance when and where I could. I mentioned what had happened to my boss in the Institute, but he advised me not to get involved, as the Cubans kept the hijackers under surveillance and considered them undesirables. I took his advice initially, but over the next few years I did make contact with several of the hijackers for a variety of reasons. I never recruited any of them as informants. I just wanted to assess the Cuban government's changing attitudes towards them and, since the Cubans required most of them to work in the fields, I picked their brains for what they saw and heard in the countryside. Oddly, TIO never seemed interested in them. I guessed the FBI would, since some of the hijackers made their Ten Most Wanted list, but I didn't work for the Keystone Cops, as we in the CIA called the G-Men.

During that year TIO wanted background information on various Cuban diplomats who might also be spies and on other Cubans who had defected to the U.S., to determine their bona fides. Could the defector be trusted, or be unmasked as a double agent only pretending to defect? Langley didn't understand how I struggled to obtain any background information on such people. The Cuban government certainly didn't publicize the identities of defectors or spies.

The U.S. denied entry visas to two Cuban diplomats accredited to the Cuban U.N. Mission in New York, Mr. Zenni and Mr. Escobar, when they tried to re-enter the U.S. after returning to Cuba for instructions. The U.S. suspected the two of assisting the Black Panthers in traveling to Cuba to receive training and political guidance and then encouraging them to return to the U.S. to put the lessons into practice. The U.S. warned the Cuban U.N. Mission of this violation and barred the two diplomats.

Later that same year, the U.S. expelled a Mr. Bonet, the Third Secretary of the Cuban U.N. Mission, on the same charges. But this proved more difficult. Bonet worked in conjunction with a man named Alberto Boza Hidalgo Gato, the First Secretary to the Cuban Mission. The Cubans had already recalled Hidalgo Gato, and he did not seek to return to the U.S. In both cases TIO asked me to provide additional information on these men, but this proved an insurmountable task with my low level contacts. It did indicate, however, that Cuban Intelligence in the Ministry of the Interior had infiltrated the Cuban Ministry of Foreign Affairs to an extent not seen before. This didn't just happen on the Cuban side, however. The CIA placed intelligence officers within the Department of State for many years, sometimes under an agreement with State but many times clandestinely. Normally, they would give a CIA officer the title of Fourth Secretary of some unknown department within the Embassy as a cover, but they were easily spotted because they flashed way too much cash, drove the best cars, and had access to the Embassy's closely guarded "cable room."

Once again that year, the U.S. warned the Cubans that they would expel one of its U.N. diplomats, a Mr. Vega, if he continued his prohibited activities. The Cuban Mission sits close to the U.N. building itself on East 66th Street in New York. Lots of dissident groups and wackos came and went from the Mission, and exiled Cubans living in the U.S. attacked it from time to time. The Mission also harbored a stockpile of weapons sufficient to start a small war. In fact, late in 1994 the Cuban Foreign Minister, Raúl Roa, pulled a sidearm in the U.N. during a heated discussion with a U.N. representative from Chile.

Then, in October, a Cuban military pilot, Lt. G. Jiménez, defected in spectacular fashion. An instructor in the Cuban Air Force, he had taken off on a routine training flight when he decided to take himself and his Soviet MIG-17 to the U.S. By the time the Cubans or the Americans realized what had happened, Jiménez had landed at Homestead Air Force Base in Florida. The radar operators in south Florida hadn't seen him coming because the U.S. had started to phase out defensive sweeps of the Florida Straits. They had placed Cuba on the back burner as far as military threats, and nobody expected to have foreign aircraft entering U.S. airspace. The U.S. offered Jiménez asylum and returned the MIG to Cuba. TIO tasked me with providing background information on Jiménez.

At this time a goodly number of U.S. citizens visited Cuba without State Department permission. One group of about 90 Americans from the Venceremos Brigade arrived to help with the annual sugarcane harvest. They arrived in two separate groups, one from Mexico and one from Canada. TIO already knew most of them, but asked me to make casual contact to determine if any of the brigade members might harbor additional agendas in Cuba. The Castro government kept them busy in the sugarcane fields and moved them around the countryside, so I found it difficult to make and maintain contact with them. I did manage to meet with some of them, who expressed solidarity with the Cuban Revolution and surprise that the living conditions they observed in Cuba looked much better than the news reports had shown back in the U.S. They didn't understand that the Cubans used their presence for propaganda purposes and that they enjoyed better conditions than the Cubans laboring in the fields.

Soon another group of individuals arrived in Cuba: a group of 13 political prisoners from Brazil and Uruguay, liberated in exchange for the release of the U.S. ambassador to Brazil, Charles Elbrick, who had been taken hostage for four days in September 1969 by MR8, a left wing group. The 13 flew to Mexico City and then to Cuba, where people welcomed them as heroes at the airport while they expressed their thanks for the support of the Cuban government. They all stated their desire to return home at some point to continue carrying out their brand of revolution. TIO asked me to keep tabs on some of the 13, but Castro spread them out across the island, which made this extremely difficult. Obviously Castro had plans for them; that was the price they paid for asylum in Cuba.

In spite of all difficulties I did score an information coup one evening at a party at one of the foreign embassies. Castro had planned a diplomatic first: to open an embassy in the jungles of Viet Nam to showcase his support for the Viet Cong as the only legitimate government in South Viet Nam. Apparently the Cuban ambassador, a Mr. Valdez, would open an embassy in either a tent or bamboo hut for publicity purposes and invite the world press. I got the word to TIO before the Cubans publicly announced it.

I also learned from social chitchat with a Bulgarian technician, who had designed the forms, that the Cuban government planned to conduct a census in 1970. TIO wanted the raw data before they manipulated it for political purposes and assigned me to obtain it.

A Marine by the name of Dostlik, from the Guantánamo base in eastern Cuba, defected. He wanted political asylum, but even the Cubans didn't know if they wanted him. He had a reputation as a troublemaker, and the defection seemed a spur of the moment decision based on drinking too much and his fear of facing a reprimand. I tried to follow up on this. Other cases cropped up at Guantánamo. Every once in a while, several Marines would get outside the wall to smoke marijuana. I guess they got so high that they didn't realize they had left a U.S. base and entered Cuban territory without the permission of either country. The Cubans detained and interrogated them for political and publicity purposes and then sent them back, having drawn attention to the fact that the U.S., having beaten the Spanish in Cuba in 1898 and signed a 99-year lease with the new Cuban government in 1903, refused to give the land back.

Two Cuban youths tried to stow away in the nose wheel cavity of a Spanish airliner leaving Havana's airport on a flight to Madrid. On takeoff one fell to his death, but the other hung on and somehow survived the flight to Spain. They found him almost frozen to death and granted him asylum. I got involved when the kid, Armando Socarrs Ramirez, later asked for asylum in the U.S. TIO needed background and asked me if they could they trust his story. I begged off because, in my book, the kid had already lived through a terrible ordeal and deserved asylum.

One day I got a call that an Englishman who represented a company selling diesel motors to the Cubans wanted to talk. We had gotten to know each other at the American Club during those Tuesday night movies. At the time he was dating a Cuban girl whom I would frequently see in the lobby and bar of the Hotel Nacional. I obtained her name from someone and got her vetted. TIO informed me that they suspected her of working for Cuban G2 (counterintelligence).

She had helped trap and convict some Cuban counter-revolutionaries a few years earlier in the province of Pinar del Rio and held the rank of captain. She must have expressed some doubts about her future in Cuba to the Englishman, and that led him to me. When we met for a drink, we took off in his station wagon and drove east of Havana to the beach known as Santa María, where we sipped Scotch. He told me that he had contacts with MI6, the British intelligence agency, and that they had warned him about the Cuban girl. He said that her single girlfriend wanted to meet a foreigner, me. He asked if I would go on some double dates with him and his girlfriend and see what I thought. I couldn't understand why he had brought this to me, and it made me nervous. Either he suspected me of working in intelligence, in which case I had blown my cover, or his girlfriend's girlfriend really had an interest in me. I agreed to play along. When I informed TIO about the proposal, they gave me the background information on the Cuban girlfriend as well on the Englishman. It turned out that he worked for MI6 as an agent or a contracted information source. TIO advised me to continue the relationship and see if it proved useful.

TIO also told me they had a new asset now in place in Havana, the cultural secretary of the Mexican Embassy, Humberto Carrillo Colón, code named José María Zaloo, and that I could use him as another source for communications. He served in Mexico's Foreign Ministry and worked with another Mexican diplomat called Sandoval who had previously worked at the airport in Mexico City, where he screened all passengers departing for Cuba. In Mexico City officials herded all passengers in transit to or from Cuba into a large room at the airport, where the Mexicans photographed them and then gave the passenger manifest and photos to our Agency staff in Mexico City. The system didn't always work, however. In 1965, Ernesto "Che" Guevara slipped through undetected with an altered appearance and a false passport. He traveled on to Bolivia in an attempt to start a new Cuban-style revolution in South America. Most of the people that I worked with thought Cuba was too small an island to allow both Fidel and Che to work together. Che seemed more popular than Fidel, and we believed the Castro brothers had decided that Che had to go. Che's attempts to put together a rebel band in the mountainous terrain did not receive Cuban help, and his effort faltered. Finally Bolivian troops trained by U.S. Special Forces ambushed his guerrillas at Vado del Yeso in October 1967, and then, in the presence of at least one CIA officer, Félix Rodríguez, executed the wounded Che at La Higuera.

This all connected when I met an Argentine married to a Cuban. He knew another Argentine, a friend and confidant of Che, and had come to Cuba to see the Revolution first hand. He fell in love, married, and, finding himself disillusioned with the Revolution, wanted to leave with his wife. The government would let him leave, but not his wife. I suggested that he try to get into the Mexican Embassy and ask for help, though I knew this was no easy project. The Mexicans gave asylum to just about anybody asking for it, one just needed to get into their embassy, but Cuban security kept watch outside the walls of the compound 24 hours a day with orders to shoot anyone trying to slip past.

I mentioned this situation to Humberto Carrillo, who offered to help. He would leave the embassy grounds in an official car, drive to a pre-arranged spot, let the Argentine climb in, and drive back to the embassy grounds with the Argentine lying on the car floor. It worked, and once in the embassy, the Argentine received asylum and the Mexican ambassador asked the Cuban government to let the wife join him. Castro refused, and after several weeks of waiting in vain, the Argentine tried sneaking out of the embassy one night by climbing over the wall. The Cubans caught him, and I never learned what happened to him or his wife.

My one-year anniversary in Cuba approached. Taking stock of my situation, I felt that I had made great progress in most areas. I had established communication links with Langley and made valuable contacts, not only with Cuban nationals but also with a wide variety of foreigners as well. I detected no surveillance out of the ordinary, and I faced only a couple of years left on my contract with the Cuban Academy of Sciences. Whether any of the information I sent to the States meant anything I didn't know, but at least it showed that I actively pursued information. However, I had no news about events back home or about the situation in St. Louis. They had told me it would take time, but I wanted a resolution. My family had indicated that the FBI continued snooping, trying to find out what I was doing in Cuba and for whom. TIO kept them in the dark. This boded well for me, because if Cuban Intelligence continued to do background checks on me, they would find nothing new. My legend would continue to hold up.

In late October, a group of five Cuban mercenaries landed on the northern coast in the province of Camaguey. The army rounded them up in a matter of hours, along with weapons that the Agency had acquired in Viet Nam. Cuban newspapers reported their interrogation and execution by firing squad. Incidents like this always left me on edge, because I knew that TIO supplied and directed most of these mercenary groups. What if they carried information on how to make contact with other of TIO's assets on the island, even someone like me? Reports like this reminded me of the constant dangers I faced.

The Associated Press had rented an office across the street from the Nacional. The authorized AP correspondent, John Wheeler, would often spend time in the bar in my hotel. I became friends with him and with James Pringle, the correspondent from Reuters. Conversations with them usually turned up good bits and pieces of information that I could use, and one day I heard about a group of Black Panthers who had come down from New York. Could they have sailed on the same ship with me? Both Pringle and Wheeler met with the group without official permission, and for this the Cubans ordered their expulsion in retaliation. I would sorely miss their companionship and the information they provided. Wheeler asked to do a story on me when he got back to the States, but I begged him not to. Thankfully, he never did.

Before he left, Wheeler suggested I make contact with a Canadian couple living in the Hotel Capri just steps west from my hotel. Bill and his wife, Ana Devine, worked for Radio Havana Cuba assisting with their English language translations and broadcasts. I got to know them and they proved useful in providing insights about how the government manipulated the news broadcasts to the Cuban people and to the world. I really wanted to use them more, but they returned to Canada in early 1970 and I lost track of them.

A Czech couple also lived in my hotel, serving as instructors to the Cuban national water polo team. They would often swim in one of the pools located on hotel property, and since I liked to swim, I often joined them. The Soviets living in the hotel would not use the pool if the Czechs got there first for one simple reason: in early 1968, the Prague Spring excited the world with the uprising against Soviet domination. After bloody street battles, the resistance lost. This couple hated the Soviets and did not socialize with them. They spoke some English and very good Spanish, so we enjoyed casual conversations and I could tell they wondered about the only American in the hotel. They politely

My 1973 VW Bug, purchased from the Swedish Embassy in Havana. I needed it to replace the MG that the Academy of Sciences had given me, as I couldn't acquire spare parts.

inquired about me, but I always managed to sidestep personal questions. As time went by, they opened up more and more to me about the conditions back home in Czechoslovakia. Once again, I found myself using friendships to add to my database to forward to TIO. I felt more and more disgusted with myself for doing this. I often wondered if I could even have a friendship without the ulterior motive of gleaning information for TIO.

As the year came to a close, I noticed a power struggle developing between the Cuban Ministries of the Interior and Foreign Affairs. It came to a head over a plane hijacked from Mexico to Cuba by a group of self-proclaimed followers of China's Mao Tse-Tung. Mexico and Cuba maintained an agreement to return hijackers. The Ministry of Foreign Affairs wanted to live up to the agreement and return the group to Mexico, but the Ministry of the Interior wanted them to stay. During this battle of wills, the Mexican government sent several strongly worded notes to Cuba demanding their return. The Cubans allowed the hijackers to stay, so Mexico broke off commercial relations on a temporary basis. Humberto Carrillo at the Mexican Embassy kept me well informed on this issue, among others.

The end of the year and its related holidays arrived, but I noticed a lack of the home decorations and festivities normally associated with Christmas and New Year's. Cubans celebrated a tradition of eating 12 grapes at midnight on New Year's Eve, but no one could find any grapes in Cuba that year due to shortages. If people celebrated the holidays, I didn't see much of it. They did it at home and in private. Anyone caught venturing into the countryside to bring home a small Christmas tree faced severe punishment.

10. A Double Life

On New Year's Day 1970, I saw Castro pump new spirit into a tired populace. Before a mass of humanity in the Plaza de la Revolución, he announced the country's goal of producing 10 million metric tons of sugar in a year to last 18 months. He told his audience that it would require hard work, additional belt tightening, and more sacrifice with fewer consumer goods. He told them the continued efforts would go on for three to four more years. In spite of this bad news, the crowd cheered and yelled "Ordene!" which translated to "Order us." He mesmerized them and he mesmerized me that day.

My projects at the Institute succeeded. Prototypes of my reusable rockets performed well, and we made plans to build a few production models. The Institute put a military helicopter at my disposal to inspect possible launch sites. With it, we flew over most of the province of Havana looking at different places. I took lots of photographs, which found their way back to TIO.

A Puerto Rican friend was divorcing his Russian wife. His roving eye had gotten him in trouble, and he could not remain faithful. The three of us had become friends, as we lived in the same hotel, so we often ate meals together and made trips to the beaches east of Havana. He worked as a machinist and I convinced the director of the machine shop to loan him to me for a year. I put him in charge of overseeing the manufacture of parts for the rockets we built. He spoke both excellent Spanish and English. His Russian wife spoke perfect Spanish and worked in the Soviet Embassy as a translator. She had family members connected to the Soviet MVD (military intelligence). One night during dinner she asked me for a favor. She wanted to know if I knew anybody in the U.S. government who would help her get to the States. She didn't want to go home and face the shame of a ruined marriage and a lost career. I didn't know quite what to say. Did her handlers ordered her to set a trap for me, or did she really need help from a friend? I told her that I would try, but that with my limited contacts I could not guarantee anything. She seemed satisfied with that. I passed the request on to TIO, but they showed no interest in her. Some months later, she returned to the Soviet Union and an unknown fate.

A new journalist arrived from the Canadian Broadcasting Corporation (CBC) in Toronto. He lodged at the Hotel Deville along the Malecón without equipment, transportation or connections. A number of foreigners lodged at the Deville, which housed a store with items for sale in U.S. dollars only. For both reasons I tried to visit the hotel each week to find out who was staying there and where they came from. I met the Canadian that way and befriended him. I took him around Havana in my MG to show him the sights. I also spoke to him about the Russian woman who wanted to go to the West. He promised to talk with his employer back in Canada, but nothing came of it. One evening as we sat on the seawall across from his hotel, a city bus, empty of passengers, raced by headed east with two police cars in hot pursuit. He asked me what was happening and I speculated that someone had commandeered the bus to steal the change from the coin box and perhaps to steal the diesel fuel as well, but something must have gone wrong. The next day, a newspaper article confirmed my suspicions.

As my Spanish fluency had improved considerably, Castro San Román asked me if I could teach an engineering class at the University of Havana twice a week. I agreed, as I had already attended classes there to brush up on meteorology and atmospheric physics. I found this additional role very useful in meeting a variety of students as well as student leaders in the FEU (Federation of University Students). This group, controlled by the Communist Party, served as the official voice of the students on campus. Attending some of their meetings as an invited guest allowed me to gain a better understanding of the direction of education in Cuba and the type of ideology pushed on them. Students had little access to printed literature, especially from the West. Much of their material consisted of Xeroxed copies of articles and texts copied or purchased in Mexico, usually of poor quality. The University of Havana always saw intense political activity. Castro had studied there himself and done a lot of his initial recruiting from the student body. In the 1970s his political lieutenants still kept an eye on things. A dozen engineering students attended the classes I taught in structures, propulsion systems, electronics, aerodynamics, and math. I found them eager to learn, and I did my best in Spanish. A few had learned English in high school and the first few years of college, so they helped me out quite a bit.

Panic attack! Another infiltration on the north coast. But this time several managed to escape and made it inland. When Cuban troops surprised and captured them, they didn't have time to destroy some of the documents they carried. More bad news: an urgent message from TIO informed me that the captured papers might have compromised Humberto Carrillo, our man in the Mexican Embassy. Carrillo lived in a house located at the intersection of Fifth Avenue and Tenth Street in Miramar. There he had strung up a 50-foot-long wire antenna from the roof to his outdoor patio to broadcast his reports and information to our listening post in the Florida Keys. Carrillo would code the reports into numbers and letters and then group them into sets of five figures. He verbally recorded the coded sets onto a magnetic tape and at a predetermined time and date would transmit the messages at a very high speed to the listening post in the Keys. Anyone lucky enough to be listening in at the right time and on the proper frequency would hear only a high pitched squeal as a ten-minute message got sent out in a "screech" lasting only a few seconds. We didn't know that Cuban counterintelligence listened in and recorded all of his transmissions. They later managed to break some of his codes and thus read them without Carrillo having a clue. Then they moved in and arrested him.

The Mexican Embassy protested and claimed diplomatic immunity. The Cubans released him and the Mexicans quickly shipped him home. An enraged Castro sent his Foreign Minister, Raúl Roa, to Mexico to seek his extradition back to Cuba. However, relations between the two countries had deteriorated over the previous year's hijacking, when Cuba had refused to send the hijackers back to Mexico. Now Mexico refused to extradite Carrillo. I didn't know how much material had fallen into the Cubans' hands, or what Carrillo had accumulated about me and others. My heart raced for days on end, alert to any changes in routine, any unknown cars following me on the street, any unfamiliar faces in my classes. I expected the Cubans to raid the hotel or my office and detain me at any moment.

Things got worse. The Cubans accused the U.S. of infiltrating the Mexican Ministry of Foreign Affairs and demanded answers. TIO assured me that the U.S. would never acknowledge anything and neither would the Mexicans. I still lost a lot of sleep over that incident, though.

Then one day a Hungarian political refugee came to see me out of the blue. He had initially fled after the Soviet invasion of 1956. Granted asylum in the U.S., he turned to a life of crime, got caught, and served time at San Quentin. Somehow he had managed to flee to Florida, where he stole a shrimp boat and sailed to Cuba. He married a Cuban girl and worked in the fields for some time. Rather than living in the Hotel Nueva Isla with the others, he and his wife shared a cramped apartment. He had heard about my assistance to some of the other hijackers and wanted money. He'd been getting by selling what he could steal from foreigners.

"See, man, I got this funny looking radio. I got it out of a Jeep offloaded down at the harbor. The Jeep had a Soviet general's flag attached to it," he said.

"Well, I might need a radio for my car," I told him. "I could let you have $20 for it." He quickly accepted.

"I got something else too." We sat in my room with the door closed.

"O.K., what's that?"

"See, I'm sitting in the Havana Libre one day. An Eastern European guy, looks like a diplomat, comes in with a briefcase handcuffed to his wrist. I see him ready to check in, uncuff the briefcase and wedge it into a couch where he sat. While he fills out forms at the front desk, I take the briefcase."

"I'd like to see that."

He brought it to me and we opened it with a knife, only to find inside a paper in a foreign language neither of us could decipher, but which looked like a list. I gave him another $20. When TIO saw the radio later, he valued its intelligence as worth a small fortune, but translated the paper as a list of things the diplomat's wife had instructed him to buy while in Cuba. Funny how things just seem to fall from the sky sometimes. The Cubans later arrested the Hungarian and deported him on a ship literally bound for Shanghai. There the Cuban crew forced him ashore, but the Chinese put him back aboard for a return trip to Cuba. I never found out his ultimate fate.

Harry Reed, an Australian political cartoonist, called it quits. He had worked under contract for *Granma*, the official newspaper of the Cuban Communist Party, but he divorced his Russian wife and got fired from his job. He wanted to sell me his Soviet motorcycle and sidecar. I turned him down, as I couldn't get parts for it. Before leaving Cuba for Mexico, he introduced me to an American journalist by the name of Lionel Martin, who had strong leftist tendencies. Martin had claimed his 15 minutes of international fame several years earlier when he became the only American to interview Captain Lloyd Bucher in North Korea. Bucher was the captain of the spy ship USS *Pueblo* when the North Koreans seized it and its crew and held them for nearly a year. Apparently at one point during the interview, Bucher struck Martin in the face after Martin insulted him. I didn't get along well with Martin, but he had close connections to upper government echelons, including Castro. I flattered his huge ego, bought us a lot of Scotch whiskey, and milked him for all I could get.

My boss at the Institute, Castro San Ramón, who also headed security at Cubana de Aviación, informed me one day that Cuba would purchase a couple of Soviet-built IL-62 passenger aircraft, paid for with nickel ore mined in eastern Cuba, site of one of the largest deposits of nickel in the world. The Cubans would have to divert the money from other domestic purchases. Castro San Román who had once worked for the Miami *Herald* and for Bacardi Rum in Miami, enjoyed talking to me about the good old times when he lived in the States. He also told me that on all Cubana flights, both domestic and international, an armed guard sat just outside the cockpit door to eliminate hijackings. He told me of several hijacking attempts that the Cubans had kept secret. He wanted to impress me with his insider information. I reciprocated by spending a lot of time at his house to hear more.

The Castro brothers numbered three in all: Fidel, my real boss, since he had instructed Antonio Jiménez and Castro San Román to hire me for the Academy; his younger brother Raúl, who headed the Army; and Ramón, the oldest, who stayed out of politics and headed a dairy farm that I visited a couple of times. Ramón, who looked just like Fidel but a lot heavier, never involved himself in politics. He was then negotiating the purchase of milking equipment for his farm from a Swedish firm called Alfa Laval. The Swedish chargé d'affaires in Cuba, a friend of mine, filled me in on all of the details. Since it added up to a multi-million-dollar deal, I knew this would pique TIO's interest. I got the feeling that this Swedish diplomat nursed suspicions about my clandestine activities in Cuba, though he never came right out and said so. He told me that if I ever needed assistance, I should go to any Swedish legation in the world and have them contact him for me. I appreciated what seemed a sincere offer. I never quizzed TIO about this, but I should have.

The Cubans also made a deal with Leyland Motors. The British firm sold something like 100 buses to Cuba along with spare parts, and the deal included a few mechanics to make sure the Cubans did proper maintenance and repair work. I got to know a few of these technicians and learned the weak spots on this model of bus; this knowledge later proved useful in sabotage attempts. To bring down the Castro brothers the U.S. resorted to economic warfare, fomenting internal strife and sabotage. We aimed to sabotage transportation systems, the electric grid, the food supply, anything that might make the life of average Cubans impossible and move them to take Castro down themselves.

TIO assigned me another secondary task: to try to find the family members of Cubans who had defected to the U.S. from other countries, infiltrated dissident Cuban groups in the States, and then returned to Cuba with that information. Some of those false defectors had information so important that they couldn't wait to get it back to Cuba, and they ended up hijacking planes in several cases.

We also looked at ways to control the amount of food coming into Havana for distribution to the public. If we could puncture tires on a truck loaded with tomatoes for the market, or if we could cause a truckload of whatever (onions, fresh fruit, meat) to become putrid or stolen or contaminated on the way into town, we would do that. In one instance, I remember a brand new secondary school had opened in the countryside. We knew when they would receive their week's supply of fresh milk. We bribed the driver of the truck. We knew where he stopped to have breakfast on his route, and simply paid him to step away from the truck for a few extra minutes and turn a blind eye to what happened next. We bought sacks of powdered cement mix and a dissident, vetted and paid by TIO, climbed on top of the truck and dumped the powder into the tank. We never learned the effects of our sabotage in this case, but I could imagine lots of kids getting sick as a result. How low had we fallen? It made me sick too. We couldn't win hearts and minds by waging war on school children. Most adults went without milk so that the children who went to school could have it, and we were doing this! I voiced my opposition to TIO, but to no avail.

TIO informed me that in March, one of our people had delivered a vial of African swine flu virus to one of the many anti–Castro groups still operating under CIA auspices. They took the vial to Navassa, an uninhabited island between Haiti and Jamaica, used before by the CIA and anti–Castro groups. They then smuggled the virus into Cuba, and less than three months later the island suffered from the first-ever outbreak of swine flu in the Western Hemisphere. The Cubans slaughtered 500,000 pigs to try to stop the epidemic, causing severe food shortages across the island as pork serves as a staple of the Cuban diet. Even the United Nations Food and Agricultural Organization, alarmed that the virus could spread to other countries, sent representatives to look for the cause of the outbreak. The U.S. never told them how it happened.

A penetration project I had begun the previous year started to pay off. The CNIC (National Center for Scientific Investigation) stored results of the most important scientific work on the island. CNIC finally gave our Institute permission to use its electron microscope to examine small particles taken from air samples. With everything in flux due to construction at the Center, they stored everything in cardboard boxes, and as we ran back and forth between the microscope and the library I found it easy to rummage through the files, gathering a wealth of information on which countries supplied what material for what dollar amount, as well as the goals of the experiments. I thought of it as another example of seizing the moment and taking advantage of a rare opportunity.

The Cubans began a massive roundup of "vagrant youth" in Havana, afraid that kids as young as 14 were falling under the influence of Western culture in their style of dress and tastes in music, as well as turning to locally grown marijuana. These young wannabe hippies hung out all over town, and the young girls would turn tricks for a pair of pantyhose or a tube of lipstick. A small bottle of perfume cost a small fortune in foreign currency. The young Cubans could buy, but didn't want, "Midnight in Moscow," a perfume imported from the Soviet Union and available for pesos. Many foreigners living and working in Cuba found this black market very appealing. Castro planted a few of his spies among the youth in order to trap the unsuspecting foreigners. Once identified and caught, the foreigner had a choice: cease activity in the black market or catch the next plane home. A chill blew through the community of foreigners on the island.

I traveled to the southern port city of Cienfuegos to check out information I had received about suspicious construction taking place there. We knew the Cubans planned a new fertilizer plant at the port, but the construction didn't seem related to that plant, so I decided to check it out. I reserved a room in the Hotel Jagua with a good view of the harbor and some of the surroundings. I could see the field they had leveled, which looked like a football field back home. Later that night I went over to the field, and seeing no guards on site I quickly stepped off the length and width and jotted these down. The size of the area and the absence of footings or post holes stumped me. I returned to Havana puzzling over what I had seen. One night at the American Club for the weekly movie, I was talking to an Englishman and somehow the subject turned to sports. During the conversation we discussed the similarities between a soccer field and an American football field. In that moment I realized what I had seen in Cienfuegos: a soccer field. But the Cubans didn't play soccer! The Russians did.

I looked into it further and discovered that indeed the Cubans planned to load and offload Soviet bloc ships at the Cienfuegos port. I reported my find to TIO, and some months later U.S. Secretary of State Henry Kissinger announced that reliable sources confirmed that the Soviets were building a naval base for their atomic powered submarines at that coastal city of Cuba. He completely changed the facts of my report. I knew that governments sometimes manipulated raw intelligence to fit preconceived ideas, but this proved it! They twisted my little intelligence coup into an international war of words, as the Soviets denied the U.S. accusations, increasing tensions and mistrust between the two superpowers. Heated discussions between Moscow and Washington played out in the papers and then, somehow, simply disappeared from the news.

The Soviet spy ship named after their cosmonaut Yuri Gagarin arrived in Havana, ostensibly on a "friendship" visit, but really to position itself off the east coast of Florida to monitor our upcoming Apollo moon shot. They invited the Soviet technicians at the Academy of Sciences to send a delegation aboard to observe the operation, and I got invited as well. I think they were responding to the successful U.S. landing on the moon the summer before and wanted to impress the Cubans with their electronic sophistication. A few days later we sailed out of Havana Harbor to take up station off Cape Canaveral. The ship was sailing in international waters, so the U.S. Coast Guard could do little but shadow it. We observed the launch and returned to base. I noted in my report to TIO that all of the antennas on board the ship swung about actively during the launch, recording all of the radio and telemetry being transmitted on liftoff. The ultra modern ship bristled with electronic communication gear. I felt very privileged to have sailed on this mission and considered it another coup for TIO. The same ship returned from time to time to Cuba, but they didn't invite me on board again.

Soon after this, hostility flared in the Florida Straits when the U.S. Coast Guard captured five Cuban fisherman for violating territorial waters and threw them in jail in Key West. The U.S. demanded an apology from Castro. Instead, he flew into a rage and called for public demonstrations around the old U.S. embassy on the Malecón not far from my hotel. About 200,000 people showed up and stayed there for two days and two nights. Castro allowed people to take time off from their work centers in order to keep the crowd huge. Cuban security guards escorted the Swiss diplomats who staffed the embassy to and from the building. The crowd broke windows and painted anti–American slogans on the walls. The whole incident blew over when the U.S. released the fisherman and their boat after a few days. When I visited the embassy a couple of weeks later, staffers told me that they had removed all secret files, including mine, every day that the demonstration took place.

Castro paid a fine to get his fishermen back, but he recouped the money, with interest, by charging huge landing and service fees for all hijacked U.S. planes after that. He would keep the hijacked planes overnight, bus all of the passengers to a hotel and feed them dinner and breakfast, and then demand to be paid before releasing the plane, passengers and crew. Castro won this part of the constant war.

TIO notified me that a British diplomatic mail pouch that was sent each Wednesday from Havana to Nassau in the Bahamas had arrived open. Nobody knew if someone purposely opened it or carelessly left it unlocked in Havana. Could the Cuban security forces have examined the contents? If they had, they'd discovered nothing on me because I hadn't sent anything that particular week, but the incident served as a warning of how vulnerable this form of communication made us and sent more chills up my spine.

Some time later, TIO told me they had received a request for contact from a janitor who worked for JUCEPLAN, the central planning center for the Communist Party. They wanted me to do some background checking on him before responding. Missions like this made me nervous. I didn't have enough people working for me or access to this kind of information. It would entail wandering around neighborhoods I had no business in and talking to people I didn't know. Castro had created the Committees for the Defense of the Revolution (CDR), and they worked on every block in the city as the eyes and ears of the Interior Ministry. A resident CDR manager lived on each block and knew everybody who lived there, where they worked, where the kids went to school, and so on. Any stranger on the block, especially a foreigner like me, immediately raised suspicions. I hated those assignments and avoided them whenever possible. I feared TIO wasn't protecting me as they should.

The CIA station chief in Mexico City, Jim Noland, sent word through TIO that he wanted more information on the supply of people and arms flowing from Cuba to the new leftist government in Chile. The Chileans had elected the socialist Salvador Allende to the presidency, and this had spooked the Chilean military. Castro responded by sending security agents to the country, as well as arms hidden in shipments of sugar. It upset me that Noland might know about my operation in Cuba, because he employed a few loose-lipped people there and they could easily compromise me and my mission. He might have learned about all this when Humberto Carillo had returned to Mexico after the Cubans ousted him. President Allende had made several private trips to Cuba before being elected and had solicited offers of support from Castro, and now he wanted Castro to make good on them. In response, I spent more time sneaking down to the port to determine the contents of crates being loaded onto ships bound for Chile.

Meanwhile, as if I didn't have enough to do, the time to test the production model of my rocket arrived. We needed to change the instrument package for a chemical payload for treating the clouds at the freezing level, as well as a parachute to return it in good shape to earth. My boss Castro San Román enlisted help from the Cuban Air Force. They offered some used parachutes that could be modified to meet the size and weight requirements I needed. I went to a base called San Antonio de los Baños to spell out my requirements and meet the people making the chutes. I visited one of the caves where TIO thought Castro had stashed away some Soviet rockets after the October Crisis of 1962 for some future use, but I never saw any evidence of this. Security there rivaled U.S. security at Fort Knox.

San Román dropped by my office one day with a problem. The U.N. was sponsoring an international conference on weather modification in Washington, D.C. Castro desperately wanted to go, and he ranted and raved about the dumb Americans and their embargoes. I wanted to inform TIO about these plans, but before I could, Castro scuttled the idea and that ended that. In a similar incident in New Orleans, Castro sent a plane with some sugar cane experts to an international conference and the U.S. denied them entry.

I got a message from TIO that Francisco Caamaño, a former general in the Army of the Dominican Republic, had popped up in Havana seeking support for a Cuban-style invasion on the eastern half of the island of Hispanola. The U.S. had ousted Caamaño with a full-scale invasion in 1965 following a

The test firing of the MARV rocket engine at the Atmospheric Physics research facility southeast of Havana. This was one of several aboveground test firings that took place before we actually fired rockets into the clouds.

failed coup attempt and had reestablished the democratically elected president, Juan Bosch. I tried to monitor Caamaño's comings and goings, but failed to gather much intel. In the winter of 1973, a few weeks into his invasion attempt, the forces of Joaquín Balaguer, who had faithfully served the long time dictator Rafael Trujillo and now ruled with U.S. support, wounded, captured, and summarily executed Caamaño, much in the style of Che's earlier fate.

A new English-speaking employee showed up at the Institute, always both an opportunity and a worry. Could I pump the person for information, or did the person's assignment include unmasking me? Miranda served as a merchant marine captain grounded because of circulation problems in his legs. He spoke good English and we hit it off immediately. He knew the ports of Cuba like the back of his hand. He talked nonstop and I made use of his knowledge of the Cuban Navy over many a beer or rum and coke. He also knew about the number of Cubans who had tried and failed to leave the island on small homemade boats. The large numbers surprised me. Apparently when caught they received prison sentences of up to six years.

The Institute farm just didn't have the instruments or materials I needed to refine the GALCIT fuel (invented by the Guggenheim Aero Lab of the California Institute of Technology during the World War II). I had planned for the rocket. The U.S. used this fuel mixture in Jet-Assisted Take Off rocket boosters, but I had only inferior materials available to me in Cuba. The Institute had arranged for us to perform experiments in the main match production facility in the western part of Havana. In the testing room on the second floor, we installed several double-walled mixing machines, tiled counter tops, and fire suppressing equipment, all separated from the production floor by glass observation windows. During one of our experiments, one of my engineering students took his eyes off the mixture being prepared in one of the aluminum mixing machines and it caught fire. The several pounds of rocket fuel burned with a fierce intensity, sending a pillar of flame into the air. It reached the ceiling and spread out like a lotus leaf. The testing room filled with toxic smoke and heat, causing the six or seven people in the room to begin coughing and screaming. I quickly opened the door and yelled for everyone to escape as quickly as possible. The dozens of women working on the production floor one story below began to yell as well, and everybody headed for the exits, even the security guards. We called the local fire department, awaiting their arrival while standing outside watching the thick black smoke pour out of the building's windows. The sprinkler system, much to my amazement, flared into action. The few pounds of fuel burned very quickly and soon petered out. The aluminum mixing pot melted down into a blob of aluminum, and the floor tiles under it all popped loose and cracked. The ceiling, though blackened, seemed

An Atmospheric Physics Institute machinist (right) and I stand next to a burned out MARV rocket engine after test firing. The test took place at the Institute's research center located southeast of Havana.

relatively undamaged. The walls just showed some smoke residue. It reminded me of similar disasters with smaller rockets at my home in Iowa.

The fire department and the local police showed up and began to question everyone about what had transpired. I stepped forward with one of my students and tried to explain. The police took notes, looked at my credentials, and told me to present myself at the local police office the next day with my supervisor. This looked bad. A North American shut down the production of matches under mysterious circumstances. I needed to talk to Captain Castro San Ramón. We all returned to the Academy headquarters in Old Havana and went directly to see him.

He questioned all of us, but the student explained what had happened and took responsibility for the accident. Most of Havana never learned what had happened, only that there had been a fire at the match factory and that production had resumed. Cuban State Security people visited me three more times over the next couple of weeks, but apparently I satisfied their suspicions. This whole episode could have exposed me, and it took time for me to feel secure once again.

Through a friend I met a Cuban girl who worked at the hotel where I lived. She only knew me as an American employed at the Cuban Academy of Sciences, where some of her friends worked as well. I never told her about my work for TIO until much later. Petite and beautiful, she spoke little English and was studying French. Divorced from a military officer, and the mother of a son, she at first seemed uncertain whether she wanted to know me or not, as relations with anything U.S., including me, could pose a risk. Her family, part of the upper middle class before the Revolution, still maintained good political connections in the government. I'm certain that her family members who could have me "checked out" did so. I must have passed muster, as she and I began dating and I included her in many of my activities such as receptions, trips, Academy events, and get-togethers with foreigners. We took many trips to the fabulous beaches along Cuba's northern coast and frequented the best restaurants and nightclubs in Havana. She filled an aching void in my life, and as the relationship progressed over the next year and a half we decided to get married.

We planned to marry in late October, and I sent word back to the States to my family about my plans, even though I knew none of them could make it to the wedding. Many influential members of the Academy, as well as foreign and Cuban coworkers, attended the nuptials. Back at the Nacional they gave me a much larger room with a small balcony at the front of the building. I informed TIO of my intentions to get married, of course, and they wanted to know all about my fiancée and her family, why I hadn't notified them earlier, and so on. I hesitated for some time, knowing that getting married to a foreigner in a hot target like Cuba where the U.S. lacked an official presence would really complicate matters. It would also tend to raise eyebrows back at Langley. They couldn't be sure that this new relationship wouldn't compromise me, either by making me more vulnerable to discovery or weakening my resolve to complete my mission.

I answered all of TIO's questions and noted that one of my wife's uncles served as a member of the Central Committee of the Communist Party in charge of internal consumption and probably met with Castro on a regular basis. As far as I knew, he harbored no qualms about me getting married to his niece. The Cubans I worked with certainly didn't seem to object; in fact, they enthusiastically supported the marriage.

TIO got back to me, encouraging me in the strongest terms to get out of the marriage. They told me they could not promise that, when I left Cuba when my contract ended in a couple of years, they would assist me in getting my wife off the island. I saw red! I certainly didn't need anyone telling me whether I could get married or not, and I angrily sent that message to TIO. I could understand TIO's stance to a point, but their refusal to help me get my family off the island just didn't hold water. My relationship with the Agency seemed to worsen each day. TIO did respond at a later date suggesting that maybe, just maybe, something could be done if I recruited my wife to gain access to Party information via her uncle. I couldn't do that and jeopardize her safety, so I reassured TIO that neither she nor anybody else would know of my CIA connection.

TIO gave me the silent treatment in response. I contemplated quitting once again, but I knew that would cause several devastating chain reactions. TIO could abandon any plans and promises they had made to extricate me from the St. Louis incident, they could refuse help when I left Cuba, they could freeze my pay, which was locked up in an account in a bank in Canada, they could refuse to renew my passport, and a host of other things. I tried to plan very carefully, but deep in my heart I knew my relationship with TIO had no future. I had developed many friends in Cuba and these friendships seemed real and sincere. I no longer viewed these people as enemies, as TIO had described them before this whole mess began. I continued to collect intelligence and information as before, but started dragging my feet, delaying sending it off as long as I could to avoid harming the Cubans. To TIO I cited communication issues, money problems, and any other factors that might seem like legitimate excuses.

A Cuban military jet crashed in Santa Clara, east of Havana. The pilot, Major Despaigne, lost control on a training mission, crashed, and died. I guessed that the defective state of the Soviet aircraft he was flying had contributed to the crash, since the Air Force had run out of spare parts; Cuba was running out of money. The 10 million metric ton sugar cane harvest that Castro had announced came up short, and I knew some important heads would roll. First the Sugar Minister, Padrón, got the boot and Lage Cuello replaced him, only to fall himself at a later date. The axe next fell on the Minister of Education, Llanusa, blamed for not drumming up enough student support for the harvest. It seemed the students wanted to go to class instead of taking long breaks to cut sugar cane. Castro replaced him with an ex-military pal, Belarmino Castilla Más, known as a man with an iron hand, and he quickly took control of the education system. The Minister of Interior Commerce, Luzado, fell next, replaced by another military man named Fernández. Castro made a habit of replacing anyone he felt was not producing at a 110 percent level with old military buddies he knew he could control. But while military people can take orders, that doesn't always mean that they can, or will, produce. Putting former military people in supposedly civilian jobs allowed Castro to surround himself with cronies and puppets. In his rage about the failed harvest, Castro fired a fourth minister, the head of the Merchant Marine, and a new military head, one Major Chaveco Hernández, took over. My friend Miranda knew this man well and confided in me that Chaveco could easily be bought. I'm not certain why he told me that, except that perhaps Miranda wanted to impress me with his knowledge of the man. I never did approach Chaveco.

Our efforts to seed the clouds over Cuba and produce additional rainfall seemed to work extremely well, but only in isolated cases. At the Institute we just scratched our heads over the results. Later I learned TIO knew why. While I conducted operations to seed the clouds forming to the northwest of the island, the CIA used technology provided by the China Lake Naval Weapons Center in California to seed the same clouds a few hours later. This excess seeding caused some torrential rains in parts of the island and destroyed crops and cost several lives. This floored me when I found out. As an engineer, I wanted my efforts to succeed and produce rain when Cuba needed it. It meant a job well done in my profession and could lead to future advancement. At the same time, I knew TIO expected me to delay, disrupt, and sabotage my own project to hurt Cuba. These two conflicting goals tore me apart and gave me many sleepless nights. I felt almost schizophrenic. I drank too much. I smoked too much. With my nerves on edge it took every bit of self-control to try to conceal my anxieties.

An earthquake in the mountains of Peru caused both a lot of damage there and a huge problem for me. Cuba and Peru did not have diplomatic relations, but Cuba joined in an international effort to aid the citizens of Peru affected by the disaster. Cuba didn't have much to offer in the material sense, but they

At the Atmospheric Physics production and test facility southeast of Havana. I am kneeling and smiling after a successful test firing of the MARV rocket engine. University of Havana science and engineering students gather around the test pad.

did hold a special blood drive, added some military blankets and a few medical teams, and sent them to Lima. The Institute pitched in and I helped prepare the materials being sent. Peru sent a liaison officer to help with the logistics, and I worked with him to prepare the planeload of supplies. He and I hit if off right away and he told me to get in touch with him if I ever visited Peru. I promised to do so, never realizing how much I would someday need his help.

Not long after that Peru and Cuba re-established diplomatic relations. Because the Academy of Sciences had played a large role in providing aid, Castro named Comandante Antonio Nuñez-Jiménez as the new ambassador to Peru. That set off a power struggle within the Academy to see who would replace Antonio and jeopardized my own status. My contract would end in a few months and I hadn't made any progress in getting my family off the island. I started to get very nervous. This year had raised a great many changes and challenges for me and strained my relationship with TIO. I didn't know what to do or how to do it. I dreaded the new year just around the corner.

11. Dirty Tricks

Along with the development of re-useable rockets and specialized anti-aircraft shells, the president of the Academy of Sciences, Comandante Jose Antonio Nuñez Jiménez, wanted a balloon-borne platform to carry weather instruments to predetermined altitudes and remain stationary for lengthy periods of time. He asked me to develop a prototype using available materials and personnel.

The Academy and the Institute (IFA) had access to lots of cylinders of hydrogen from the state's welding and hospital supplies consortium. We also obtained rolls of black polyethylene of various thicknesses. I needed a heat sealer, and the Academy bought me one in Canada. When all of the materials were in place, I designed a dirigible that measured about 2.5 meters in diameter and 5 meters long. To it I attached three vertical and inflatable tail fins for stability. I added a 300-meter nylon rope at one end and a hand-operated winch at the other. Joking around, I grabbed some white paint at the last moment and painted a shark's mouth, full of teeth, on the balloon's nose. Now to try it out.

I chose an almost windless morning. We gathered at the Institute's vacant lot and filled the sack about three quarters full with pure hydrogen. Vladimir slung an aluminum radar reflector about one meter below the blimp and we slowly uncranked the winch. The balloon rose slowly in the air and began to expand as the surrounding air pressure dropped. When it reached an estimated altitude of 800 feet, however, the nylon tether broke. The balloon took off and spiraled ever upward. When it reached about 4,500 feet, the prevailing winds grabbed it and blew it to the southeast. We jumped in the Jeep and gave chase.

We soon lost sight of it, but continued in the same general direction with one eye on the sky and one on the road. When we came to a small village, we stopped and used a telephone to let the authorities know about the runaway balloon lest we cause an international incident. When we found the phone, we also found the headmaster of the local school using it to call CDR headquarters and tell them about the thing that had fallen from the sky into the school courtyard. He told them that some students saw the thing falling and described it as a black demon with sharp teeth. It landed in the school courtyard and, still containing hydrogen gas, it lurched left and right with every gust of wind. The school gardener, a campesino, heard the children yelling, so he grabbed his pitchfork and attacked the demon, repeatedly stabbing at it until it deflated and lay limp on the ground.

The students had all run out of their classes, and when we arrived we found them gathered around the dead demon. Simultaneously, a Jeep carrying two military officials arrived. The lieutenant began asking questions while his driver took pictures. I stepped forward to offer an explanation. The officer listened attentively to my story, but he struggled to understand my broken and heavily accented Spanish. Finally, with the help of my driver, Eliseo, we got the whole story out. The officer couldn't believe that an American, in Cuba, working on classified projects for the government, had caused all of this commotion. He placed several phone calls before allowing us to load up our dead demon and leave. By now the students had stopped laughing and several began to ask questions about our work, my presence in Cuba, and so on. I told them I would come back one day and talk to them. With that we jumped into the Jeep and departed. These events have grown in legend, and Cubans there recount the story to this day.

Some weeks later we received a visit from several high level military officials and a State Security Officer (DGI), who reviewed the entire process and told us how close they came to scrambling a couple of aircraft in response to the panic calls. We promised to give them lots of warning before our next launch.

In the mid 1960s, the United States anchored a Liberty ship about five miles off the port of Havana. They had converted the USS *Oxford* into a floating espionage platform to monitor all shipping traffic coming and going from Havana. The U.S. barred all commercial shipping vessels from entering U.S. ports if they had docked in Cuba in the last five years. On station for several years, the *Oxford* was visible at night on the horizon with all its lights burning. The Cubans grew accustomed to its presence, and several told me that Cuba would face real trouble the day that the *Oxford* left its station.

The Academy ran an old 3.2 cm radar unit on a spit of land jutting into the Gulf of Mexico a few miles east of Havana. We used the unit to detect the freezing level in clouds approaching Cuba from the northwest. This radar van also offered an unobstructed view of the USS *Oxford*.

A Russian, Vladimir, staffed the radar unit and often left the institute at Cuatro Caminos and spent the day out there. He always claimed he needed to clean and calibrate the equipment. Since he didn't have personal transportation, our driver, Eliseo, would accompany him. One day when Eliseo had taken the Jeep to run other errands, Vladimir asked me to take him to the site. We left

I (far left) am loading a MARV rocket onto a mobile launch pad in western Havana province. Cuban military personnel oversee the test firing in the background.

the institute early and drove to the north coast and parked near the unit. Vladimir unlocked the door to the trailer, and when we entered, the built up heat hit me like a hammer. He punched some switches to start the rooftop air conditioner, and only after the room cooled did he close the entry door.

He showed me the control panel and explained the simple controls that operated the equipment. He then ushered me to a tightly sealed 55 gallon drum located in one corner of the unit. It contained 200 proof pure alcohol. used along with a lint free cloth to clean the solder contacts of the radar electronics, and that's why Vladimir would spend one day a week here. He pulled out a loaf of black Russian bread, opened a tin of meat similar to Spam, produced a couple of glasses, and proceeded to scoop out some of the pure alcohol from the large drum. He told me to eat the bread and meat first and then sip the alcohol. I almost gagged to death trying to swallow the potent drink. Laughing, he proceeded to show me how to drink strong spirits, something that all Russians learn at an early age. You either fill your lungs with air or empty them first. You then chug-a-lug the shot of booze and upon doing so, slowly count to 10. Only then can you breathe either in or out. I followed instructions: no ill effects! Normally a person breathes in or out after downing a shot of potent alcohol;

the passage of air over the remnants of alcohol on one's tongue causes the alcohol to evaporate, and breathing these fumes causes the gagging sensation. Waiting just a few seconds for the alcohol to evaporate before breathing eliminates the gagging completely. We spent the rest of the day eating bread and downing shots. By midafternoon we were in the mood for mischief, so we pointed the antenna of the radar in the direction of the *Oxford* and turned it on. It didn't take long for the radar operators on the ship to point their antennas at us and begin to sweep us with their beams. By turning our unit on and off, we used simple Morse Code to send them greetings.

The *Oxford* radar operators quickly picked up our coded greeting and responded in the same way, asking us our names and what we wanted. We toyed with them for about 30 minutes before shutting down. We laughed all the way back to Havana just thinking about the mad scramble taking place on the ship. To this day I don't think the sailors imagine that they were communicating with a Soviet scientist and a U.S. intelligence officer, both quite drunk.

Not long after, TIO briefed me on several assassination attempts aimed at Fidel Castro while he made an official visit to Chile after Salvador Allende's election as president. In the first attempt in Santiago, a man carrying planted papers indicating that he was a Castro agent who had been turned, failed when the agent got sick and missed his chance. Another opportunity arose in northern Chile at one of the country's large copper mines near Antofagasta. Agents placed an old car loaded with explosives along the road leading to the mine, planning to detonate it when Castro's car passed by, but when Castro's entourage drove by and agents tried desperately to detonate the bomb ... nothing happened. It was a dud.

They tried again at the airport in Lima, Peru, where Castro's plane stopped so that he could have dinner with Peru's dictator, Juan Velasco Alvarado. Assassins maneuvered a U.S.-built twin engine Beechcraft outfitted with a cannon in an attempt to take a shot at Castro as he left the plane. They positioned the Beechcraft so the pilot could head straight for the runway and take off before anybody could react. This plot failed when Castro's plane taxied to a more secure area and the pilot of the Beechcraft couldn't reposition his plane.

TIO told me that the funding for these attempts to kill Castro came through a CIA front organization called the Castle Bank and Trust, Ltd. located in Nassau, the Bahamas. The Mafia used the same bank to fund many of its operations and kept those activities secret because no laws regulated offshore international banking. I don't know if the Mafia knew that Castle Bank fronted for the CIA, but it served as one of many such fronts in south Florida and the Caribbean.

The Agency and exiled Cuban groups continued to send armed squads to Cuba's north shore. These groups brought radios, weapons, explosives, and propaganda. They served to keep Castro's military busy and let the Cuban people know of an active campaign to bring Castro down.

After the Bay of Pigs in 1961, the CIA had started Operation 40, based in Miami and intended as a super-secret operation. They meant to keep the rest of the CIA in the dark about the agents involved, their location and their exact mission. An exiled Cuban named Joaquin Sanjenis headed the operation with his deputy, Felix Gutierrez, both veterans of the ill-fated invasion and both rabid anti–Castro agents who actually spied on the rest of the anti–Castro Cubans in south Florida for the CIA. Joaquin had run Operation 40 since its inception and had launched the vast majority of the small, fast boats carrying counter-revolutionary agents to Cuba. Operation 40 did the CIA's dirty work unknown to the Cuban community in Miami. I knew that the Cubans quickly captured, tried, and shot the squads sent to the island, and I kept telling TIO to distance my mission from the debacle of Operation 40. TIO assured me that Operation 40 would not compromise my cover.

In mid–December, one of the CIA's mother ships, called the *Johnny Express*, came under attack by a Cuban patrol boat. It was similar to another CIA supply ship, the *Lyla Express*, that the Cubans had seized only 11 days earlier; both ships were running people and equipment to counter-revolutionaries on the island, The CIA operated these ships and registered them in Panama. The seizure of the first ship had hardly made the news, but now the *Johnny Express* focused international attention. The Cuban patrol boat opened fire on the ship and pursued it north into the Bahamian island chain. They wounded a couple of the crew, and the captain, José Villa, also wounded, put out a dramatic radio call, as reported by William Montalbano of the Miami *Herald* on December 16, 1971: "The deck is covered with blood. I am dying, chico. Tell the Coast Guard to come quickly. Tell them there are dead and wounded here."

The Cubans eventually rammed the *Johnny Express*, boarded her, and towed her to a Cuban port where hospitals treated Captain Villa and the wounded crew members. The U.S. accused the Cubans of piracy in international waters, while the Cubans presented photos showing a "fast boat" on the upper deck of the *Johnny Express*, one used in previous years by the CIA to land agents, explosives, and weapons in Cuba.

TIO also worried that one of the CIA's longest running operations might close. The Swan Islands, two small islands claimed by both the U.S. and Honduras, lie south of the western tip of Cuba. The larger of the two featured a landing strip, radio transmitters, and housing for a couple hundred people. The CIA had used the transmitters during the failed 1961 Bay of Pigs invasion, not only to broadcast instructions and information to the 2506 Brigade members (the invading anti–Castro mercenaries), but also to broadcast misinformation to confuse Castro's forces. The station, known under different operational names such as Radio Americas and Radio Swan, beamed anti–Castro propaganda and coded messages into Cuba. The Cubans, for their part, worked to jam these broadcasts. Congress attempted to shut down Radio Swan in 1968, but it survived and continued to operate until at least 1975. TIO told me that they used the transmitters there even while I was operational on the island, though I neither sent nor received transmissions from Swan Island.

My wife's family slowly accepted me into the clan. I would spend as much time as I could with them, and I did what I could to help them with material goods. They never lacked food or coffee or items that I could purchase at the technicians' and diplomatic stores. As I grew closer to them, I would often curse myself when alone with my thoughts for the double life I led. I couldn't tell them my real mission on the island or why I was working for the Castro government, and I always felt they didn't really believe my legend that I had fled the U.S. for political reasons and supported Castro and the Cuban Revolution. My Cuban mother-in-law had a couple of brothers who worked in state security, and she would inquire from time to time if they knew of any investigations focused on me. They always assured her not to worry, but I didn't know whether they would have told her the truth about that or not, and I always worried.

Through my family and Cuban friends I saw how the average Cubans lived, forced to get by on what little the Revolution provided and what they could barter for in the extensive black market. Each Cuban got two ration books, one for food and the other for manufactured goods that included everything from clothing and shoes to light bulbs. Cubans could go only to the food store, bakery, clothing store, and hardware store nearest their dwelling. Only at these places could they use their ration books. People eked by on skimpy rations indeed. A Cuban man, for example, could only purchase two pairs of pants between the years of 1963 and 1970. An adult woman could only purchase three bras during the same period. If you needed something and your designated store didn't have your size, you were out of luck. This crazy distribution system gave birth to the black market.

I learned that the average Cuban housewife would take the month's supply of cigarettes, cigars, and any excess sugar or rice and head out on the streets to barter those items for things she needed more. She would trade two cigars for a can of condensed milk, or excess sugar for evaporated milk. The average Cuban could not purchase a new refrigerator, repair an air conditioning unit, or buy a new car. No one could find anything brighter than a 60 watt light bulb. A newlywed couple could go to a special store where they could rent a wedding dress and a man's suit and shoes. They could purchase a special order wedding cake along with some additional small pastries. Flowers were available all the time.

The scarcity of almost everything increased with each passing year, so the black market grew by leaps and bounds. The government, aware of the situation, allowed it because it met the pent-up demand for most material goods. People who protested faced arrest, charges of anti-revolutionary activities, and fines. The government prohibited travel to the countryside to trade clothing, rum, or cigars for fresh meat or beans, and the police stopped and searched private autos traveling the few highways that existed, looking for contraband.

People began to pilfer from their work stations. A truck driver hauling freshly kilned bricks would trade a few of them for a bottle of rum. Anyone delivering paint would trade a few gallons for a new door or whatever else he needed. Foremen at construction sites found a shortage of materials on each and every project under their supervision. They knew what was happening, and they often just looked the other way. Sometimes they built structures without enough cement powder in the concrete mix to ensure safety. They covered buildings with a whitewash instead of missing paint. When sheets of plywood went missing they struggled to find a substitute. Castro spoke about this once during his annual State of the State speech. He said that in Cuba, where communism should exist, the country boasted 12 million capitalists instead!

The black market did not go unnoticed by the foreigners living in Cuba either. Many foreign technicians assigned to houses that wealthy Cubans exiles had left behind found that they could not find simple repair items legally. To replace a window, for example, they paid a Cuban under the table with goods acquired at their respective embassy outlets or from the foreign technicians stores or from the diplomatic stores. This practice grew rapidly, and the Cuban government issued warnings to the different embassies that foreigners caught dealing in the black market would have to leave the island. This drove the transactions further underground and raised the barter rates. This black market activity also took place on another level altogether. The Soviet Bloc foreigners did not have freely convertible currencies, and they also wanted the stuff available from the diplomatic stores. Persons like me, with U.S. dollars, sat at the top of the hill so to speak. For a bottle of Johnny Walker Red Label Scotch I could obtain almost anything I wanted from a Bulgarian, Czech, or Russian. I amassed large quantities of chocolates, vodka, bolts of cloth, and other items. On the one hand, I felt ashamed to participate in this illegal activity, but I made extra cash and endeared myself to many foreigners, including diplomats, whom I could quietly pump for information.

The Cuban diplomatic service organization CUBALSE (Cuba al Servicio al Extranjero) issued the diplomatic cards, and they soon cut back on the number of cards issued by reclassifying many foreigners. Many of the foreign embassies issued warnings to their nationals living and working in Cuba about the consequences of getting caught playing the black market, but few heeded these warnings. At times I felt that everybody on the island, Cubans and foreigners alike, relied on the black market in one way or another.

This type of internal fiscal policy played directly into our hands. With each passing year the scarcity of material goods grew while disillusionment with the Revolution grew. Officials cancelled celebrations for Christmas, Easter, and other religious holidays, marked as subversive anyone espousing a religious belief, and barred practicing Christians from the Communist Party and from the labor union. If you did not "volunteer" for the annual sugar harvest, you would not have a chance for a new house or apartment down the road. The government subjected all young men to compulsory military service, and any advancement depended on whether or not one belonged to the Communist Party. Castro tightened his hold on the citizens of Cuba. Possessing foreign currency became punishable by imprisonment. Those who sought passports got a one-way trip out of Cuba, with no right of return.

In the fall of 1971, issues in Chile and in the U.S came back to bite me in Cuba. Nixon, Kissinger and the secret Committee of 40 gave the chief of CIA covert operations for Latin America, Bill Broe, the green light to do whatever he could to stop Salvador Allende from becoming Chile's next president. He targeted disrupting the Chilean economy. The CIA financed a truckers' strike and sabotaged food supplies until shortages struck the larger cities. The Chilean military, as was its custom, stayed out of the fray and let the democratic process continue. The privations and strikes didn't stop Allende from being sworn in as president in October. Almost immediately the CIA started a clandestine campaign to deny credit to the new leftist government while increasing aid to the Chilean military almost seven times in 1971 alone. Nixon and the CIA thought that only through the use of the Chilean military could they destabilize Allende's government. TIO asked me to increase my activities to gain intelligence about Cuban aid to the new government in Chile. I saw that the CIA had now fixed a new target in the crosshairs.

Back in the U.S., family and friends informed me that the FBI continued to show up at their homes and places of work to ask if they had heard from me and if so, could they copy any letters. This intimidated people and made them fear having any contact with me at all. It also showed me that the CIA had not shared the truth with them. But if the CIA was sharing information with the FBI, then perhaps they only continued the practice knowing that the Cubans intercepted all personal mail and so would remain confident in my outlaw legend! I didn't know what to believe. TIO would not, or could not, confirm any of this. As the end of the year approached, my anxiety only increased, leaving me a nervous wreck.

12. Going Dark

1973, which changed my life in so many ways, began much as previous years had, with Castro giving speeches that blamed the U.S. blockade for most, if not all, of Cuba's ills. He also blamed the vagrants, the bureaucrats at all levels, worker indifference, and the fact that most Cubans didn't embrace revolutionary fervor to the fullest. He blamed mistakes on some former leaders of the Revolution. I could understand all of his arguments, and I knew that many of the economic problems facing Cuba could be laid at the feet of people given high places of authority who lacked the education and experience to manage their ministries.

When Castro's "barbudos" (bearded ones) rolled into Havana after the Revolution drove Batista from the island, these people, mostly uneducated campesinos who could barely read or write, became, because of their loyalty to Castro and the Revolution, the new leaders of the country. They took charge of the sugar mills, factories, banks, postal service, farms, schools, and so on. Their lack of education and experience soon showed up in shortages, breakdowns, mismanagement, theft, and nepotism. Case in point: when Ernesto "Che" Guevara became the Minister of Industrial Development, he wondered why Cuba imported foreign manufactured goods like table silverware that could be made in Cuba. He ordered new factories built, machinery installed, people trained, and material purchased, and then he placed the shop into production. But the unskilled workers and inept supervisors insured low production and poor quality. Finally others pointed out to him that for a pound of sugar, he could import complete sets of silverware from China for a fraction of the cost. To this day his new factory sits empty and idle.

Another example of stupidity came to light when someone ordered a quitanieve (snow plow) grader, mistaking it for a niveladora (road-grader). Castro let it sit on the dock for years, rusting, as an example to everyone of what not to do. This kind of mismanagement and waste of money happened again and again, and despite all of Castro's good intentions, things just kept going from bad to worse.

Castro thought that perhaps rewarding his most loyal servants with some-thing nice would induce others at lower levels to aspire to improve things so that they too could move up and attain special privileges. He purchased several hundred new Alfa Romeos, compact, well built and fast. Only the most loyal received these cars along with chauffeurs. You could see them speeding down the streets, showing off their occupants' special relationship with Castro. Soon, however, notices began to appear in *Granma* and by radio bemba (lip, or street gossip) that the owners of the cars were dying at a horrendous rate, as a result of speeding on Cuba's narrow and badly kept highways. TIO once told me that giving out the Alfas did more to decimate Cuba's leadership than the CIA!

Apathy on the part of Cuba's population reached new levels almost daily. During the ill-fated 10 million ton sugar harvest that only reached 8.5 million tons after an 18-month year, *Granma* published the number of tons processed daily and put it in large print at the top of the paper. The Party noticed that daily newspaper sales increased dramatically. They claimed this showed the public's interest in the fate of the harvest. They misjudged. The Cuban people, with no other source for toilet paper, turned to the newspaper instead. Since the paper used red and black ink, the colors of the July 26th Movement that had started Castro's revolution, people became known as potos revolucionarios (revolutionary asses) because the ink stained their butts.

The people also used the numbers appearing at the top of the daily edition for gambling, as in a lottery. The day before the edition came out, people placed huge bets on the next day's production numbers. When the Party finally real-ized the connection, they stopped publishing the production numbers. Sales of the newspaper fell dramatically.

The U.S. economic warfare against the Allende government in Chile caused shortages throughout the nation. Demonstrators took to the streets of the major cities. In a botched kidnapping attempt, members of Chile's military assassinated their own Army chief of staff, René Schneider, with machine guns supplied to them by the CIA. General Schneider had kept the Chilean military out of politics, but with his removal, coup rumors stirred. Chile had a long rep-utation as a democracy, and few, if any, thought a coup likely. Cuba diverted to Chile food and material goods destined for the Cuban people to shore up Allende, as well as military advisors, arms, and bodyguards.

It appeared that once again Castro wanted to export his brand of revolu-tion to South America. He had failed in Bolivia in 1967 with Che, but didn't propose to make the same mistake in Chile. Apparently, during his visit to Chile a year or so earlier, Castro had mentioned to President Allende that Cuba had sought the help of foreigners to fill in the gaps left by all the professionals who had abandoned the island. He suggested that Chile might do the same. In response, Chile issued a call for foreign professionals to come for two years as professors, engineers, technicians, and so on. This invitation came to the Cuban Academy of Sciences and reached my desk.

I thought it looked like an interesting possibility in a couple of ways. I didn't know how long my job in the Academy would last, and I thought, since Chile now aligned itself with Cuba, that maybe, just maybe, I could take one of these new contracts and have my family join me. Cuba would find it harder to say no in this case. I couldn't decide if I should tell TIO about this opportunity. Then another chance came up to return to the Soviet Union with the Academy. I knew that my efforts to design and build cloud seeding delivery systems had basically stalled out, but maybe I could get the Soviets to provide the silver iodide that I needed to continue the project. This trip would only last one week; it could give me one last chance to save the project and buy me more time with the Cubans.

I made the decision to quit the Agency that year if they continued to stonewall my efforts to leave the island and take my family with me. How to handle all of this provided multiple challenges. I worked hard to convince the new Academy president that going to Moscow merited their financial support. He reluctantly agreed, so I made plans to go in the spring. I spoke to my Soviet contacts in the Academy and asked them to write letters supporting the cloud seeding experiment. Armed with the letters and my material requests written out in Russian for presentation on arrival, I boarded a flight to Moscow.

The flight passed uneventfully and I saw a few Soviet technicians that I had known in Cuba on board. Their two year contracts had ended and they were now headed home. I sensed a reluctance in their voices. They had lived well in Cuba, enjoying many more material goods than they would have in Russia, as well as more freedom to meet and know a variety of people from different countries. Back home their lives would return to a dull daily routine and they would not have the possibility of exchanging views freely with foreigners. I felt their pain.

Once in Moscow, I returned to the hotel where I had stayed before, and my contact with the Soviet Academy of Sciences came by to pick me up the next day. I spent two days at different offices talking to numerous department representatives and dispersed all of my support letters, which they received with grace and understanding but no promises of immediate help. I spent a couple of days sightseeing and then headed back to Havana. The flight stopped over in East Germany, so I planned to stay in East Berlin for a couple of days. Once I arrived, I contacted an East German technician I had befriended in Havana and asked his help in getting a hotel room. He happily obliged, but told me that he needed to clear everything with the infamous Stasi, the Ministry for State Security (Ministerium für Staatssicherheit). This government spy agency kept files on everyone, including themselves! Here, in possibly the world's most severe police state, nobody trusted anybody, sometimes not even their own family members. I waited at the airport for my colleague to arrive, and after several hours he showed up with some paperwork that allowed me to leave the airport. We drove to a modest hotel and once again he needed to present paperwork provided by the Stasi. We then went out to eat at a restaurant located in a TV antenna tower in East Berlin. The East German government, headed by Erich Honecker, tried to counter the allure of the glowing night lights of West Berlin with several sites aimed at providing food and material goods to foreigners, including this restaurant with food as great as the wine, the vodka, the beer, and the presentation. The average East German citizen could not access this place, so my friend really enjoyed himself. The next day he drove me around in his East German-made car, a two-cycle Trabant, probably the worst car ever designed and put into mass production. When East Germany collapsed in the '90s, people abandoned them by the hundreds. They carried no value as sale or junk. I understand the owners would just leave them on the street with the keys in them. Any passersby could just get in one and drive it away.

We drove close to the famous Berlin Wall and Checkpoint Charlie. Here the Stasi inspected all vehicles coming and going from East Berlin to make sure no one brought anything in or out without permission. They also inspected each car to make sure an East German hadn't hidden aboard in a secret compartment to be smuggled out of the country. The Allies had divided Berlin into four segments after World War II: one for the Soviets, one for the U.S., one for the British and one for the French. Even though Berlin sat deep inside East Germany, westerners could drive from West Germany along a unique highway, and though the East Germans prohibited them from stopping or picking up passengers, the Stasi staffed control stations every so many kilometers checking cars and trucks. It was a very tightly controlled country and city.

My time in Berlin ended, and I boarded the flight to Havana in much the same state of despair with which I had left Cuba. I didn't believe my trip had accomplished anything at all, exchanging one prison for another.

Back in Havana and back at work, I could sense a demoralization among the workers. The Institute existed for the cloud seeding program, to take measurements of atmospheric particles and do all the other research associated with the project. With the apparent demise of the seeding program, no one had anything to do. Maybe they blamed me for this. Everyone knew that the money for the program had dried up; I could only hope I wouldn't take the fall for the failure.

At the Atmospheric Physics research center southeast of Havana. I am holding the High Altitude Research Vehicle (HARV) just outside the assembly building.

My wife sensed my pessimism and tried her best to cheer me up. She also knew that if things didn't work out for another contract extension with the Academy, I would face a choice to leave without her or try to stay without work. She knew that she would have problems trying to get an exit visa for the U.S., but she never made me feel responsible for what could happen. I felt anxious all the time, but tried to hide my concerns from her, though I probably didn't do a very good job. She saw me drinking more, smoking more, and unable to sleep.

I continued to collect some intelligence, but I told TIO that my mission had become harder and harder. I don't know if TIO noticed any change in my attitude, but if they did, they said nothing. They still played the waiting game with my family, and my anger grew with each passing month. Word from the States showed me that nothing had changed there. TIO had lied to me, and they knew that they had me by the short hairs. I spent many a sleepless night over the situation, and I finally decided to push the application to take a contract in Chile by going to their embassy in Havana. In July I received the invitation from the Universidad Técnica del Estado in Santiago, Chile. They expected a couple of professorship openings in mechanical engineering and suggested I come for an interview. I arranged to make the trip and it took most of my savings. The Academy wouldn't pick up the tab, so the expenses landed on me, but it seemed a solution to many problems and I decided to take the risk.

I told my wife about my plans to seek employment in Chile and then seek a temporary exit visa for her to accompany me. She appreciated the unique possibilities and agreed. She thought that perhaps I could directly approach an official in the U.S. Embassy in Santiago instead of going through the Swiss Embassy in Havana, and that maybe I could resolve our future that way. I assured her I would try.

I decided to tell TIO about the offer in Chile and try to convince them I could serve as their new eyes and ears in Santiago. I didn't know if they needed additional assets there, but by telling TIO about my plans, I hoped to throw them off suspicions that I might renege on my mission. They didn't have much to worry about, since they held all the keys to clearing my name and protecting my family.

Initially TIO didn't seem to favor my plan, so I tried to convince them that several other foreigners were taking up the offer and my participation would provide inside information on the individuals invited, where they might work and what they might be doing. TIO finally agreed and asked me to make contact once I arrived in Chile by going to the U.S. Embassy and registering, seemingly a normal move for a U.S. citizen in a foreign country. TIO would not inform the CIA in the embassy there about my mission and real identity, only that they could expect a contact from me regarding my concerns about my family in Cuba. I worried about this, as the legal attaché in each embassy usually worked for the FBI and the FBI was looking for me. I told TIO that we needed to make other arrangements. They never did.

I planned to travel to Chile in late August for an interview in early September. I checked my passport, which had been issued in September 1968, and saw that it didn't expire until the end of September 1973. This would cut things very close. I hoped to renew my passport via the Swiss Embassy once I returned to Havana. I flew to Santiago on Air Cubana. A university representative met my flight and took me to a downtown hotel. I spent the next two days in an interview process in which they examined my credentials as well as my capacity to speak Spanish sufficiently to teach in a university setting. Allende's government had several representatives on the interview panel who seemed happy to see a foreigner from Cuba, especially a North American, applying for the job. I impressed a few on the panel with my language skills and my engineering credentials, but they didn't seem to share Allende's politics. I didn't know which faction would win the final decision on my application. I stayed in Santiago a couple of extra days to get to know the city a little and noticed an increased sense of apprehension. Soldiers and police patrolled each street and plaza. I planned to head back to Havana via Lima, Peru, on September 9.

Word reached me that Castro planned to attend the Fourth Conference of Non-Aligned Nations in Algiers that same month. This non-aligned bloc consisted of more than 70 different countries in Asia, Africa and Latin America. The name "non-aligned" didn't mean neutrality in any sense of the word. Castro wanted his friend Salvador Allende to back him in promoting the Soviet Union as the only true friend of the non-aligned bloc, but Allende, facing increasing opposition back home, declined. Representatives from the more moderate nations like Algeria and India wanted to express their displeasure with all the super powers for not giving enough assistance to Third World countries. The Libyan Supreme Leader, Muammar Gaddafi, came out with strong statements against Castro, claiming that Castro was indeed aligned with the Soviet Union and a communist while he, Gaddafi, sought a truly non-aligned path as a socialist and not a communist.

The non-aligned meeting reached no consensus, and Castro took it as a personal defeat. He had always wanted to travel to North Vietnam, so his return flight went from Algiers to Baghdad and then on to New Delhi, India. There, on September 11, 1973, he learned of the coup d'etat in Chile and the death of Salvador Allende. Luckily I got out two days before the coup, because the Chilean military detained all Air Cubana flights for several days and investigated all foreigners in the country. If they had swept me up they would have contacted the U.S. Embassy and I would have had more problems than I could handle.

The new military government put all of Chile under martial law, and the junta elected General Augusto Pinochet as the maximum dictator. They rounded up everyone with a socialist, communist, or leftist leaning past. They killed thousands outright, "disappeared" many and tortured more. I didn't know what might have happened to the professors who had interviewed me just days before. The country descended into chaos and barbarism, and the heavy hand of the CIA moved behind it all. Secretary of State Henry Kissinger publicly denied a U.S. role in the military coup, but, as reported by Amy Goodman, in "Ask Kissinger About Pinochet," *Democracy Now*, December 14, 2006, stated: "I don't see why we need to stand by and watch a country go communist due to the irresponsibility of its people. The issues are much too important for the Chilean voters to be left to decide for themselves."

The coup in Chile represented a disaster for Castro. He could no longer count on an ally in the Americas. He secretly sought aid from Europe to offset the loss of trade with Moscow. However, the decimation of the European beet crop caused a worldwide shortage of sugar that would see the price rise to an unheard-of price of 65 cents a pound, well above what the Russians would pay. For a short time, Cuba enjoyed new riches.

I saw my trip to Santiago as a disaster as well. With the fall of the Allende government, the university dropped its search for foreign professors. In fact, the new military junta in Chile broke relations with Cuba, so any ideas of going to Chile to work died, as did any chance of getting my wife out that way.

To make matters worse, when I went to the Swiss Embassy to get a new passport, I turned in my old one that would expire in a few days and filled out an application for a new one. The Swiss told me that it might take a week or two to get it and that I should return. I waited for over two weeks and went back. The Swiss diplomat told me that the U.S. had confiscated my passport and issued instructions that I receive a "temporary" passport valid only for a direct return to the U.S. I left the Embassy in shock. What had just happened? I couldn't quiz this Swiss person because I didn't know him and he probably didn't know who I really worked for. I didn't know what to do. I went home and contemplated my situation.

I would soon be out of a job. I'd lost my passport, so I could not travel internationally. My money was almost gone. TIO had failed to resolve the St. Louis situation. The FBI wanted to arrest me and I saw nowhere to turn. My job with the Academy did have another year to run, so I drew small consolation from that, the only bright spot I could see. I could bet that TIO knew about my situation and my problems. In fact, they probably caused most, if not all, of my problems. What did they want from me? They had wanted me to divorce my wife, but they seemed to eventually accept the marriage, so something else must have upset them. For the life of me, I couldn't figure it out.

I had considered breaking with the Agency for a long time and now I finally made the decision. I resolved to write a letter of resignation and send it via the diplomatic pouch. Could I take that risk? The Cubans, we thought, sometimes intercepted, opened, and read material being sent out of the country. If they intercepted my letter I would lose even my relative safety in Cuba. I saw no other choice, so I wrote the letter and dispatched it. I then literally sat down to await the response I knew would come. I dreaded it, but I also finally felt free from my long relationship with the CIA, a bad bargain from the very start. I went dark.

13. Trapped

The year 1974 saw many changes at home. President Nixon removed my former boss at the CIA, Richard (Dick) Helms, and named him ambassador to Iran to get him far away from Washington and the press. Lyndon Johnson had appointed Helms after firing Admiral Bill Raborn in 1966 because he just didn't fit in the intelligence community. James Schlesinger replaced Helms in February, but he didn't fit in either, so in July Nixon chose William Colby. With all of these changes going on, I could bet no one would pay a great deal of attention, if any, to my situation. Late in 1974 Operation CHAOS became public, and the details caused a firestorm with the press and the public. Operation CHAOS had originally recruited me back in 1965. Then President Nixon resigned and Gerald Ford took office. As for me and my situation … I sat and waited and hoped for TIO to act on my resignation letter. I hadn't shared my plans with any of the informants that I had cultivated over the past years, as I still wanted to collect intelligence to barter if I needed it. This way I could also learn whether TIO relied on someone else in the Havana area, either to provide intelligence or to watch me. When my informants and communication links stopped responding to me, I would know.

Work at the Institute ground to a near halt. Several of the Cuban technicians tried to move to the Institute of Meteorology to continue our work. No new Soviet technician arrived to replace Vladimir. Our new director, Nestor, confided in me that things just didn't look good beyond the end of the year. I told him about my problem of trying to arrange for my wife to leave with me when my contract ran out. He became a friend, and I think he really felt sorry for me because of the paperwork nightmare the Cuban government had placed in front of my wife. He offered to help by using his connections, but he couldn't promise anything.

I considered going to the Cubans and asking them if I could remain in Cuba, perhaps with a different job, until another country friendly to Cuba might take me and my family. I even contemplated using a go-between to ask the DGI if they would cut a deal with me if I revealed information about my mission and the CIA. Every time that thought came into my head I struggled to forget it. The consequences attached to that solution seemed unpredictable at best and dangerous at worst.

I was drinking and smoking way too much and I knew it. My situation set my nerves on edge, and all of our friends noticed. I went through the motions of going to work, even though I really had nothing to do. I taught English to the remaining students at the Institute and I continued to teach some engineering classes at the University of Havana. I thought that perhaps I could go to the leadership at the University and propose they hire me, so I sought out contacts who I felt could help me. But the University employed native-born Cubans who had joined the Communist Party. I didn't fit those two basic requirements, so the prospect seemed doomed from the start.

Back in 1973 the Castro brothers had had a long discussion with the leaders of the Soviet Union about how to move the Cuban economy forward after years of stagnation with Fidel Castro calling the shots. He had named himself and his brother Raúl as generals instead of majors, but that didn't do much for the average Cuban worker or peasant. For years the Soviets told Castro he needed to appear to give more power to the people. But Castro didn't have a good cadre of educated and dedicated communists that he could rely on to make difficult decisions. Finally the Soviets convinced him that, if he continued down the same path, the Revolution would fail. Castro finally announced that he would allow the formation of a "National Congress" to be made up of elected officials picked by the workers. Of course, the Communist Party would vet all the candidates. Supposedly selecting candidates in a secret process, the well oiled Communist Party, in conjunction with the local street spy networks (CDR's), made sure all of the nominees walked the straight and narrow and assured Castro of "reliable" candidates.

He structured the Municipal Assemblies so that these local groups dealt with such matters as who was allowed to operate a taxi, how and when to repair a street, where to locate food distribution centers, how to allocate scarce material goods, and mundane things like this. In fact, the average person in Cuba worried about these things more than foreign relations or the national budget. These Municipal Assemblies, in turn would choose delegates to represent them at the National Assembly for terms of up to five years. The National Assembly members, all scrutinized by Castro, then would select delegates to the all-powerful Council of Ministers who ran the Council of State. Castro led both councils, so real control still rested in his hands. The people, however, now felt that they had a say in decision making, not only at the local level but nationally as well. In 1975 the first Party Congress voted this change to the Cuban constitution. The people, gathered in the Plaza of the Revolution, roared their approval.

In reality, the legislative process worked in reverse. Sure, the Municipal Assemblies bumped some small issues up to the Council of Ministers for action, but these had little consequence. The real issues began in the Council of Ministers and got shoved downward to the street level. Not much changed, except that decisions took more time for implementation and, indeed, some issues forced downward did not get approved or implemented. Small victories for the Cuban democracy promised by Castro right after he won power in 1959.

Impressed with these changes, foreign leaders, even those in the West, came calling, and Castro wined and dined leaders from Canada, Mexico, East Germany, Bulgaria, and even some business people from the U.S. In April 1974, the Senate Foreign Relations Committee called on the Ford Administration to end its blockade of Cuba. With Nixon gone, President Ford made it known that the U.S. would no longer oppose letting Cuba rejoin the Organization of American States (OAS). With the deaths of Che Guevara and Salvador Allende, Castro seemed resigned to ending his attempts to export his revolution to South America. This new attitude seemed to please many nations, and some that had broken diplomatic relations with Cuba now re-established them in quick succession, including the Bahamas, Jamaica, Panama, Honduras, Ecuador, and Venezuela. When Venezuela once again recognized Cuba it marked the end of an era, as Venezuela had first proposed Cuba's expulsion from the OAS. Word had it that if Venezuela would once again supply petroleum to Cuba, the Soviet Union would fulfill Venezuela's commitments in Spain and some other countries.

Vice President Carlos Rafael Rodriguez, always close to Castro, assured the European press that Cuba no longer supported guerrilla movements in the Americas. This statement sent a message to the West and to the rest of Latin America. The Castro brothers hoped to breathe new economic life into the Revolution. In July 1974, Mexican President Luis Echeverría said that he would lead the rest of the Americas in an effort to persuade the U.S. to end its economic blockade of Cuba. In fact, President Echeverría did his best to convince the rest of the Latin American nations to vote for him as a possible Secretary General of the United Nations. He visited over 15 other countries trying to encourage support for his nomination. It never happened.

While Cuba seemed to have ceased its export of revolution to the Americas, it did nothing to stop Castro from looking east at Africa. His interest really picked up in April 1974, when a small group of military officers staged a coup against the Estado Novo dictatorship in Portugal. This triggered an almost immediate response among the Portuguese colonies and territories worldwide, beginning in Angola where three guerrilla movements vied for primacy: the Popular Movement for the Liberation of Angola (MPLA), the National Front for the Liberation of Angola (FNLA), and the National Union for the Independence of Angola (UNITA). The U.S. ultimately backed the FNLA, while Cuba and the Soviet Union supported the MPLA. To avoid a direct military confrontation with the U.S., the Soviets advised the MPLA to ask Cuba for men and training, with the Soviet Union providing weapons. Things quickly got messy in Africa.

By the middle of the year I still had had no news from TIO concerning my resignation or the situation in St. Louis. I didn't know what to do. I had stopped providing information and had quit seeking input from my informants. TIO must have noticed my lack of activity. I felt certain that if the Cubans knew of my activities, they had also noticed that things had really cooled between me and Washington. If they did notice, they must have scratched their heads about the lull in my activities, and if they worked as hard as I assumed, they must have also noticed what had happened to my application for a new passport and my inquiries as to how to get my family off the island. If so, they wouldn't wait too long before knocking on my door. I checked but could not detect any surveillance by the Cubans, so perhaps they really hadn't tumbled to my clandestine activities. Maybe my fantastic luck held.

I received word that, with the arrival of the Soviet leader Alexi Kosygin in Havana for talks with Castro, the Cubans had rounded up most of the airline hijackers and confined them to a immigration detention center just a few blocks from my home in Miramar. The center, at 16th Street and First Avenue, sat adjacent to a hotel frequently used by Soviet technicians. I went by the place to see if I could catch sight of one or two of them, as I'd made some black market deals with them earlier. One of the guards allowed me to talk to one of the detainees and I asked him what had happened. He said that the Cubans had arrested the majority of them early in the morning at the Hotel Nueva Isla in Old Havana where they stayed, and brought others into the city from the farms they worked on. The Cubans told them they all faced deportation. A couple of days went by, and then one of the Puerto Rican hijackers who had been picked up later than the others told them the real reason: with the Soviet leader visiting, the KGB insisted on the detention of all "delinquents" for the duration.

The hijackers' family and close friends didn't know what had happened, why, or how long the Cubans would keep them. My contact asked me to get word to his Cuban girlfriend, who would then let everyone else know what was going on. I agreed, thinking that someone should know in case the Cubans planned a mass deportation or something worse.

I found his girlfriend sitting across the street from the hotel. She recognized me from a prior meeting. I told her what had transpired and that I thought the Cubans would release the hijackers as soon as Kosygin left Cuba. I urged her and others to go to the detention center and demand to see their significant others, as this would probably prevent the Cuban security forces from pulling off any surprises. She and about a dozen others showed up that same afternoon demanding visitation rights. The Cubans allowed the hijackers to see their families and friends and confirmed that all would get out in a couple of days. The girlfriend never told the Cuban security people how she found the detention center. If she had, they would have come looking for me.

Later that year I noticed that my drop boxes and dead drops contained nothing new. TIO must have told my informants of my resignation letter and ordered them to cut all communications with me. TIO also refused to respond to my communications, and the shoebox signal in the old U.S. Embassy no longer appeared in the window. They had cut me off.

Osvaldo Dorticós, who had been appointed president of Cuba under Castro, gave an address to the Cuban people assuring them that Cuba would no longer seek huge gains in its yearly sugar production, as attempts to do so had failed again and again. Instead, he said that Cuba would try to show small incremental increases in production of refined sugar while using the remaining cane in the agricultural field to produce feed for the cattle industry. This change in the economy signaled that Cuba would try to boost hard currency reserves by selling other products, such as nickel, tobacco, rum, and perhaps coffee. But this would affect the consumption of these products at the national level, and the average Cuban feared a decrease in the monthly ration. I expected this to lead to more protests and the theft of these products between the factories and the local outlets.

In late December, two lieutenants, Pupo and Nelson, came to my house late one evening and asked me to accompany them. I saw no way to refuse. By doing this late in the evening, they had eliminated any possible interference from anyone at the Institute. After they had packed me into their waiting car, we took off toward the National Security Headquarters located south of Havana in an area called Vento. My anxiety spiked as we sped away.

At headquarters they ushered me into a small room containing a table and three chairs. It looked like an interrogation room anywhere in the world. I demanded to know why they had picked me up in the middle of the night. Lt. Pupo said that I already knew why, but that they would happily explain. For the best part of an hour they told me how they had placed me under surveillance several months back and, as a result, they had caught me trading on the black market. However, their real interest lay in my use of dead drops and diplomatic pouches to communicate with the U.S. government. My worst nightmares were realized. They accused me of ties to several Cubans they had already arrested

This is a street scene of Old Havana. I did a couple of Cuban street scenes just in black on a white background. The Calle Emperadero in Old Havana runs east-west and goes to the Cathedral of La Habana, but the street is better known for the Bodeguita del Medio (nickel store), which is one of the best known restaurants in La Habana.

for espionage against the state, and ties to foreigners like Humberto Carrillo Colón, the Mexican diplomat they had expelled for spying for the CIA.

They showed me photographs of the dead drops, of people accessing them, of me accessing them, and of me meeting with people already under surveillance for activities against the state. It wouldn't do me much good to deny the evidence, but I did anyhow. Once they showed me what they considered enough, they also said that they had monitored my phone calls, telegrams, and mail. This didn't worry me because I always took great care not to say anything using those types of media. They told me they had also monitored my contacts at the old American Club, with foreign diplomats, with some of the Cuban leaders, and with known foreign intelligence agents. I told them I had friends, went to clubs, and talked to all kinds of people and this proved nothing. In fact, as a foreigner I naturally wanted to stay in touch. I stressed that all foreigners discussed the pros and cons of the Cuban Revolution, a natural conversational item at any gathering. They continued to say that my activities raised suspicions and they wanted to give me the opportunity to explain my actions and activities. Clearly they didn't know a lot in some areas, but they did know all about the dead drops and some of my contacts. I didn't know how to explain those things away, so I tried to shift the focus of the interrogation toward other topics, but to no avail.

We went back and forth until the wee hours of the morning. They asked nothing about my family, and that told me they didn't suspect them of anything. They didn't mention any formal charges being lodged against me yet, but when the meeting ended, they told me they would detain me for the time being. With that, they left and a guard took me to a cell located a little deeper in the building. My heart pounded. I couldn't contact my wife or people at the Institute to let them know what happened. I fought down a rising sense of panic. With no official cover or representation. I could not claim diplomatic immunity or U.S. protection. Things did not look good, and I spent the night tossing and turning.

The next day started badly. After a quick breakfast of bread and a cup of coffee, we returned to the interrogation room and the questions flew once again. We covered some of the same ground from the previous night, but in greater detail. I demanded to know the whereabouts of my family and if they knew where I had been detained. My demands went unanswered. Finally I refused to even talk with Lt. Pupo and his assistant unless they answered my questions. We had reached a stalemate. I would divulge nothing and neither would they. We must have skipped lunch, for when they escorted me back to my cell it was late afternoon. My anxiety continued to rise and my mind went in 20 different directions at once. I didn't know how I had ended up here. Had someone turned against me? Had I made a mistake? Had they infiltrated some of my informants? I just didn't know, and that only made things worse.

As dinner time arrived, I tried to see if I could determine how many others were being detained in the same building. I listened to hear how many doors opened and closed and what languages I could hear. I strained to hear the voice of someone that I worked with or knew and so get some idea as to what started all of this, but I listened in vain.

We repeated this same routine for five more days. Their field of questioning expanded daily. On the third or fourth day their questions turned to the hijackers that I knew and in some cases had helped support. They wanted to know if any of them really worked for U.S. intelligence and simply were posing as exiles. They asked me about a father who had brought his young son with him in a small airplane from the U.S. I didn't know anything about the case except what I had read in the papers. They asked me about some individuals who had hijacked commercial flights to Cuba. Again, I knew nothing about these cases and told them so. They asked about the Venceremos Brigade members I had interacted with, as well as members of the Pastors for Peace movement that was just getting started. Again, I told them I didn't know about the groups or people other than what I had heard on TV and read in the newspaper.

They told me that they would be sharing their suspicions with the leadership of the Academy of Sciences as well as with the leadership at the Institute, clearly threatening me that even if I got out of this, any future with the Academy had closed. They would intimidate anyone who knew me to the point that they would probably avoid any contact with me at all. The noose just got tighter and tighter.

I had always known that the Cubans could react harshly to someone like me, especially since they had invited me to Cuba to help them. To learn that my mission meant to harm them, made it a blow below the belt. I didn't know whether they would turn me over to a military court or a public court, or deal with me in some other manner unique to the Cuban sense of justice. About the only thing I did have going for me was the fact that I had resigned from the Agency almost a year before and I knew they must have also learned that. I could only hope that my marriage to a Cuban woman whom I did not involve in my clandestine activities would also be a mitigating fact, but who knew? What if the Cubans tried to "turn" me at some point? How would I react to such an offer? They could also deport me without my family, not only causing heartache for all of us but also raising suspicion on TIO's part, thinking that maybe I gave up a lot of secrets in exchange for a measure of mercy. To reinforce that move, they could easily round up some of the informants I had used, knowing that

TIO would get the word and that this would only serve to feed TIO's suspicion that I had turned. The walls closed in on me and I saw only a true lose/lose situation.

If they deported me, what would happen to my family? Would I ever see them again? If the Cubans denied me re-entry to the country in the future and never allowed my wife and son to leave the island, that meant the destruction of my family. If they didn't allow my family to leave, TIO might see that as the "Sword of Damocles" to be held over my head for future blackmail. If they deported me and TIO picked me up, the long debriefing sessions, conducted in secret, of course, might take months or even years to complete. Like another Sword of Damocles, the St. Louis incident hung directly above my head at each and every step. I couldn't sleep and I paced the floor of my confines endlessly. I aged 20 years during those five days.

After I had spent a few more days in isolation, Lt. Pupo said he would release me that afternoon. He offered no explanation and I didn't ask for one. Release meant seeing my family and escaping prison or deportation, at least for now. After lunch, they put me in a car with two body guards and drove into Miramar where I lived. We drove through a driving rainstorm to within three or four blocks of my home. There they opened the door and shoved me out with one final caveat: "Vamos a retornar," we'll be back.

I made my way home, but found the house empty. Thinking that my wife must have gone to her mother's, I went next door to Comandante Baldezia's house and asked his wife if I could use their phone. She had no idea of where I'd been or why but she must have wondered why I now stood outside soaked in the rain, so I told her that my car had broken down and that I didn't have a key to get in. I called my mother-in-law, and when she answered she let out a shriek. My wife then answered and shot me non-stop questions. I told her I would explain everything to her, but I needed her to drive home. She arrived within 30 minutes.

I spent the next several hours recounting to her and my in-laws the events of the last six days. They just sat there unable to believe my words. They told me that they had used all of their connections in the government with the several agencies where they had good friends or family members to try to find out what had happened to me. They found out the day before counterintelligence cut me loose. That told me that someone had used his influence to get me released. I thanked them profusely.

I told them I didn't know what the future held for me and my wife. I didn't tell them everything, but I don't think I needed to. I'm sure they harbored suspicions about some of my extra-curricular activities. I also knew that all of them wondered, inside, how all of this would affect them. However, for the moment, we concentrated on what to do over the next days, weeks or even months before the inevitable happened. We went over most of the possible options and tried to narrow down the possibilities. We even considered buying a boat that would allow the whole family to leave the island, but knew that my son's biological father, an Army officer, would not allow him to leave. We left nothing unsaid or un-discussed. We spent the rest of what remained of the year exploring options, but most of them meant splitting up my family and none of them guaranteed us ever getting back together.

14. No Way Out

With the start of 1975, I threw myself into the task of resolving my situation and that of my family. I visited several diplomat friends who I thought might help me, knowing I needed to share with them the truth of my relationship with TIO, my resignation, and the suspicions of Cuban counterintelligence, not an easy or fun task. Knowing that I had planned and carried out clandestine operations against Cuba would give pause to a diplomat even considering offering any kind of assistance. They could earn the enmity of the Cubans and the U.S. by aiding me. Going to the Cuban government to ask for exit visas for my family would place them in the position of supporting me rather than remaining neutral. I bounced back and forth for weeks trying to put together a solid plan that would work in the long run. Each time I thought I saw a possible solution, something would happen to close that door. I felt frustrated on every side. Although the DGI probably followed every step I took, I had to thank them for allowing me the opportunity to at least explore some way out. At the same time, they knew the difficulties I faced and they apparently did nothing to alleviate any of them.

In April the DGI officers returned, along with an immigration agent. They once again detained me and this time drove me to an immigration detention center, a house located at the western edge of Siboney on 228th Street that had been confiscated by the government when the original owner left the island. It stood next door to a military training base for the Cuban army. Again, they told no one where they had taken me or how long they intended to keep me.

A high wall surrounded the house, the only structure on the wedge-shaped block. It offered only two entries, one for cars and another for foot traffic. I could see two guards; one stood at the front door while the other patrolled around the building every hour or so. A cook came in during the morning to prepare breakfast and make something that we could heat for dinner. They placed me in a room on the second floor with a window that looked out over the military base just across the street. The wall stood about 10 feet high but didn't have the imbedded glass shards on top like so many others.

It looked like the immigration people ran the facility and not the DGI, with more moderate security. After scoping out the facility and watching the guards' rotation and duties for a couple of days, I knew I could easily slip out without getting caught. I liked the idea of escaping, at least for a few hours, to notify my wife, because detention here meant probable deportation at a moment's notice. I needed to act quickly.

I stayed awake for two nights carefully watching the guards and observing their routine. After the evening meal, they would both gather in the downstairs living room to watch television and drink a little rum from a bottle that was hidden away during the day. One or both would then doze off. They never made their rounds after that. I shared the building with a low priority detainee, a sailor who was waiting for the next merchant marine ship bound for his home country. He had jumped ship and remained in hiding until after the ship had sailed and the captain notified Cuban authorities.

Throughout the next day I planned my escape route and tried to estimate the time needed to make it over to Fifth Avenue, find a phone, place a call to my wife, and then return before anyone noticed: about three hours. If everything went as planned I could do it with time to spare.

In my pocket I found a few coins that I could use to make a call if I could locate a working public phone. This was not always easy, since when things broke down in Cuba, they often didn't have the spare parts to fix them. I decided to risk it. I planned my escape for 1:00 a.m., hoping to return by 4:00, two hours before bed check at 6:00. After dinner, I sat and waited. I hadn't noticed any barking dogs in the area and took that as a good sign, although it seemed strange with the military installation just across the street.

At 1:00 a.m. I crawled out my window onto the narrow ledge at the top of the wall. I inched my way forward, constantly feeling for loose stones or gravel that might fall and alert someone. My trip took me just above the front entrance, where an orange tree grew next to the front door. I prayed it would support my weight as I climbed down and then again when I climbed back up. As I passed over the window of the ground floor kitchen, I could hear the television but no sounds of human activity. I slowly let myself down to the ground and, once there, moved quickly away from the building. I wanted to break into a run, but decided against that because any passing police car or military patrol would see that as awfully suspicious. With my heart beating loudly in my chest, I began walking toward Fifth Avenue, about one mile to the north.

I recognized the area as close to the residence of the Canadian Ambassador, and for a fleeting moment I considered waking him up and asking for protection. However, I knew that the Cubans stationed a guard near the front door, and my arrival at this time of night would cause an alarm. I crossed 226th Street, still headed for Fifth Avenue. I had seen a public phone at 146th street near an old amusement park in an area known as Coney Island. Several Cuban coworkers from the Academy lived near there, but I decided not to approach them either. Here it seemed dark enough to hide my movements, so I ran one block to save time and then walked the next. I reached a neighborhood called Nautico and lo and behold, I saw a public phone mounted near a bus stop. I deposited my five cent piece and dialed my home number. It took forever for my wife to answer.

I tried desperately to calm her to the point that I could tell her where they had taken me and what I thought might happen next. I told her to come to the facility first thing in the morning and demand to see me without revealing how she knew my whereabouts. I told her they would probably deport me within a couple of days and that she should demand to see me. I told her to contact Lt. Pupo of counterintelligence and see what he could do. After just a few minutes I hung up, and almost immediately I noticed that my heart rate slowing considerably. Calmer now, I didn't care who saw me. I turned and retraced my path towards 228th Street. Oddly, I saw no one from the local CDR units out doing their required vigilance, or they would have spotted me at least a dozen times before I made it to the phone. I walked briskly back to the building and arrived at about 4:00. My planning had worked out exactly as I had hoped. Now to get back on top of the wall and creep back to my room.

I climbed the orange tree rapidly and once again crawled along the top of the wall. They still had the television on, but I didn't see or hear the guards. I didn't see any cars outside the house, either, so I guessed they hadn't missed me. I made it back to the window and climbed inside. I examined the small piece of tape I'd taken from a poster of Castro on my wall and placed over the space between the door and its frame. No one had entered. My heart started to beat rapidly as I recalled my escape and return. Now to try to sleep and wait for my wife to show up in the morning.

I heard the sound of the VW engine before I saw it. My wife drove the car slowly along the street separating the building from the military installation so I could see it. She told the guard that she knew I was there and demanded to see me. He neither confirmed nor denied my presence, but called his superior, who in turn called farther up the ladder. In less than 30 minutes a couple of cars arrived and I saw Lt. Pupo in one. I could just make out the sounds of a heated discussion taking place downstairs. Soon after, Pupo showed up at my door demanding to know how my wife had found me. I just shook my head, acknowledging the mystery of this turn of events. He seemed to think some well connected family members must have told her, and said he would allow the two of us some time together later that evening at a different facility. He left and I sensed that I had won this round but would still likely lose the war.

Around midnight he returned to drive me to yet another immigration center, this one nearer my home in Miramar. About an hour later my wife arrived. They told us we could have an hour together and that they would deport me that same day. What do you say to your wife when you don't know if you will ever see her again? She had all of the contact information of my family back in the States, as well as contacts with friends who lived in Canada, Sweden, England, and elsewhere. I instructed her to let my family in the States know that I had left the island and to tell them that I would contact them just as soon as I could. She brought me some clothes and about $100 in U.S. bills, all that we had in the house. The Cubans gave me nothing, not even telling me where they would send me. The hour passed too quickly. I swore to her that I would find a way to reunite as soon as I could, that she should not lose hope. We both cried as she left.

A few hours later Lt. Pupo showed up with more guards. He handed me a one-way plane ticket to Kingston, Jamaica, and $25 in old U.S. dollars. Such generosity. He told me he regretted what he needed to do, but reminded me that the government could have done much worse. Luckily for me, Cuba wanted to improve relations with the U.S., and perhaps Washington would view my release as a signal. With that, they drove me to Rancho Boyeros, the international airport located south of Havana, for an 8:30 a.m. flight. An hour before departure, they escorted me onto the plane and stationed a guard at the door to make sure I didn't get off. Shortly after that, one other passenger boarded and we recognized each other immediately. Cecil Collier, the Jamaican chargé d'affaires in Cuba, rented an office just a few blocks from my house, and we had met at several dinner parties. He took a seat near me and immediately asked me why I was going to Jamaica without my wife. I quickly told him my predicament and explained I had no visa, little money, and no idea what to do next.

He told me he had long suspected me of doing more than seeding rain clouds and wondered if I worked in intelligence as well. He advised me to stay by his side when we arrived in Kingston. He promised to do what he could to help me, and I jumped at his offer. He also said that upon his return to Havana in a week or so, he would personally see my wife and let her know that we had shared the flight and that I had gotten out okay. He asked me if I wanted him to inform other diplomatic friends in Havana of what had happened. I asked him not to. He just nodded without asking for an explanation.

Landing in Kingston, I stuck close to Cecil and, as we approached customs and immigration control, the authorities recognized him and waved us through. Outside the terminal, he instructed his driver to take me to the Pegasus Hotel on Halfway Tree Road, where the Jamaican government maintained several rooms for visiting dignitaries. They allowed me to stay for free in the hotel for the next several days while I planned my next move. Without funds or a passport, I saw few options.

First I needed to find out what was happening back in Cuba. I scoured the local newspapers and television broadcasts, but found no news of anyone arrested for espionage. If the Cubans had rounded up my former agents and contacts they had done it on the QT. I tried calling my family in Havana, but couldn't get through. The very same day, while downtown in Kingston, I ran into someone I had trained with at Camp Peary. His face turned white when we ran into each other on a street corner. He quickly headed down a side street, and I followed. He asked me what I was doing in Jamaica and I told him my story. He said that because several of my contacts had gone silent, TIO thought the Cubans had turned me and that I had ratted them out. I assured him I hadn't, but how could I convince TIO? My friend offered no solutions, but suggested I find a hole to crawl into because TIO was looking for me everywhere. He also promised not to tell anyone about our meeting. I thanked him and we parted.

I needed to make a quick decision. I knew he would eventually tell his superiors he'd seen me. With no way off the island, I decided to ask an old friend in Canada for help.

Dan Bjarnson worked for the Canadian Broadcasting Company (CBC) and I had befriended him in Cuba a few years earlier, showing him the real Havana and its secret hide-a-ways. Upon departing, he had invited me to contact him if I ever needed any help and to definitely come see him if I made it to Canada. Since his offer seemed sincere, I contacted him now and brought him up to date. I told him I needed a place where I could think as well as make contact with my family. He suggested I join him in Winnipeg. He told me about his contacts with the RCMP Intelligence Division, who would definitely like to talk to me. I quickly accepted and made plans to fly to Canada on the next flight. Not having a passport posed no problem, as U.S. citizens didn't need a passport to visit Jamaica or Canada.

Canada worked well as a place to get my thoughts together and decide on a plan. Canada had resisted the U.S. mandate to isolate Cuba and had never broken relations with the Cubans. Maybe I could get my family out of Cuba and to Canada with less hassle than going directly to the U.S. Perhaps talking to the RCMP would also allow me to re-establish myself in Canada and open an opportunity to work things out back home. At the time, it seemed the best course of action.

I arrived in Winnipeg, met with Dan, and agreed to meet with the RCMP, whom he had already notified. They had convinced him that they really wanted to talk to me. I rented a room in a boarding house and tried to contact Havana. Eventually I did get through to my wife, and she informed me that right after they deported me, the DGI had arrested several people who had worked for me. I felt terrible. My work for TIO had endangered all of them. Now they were paying the price.

I told her what had happened over the past several weeks and said that she shouldn't despair, as I would try working with Canada to get us back together. Then I contacted the RCMP officer that Dan had spoken to. He told me to show up the following day at his office and assured me I could trust him. I found it hard to believe, but what else could I do?

With trepidation, I approached the meeting at RCMP Headquarters at 1091 Portage Avenue. Was I walking into a trap? Would I find TIO there waiting for me? My hands shook uncontrollably as I entered the building.

The two officers I met, Paul Walnuchuck and Gary "something or other," seemed friendly enough. Though it was still early in the afternoon, they invited me to have a Scotch. My hands stopped shaking. They told me that they had no agenda and that we would arrive at mutual goals without any deadline. I explained that my agenda included getting my family out of Cuba, coming to some sort of understanding with TIO, and cleaning up all this mess. They assured me that, depending on the value of the information I could provide them, they would go to the Minister of Defense if necessary to sponsor me as a landed immigrant, usually a lengthy process. Until they found a solution, they assured me that I could feel both safe and free in Canada and that I should not fear extradition or kidnapping. They also told me to let them know if I needed any emergency funds. Based on these commitments, I agreed to talk to them without legal representation. We laid out an outline of subjects to cover in the next few months, including my first stay in Canada, TIO's activities, known and unknown to the RCMP, the location of safe houses in Canada, operations still underway, and a host of other topics, including DGI operations against the Canadian Embassy and its personnel in Havana. When I walked out of that first interview into the heat of the summer sunshine, I felt as if they had lifted the weight of the world from my shoulders and that perhaps my planning would yield results. For the first time in a long time I actually felt hopeful.

I feared that once TIO knew my location and activities he would become infuriated and pull out all stops to get me. My paranoia returned and I started to look for alternative places to get further from his grasp. I considered Peru, which was re-opening diplomatic relations with Cuba. That might increase my chances for survival, especially because my old boss in Havana, Comandante

Antonio Nuñez Jiménez, now served as the Cuban Ambassador to Lima. With this in mind I went to see the Peruvian consul in downtown Winnipeg.

The consul, Vaughn Baird, who was a partner in a prestigious law firm, served as both an honorary consul and a barrister. During my first meeting with him, he called in G. Campbell McLean, the senior partner in the firm, to join the session. They both listened intently to everything I said, and when I finished they both offered their help. Vaughn would take my case to the Canadian courts to seek landed immigrant status, just in case the RCMP didn't follow through. If nothing worked out legally he would help with a safe conduct to Peru. McLean promised to use the power and prestige of his firm to open doors a little faster than usual. In fact, he offered me a job at his resort, located a few miles east of Winnipeg, and also offered to do all the paperwork to get me permission to work in Canada. I couldn't believe that my luck was finally turning: the RCMP had guaranteed my freedom of movement and stability in Canada, the Peruvian honorary consul had offered to help, and a prestigious lawyer was throwing his weight around to open doors and now was offering me a place to live and a job! Coming to Canada seemed like it had been a good idea after all.

I left my rented quarters in Winnipeg and moved into the Lake Riviera Resort about 30 miles southeast of the city. The couple taking care of the place lived in a trailer that served as their quarters and office. They gave me the spare bedroom and expected me to help the overseer whenever he needed it. McLean saw that I needed a car to travel to and from Winnipeg for legal conferences and court appearances, so he bought a small convertible from his secretary and told me to use it. It needed some emergency repair work that I offered to do in exchange for its use. The summer guests at the resort arrived in their motor homes and campers and eventually filled the park. I helped lay out and pour the concrete for a tennis court, and then later offered free instruction to the guests. Word spread that I had served in the CIA, and I continually turned down offers of meals and drinks to tell my story.

My family came up from the States a few times to visit. I enjoyed every visit, but it pained me to hear their stories of FBI harassment and the questioning of everyone in my home town. Other than what they remembered from my childhood and school years, they really couldn't add anything. The FBI knew this, but used the very public exercise to spread the word that they considered me a fugitive from justice, armed and dangerous, slightly psychotic, and a threat to national security. I doubt that most of the people in my small central Iowa town actually put any stock in this contrived story, but my family did tell me that the local police made frequent trips past the house looking for me. I guess it amounted to the only 15 minutes of fame those cops would ever get.

The FBI cast its net wide enough to take in everyone who knew or associated with me. When a couple of FBI special agents come knocking on the door, they are intimidating to say the least. Most average citizens don't know that they don't have to talk to the FBI, and of course the Bureau doesn't advertise that simple, basic fact. The agents know that their visit to a home or workplace leaves a negative impression on neighbors and coworkers.

In Canada, the RCMP Intelligence Division instructed its highway patrol officers to come by the park from time to time just to look after me. At least they wanted me to believe they had my best interests in mind. They had probably received instructions to keep an eye on my whereabouts and doings as well. The local RCMP boys became fairly good friends and would often invite me to join them on patrol. They asked lots of questions about my past, and I would throw them a tidbit from time to time.

The summer passed quickly, filled with trips to Winnipeg for meetings with the RCMP and with my attorneys. Baird presented my case for landed immigrant status to the Canadian government. He also sought a minister's discretion from the Minister of Defense, James Richardson, making this a two-pronged effort to keep me safe in Canada. But Richardson said he wouldn't act until the courts and the government had made their decision. My lawyers suggested we go public with my situation to garner public support. I agreed and met with a reporter, Harry Marsden from the Winnipeg *Tribune*. We spent several days going over the series of events that had brought me to Canada once again. The story made the front page and continued on several interior pages as well. Phone calls of support arrived. A reporter from the Des Moines *Register*, Michael Pauly, traveled to Winnipeg to follow up for readers in my home state The two newspaper articles caused quite a stir, but the new interest in my case brought trouble as well.

I visited the U.S. Consulate in Winnipeg to request a new passport. My old one had expired in 1973, and when I sought renewal via the Swiss caretakers of the U.S. Embassy in Havana, they refused. They had offered me a safe conduct for direct return to the U.S. back then, but had made no provisions for my wife and son. The Swiss kept my expired passport on orders from Washington. Now, in Canada, I had no supporting documents, and that unnerved me, to say the least. Without a passport I couldn't travel. The U.S. Consul Dareslav Vlahovich called me in one day and told me that Washington had denied my application without offering any explanation. I asked if he had received any word from the Justice Department concerning me. "They've told me nothing," he said.

Both Baird and Walnuchuck informed me that the U.S. had told them it would not seek my extradition. This surprised me. How could they not want to get their hands on such a dangerous fugitive? They would seek the extradition of a person stealing a loaf of bread in the States and fleeing to Canada in a matter of days, if not hours, yet they would not extradite a notorious criminal like me? Obviously they were making other plans. Baird speculated that they wanted to avoid an extradition case that would require coming to Canada and presenting a case. Shining a light on U.S. intelligence agency business in Canada would create quite an international mess, a mess that the U.S. and TIO wanted to avoid at any cost.

A few days before Christmas, an unmarked car pulled into the drive in front of the trailer at the lake. Two RCMP officers I didn't know came to the door. I invited them in, and after some small talk they asked me to identify some photographs in their car. I agreed, but once we were in the car, they told me we were headed to Winnipeg, locked the doors, and sped away.

As we approached Winnipeg from the east, they pulled into a service station near several cars closely parked together, all with their engines running. As soon as our car stopped, several people came running from the waiting cars. I didn't recognize anyone. I immediately sensed a kidnapping. They had planned well: on a weekend, late in the afternoon, with everyone out of their offices and probably out of touch. Once the car was loaded with more officers, we sped south toward the border. Panic set in.

One RCMP officer at my side, a Sergeant Howard Comba, didn't seem quite convinced that this was all above board. I quickly explained to him that he should contact my attorney, Mr. Baird, as well as Paul Walnuchuck of the RCMP D Division, to verify the information I had given him. He made a few calls, stopped the car he was driving, turned around and headed back north. All the cars in the caravan did the same, and Sgt. Comba explained his move over the radio. The conversation grew animated and visibly upset the sergeant.

When we arrived at the RCMP patrol division headquarters in Winnipeg, I caught a glimpse of Baird and an RCMP D division officer whose name I didn't know waiting for us. The ensuing conversation got loud and chaotic. The facts that emerged made clear that FBI Special Agent Merle Nelson, from Grand Forks, North Dakota, had come to Winnipeg and, with his close friend the chief of police of Winnipeg, had hatched the scheme to grab me using local highway patrol cops, drive me to the border, and hand me off to FBI agents waiting on the other side. They would have succeeded if not for the professionalism of Sgt. Comba. The FBI agents returned to North Dakota empty handed and reprimanded. It took several days for my nerves to calm down.

This incident made clear to all of us that TIO would now get down and dirty. They wouldn't seek extradition publicly. Their kidnap scheme had gone bust. They would now use direct diplomatic efforts to convince Canada to kick me out, with hopes of snatching me elsewhere. A few short weeks later I

Department of State

```
                    LIMITED OFFICIAL USE    3224
PAGE 01  OTTAWA 01014  112129Z                        ACTION
12
ACTION PPT-01

INFO  OCT-01  SCA-01  ISO-00  PPS-01  L-03  JUSE-00  EUR-12  /019 W
        ------------------------              096453
R 112611Z MAR 76
FM AMEMBASSY OTTAWA
TO SECSTATE WASHDC 9102
INFO AMCONSUL WINNIPEG
```

LIMITED OFFICIAL USE OTTAWA 1014

F.O. 11652: N/A   **URGENT**
TAGS: AINF, CPAS, PFOR
SUBJ: CPAS (LYON, VERNE ALLEN)

REF: A. DEPT'S OM DATED OCT. 15, 1975

B. WINNIPEG'S A-1 OF FEB. 19, 1976

1. AS PER REF OM, DEPT DISAPPROVED VERNE ALLEN LYON'S U.S.
PASSPORT APPLCATION OF AUGUST 19, 1975, UNDER THE PROVISIONS
OF SECTION 51.70(A)(1). DEPARTMENT'S DISAPPROVAL BASED ON
OUTSTANDING WARRANT OF ARREST FOR VIOLATION OF TITLE 18
USC SECTION 32 (AIRCRAFT DESTRUCTION).

2. MEDIA (PRESS AND CBC TV) HAVE EXPRESSED INTEREST IN
LYON CASE. WINNIPEG CG INFORMALLY INDICATED OUTSTANDING
WARRANT OF ARREST AS BASIS FOR PASSPORT REFUSAL.

3. IT IS UNDERSTOOD THAT WINNIPEG LOCAL PRESS AND CBC TV
ARE AWARE OF LYON CASE AS RECOUNTED IN WINNIPEG'S A-1.
EMBASSY WOULD THEREFORE APPRECIATE CONTINGENCY GUIDANCE RE
HIS ALLEGATIONS AND TO HELP REPLY TO SUCH POSSIBLE PRESS
QUESTIONS AS TO WHY THERE HAS BEEN NO REQUEST FOR LYON'S
EXTRADITION.
ENDERS

                                    PASSPORT OFFICE
           URGENT   MAR 15 1976

           LIMITED OFFICIAL USE   PT/U
                7
```

Here the State Department asks why there was no extradition request during the 15 months I lived in Canada and was in almost daily contact with the U.S. Consulate. If the U.S. had requested my extradition, I would have had the opportunity to defend myself in Canadian courts and the U.S. would have been obligated to provide me all the documents that I asked for. The CIA could not allow that.
```

received a letter from the Canadian government informing me that they had denied my application for refugee status and that I should leave Canada within the next 60 days. We contacted the Minister of Defense, James Richardson, to ask for a ministerial waiver. The minister told us that Washington had apparently made it clear to Ottawa that the U.S. would view any asylum granted by Canada in a very dim light that could seriously affect relations between the two nations. The fact that thousands of young men from the States went to Canada and received asylum during the Vietnam War had frayed relations between the two countries, and a fragile kiss-and-make-up atmosphere hung in the balance. I couldn't remain in Canada.

My attorney and I discussed the possibilities at length. He reminded me that Peru represented perhaps my best choice for the moment, since a request sent to the Swedish government through their consulate had produced no response. In fact, the timeline now imposed by the Canadian government foreclosed further waiting. I remembered that a Peruvian government official had offered me help some years earlier during the devastating earthquake there in 1973. Baird offered to intercede for me in contacts with the Peruvians. He sent a letter to Lima seeking a safe conduct passport for travel to Peru. Word came back from the Peruvians that Baird, as honorary consul of Peru in Canada, could issue me a safe conduct pass. We made plans for me to fly to Lima that very month.

15. Flight

I didn't want to leave Canada. I had run through the gamut of feelings and hopes during my time there. I had arrived with great expectations of starting a new life, getting my family out of Cuba, and removing myself from politics and TIO's grasp. All those hopes and dreams flashed by as Canadian Pacific Flight 522 lifted off from Toronto on August 5, 1976, bound for Peru. The flight went without incident and we touched down at the Jorge Chávez International Airport around noon the following day. When I approached immigration and customs control in the airport and presented the diplomatic safe conduct pass, they asked me to wait in an adjoining room for a few minutes until a Captain Ramírez of the Peruvian Servicio de Inteligencia Nacional (SIN) arrived. He told me that Peru would honor the safe conduct pass, but he added some conditions. He told me that I could not carry a sidearm and that I should not engage in politics of any sort. He also admonished me not to advertise my presence in the country and to keep SIN posted on my whereabouts. He suggested a few places that I could look for lodging in Lima and warned me to stay away from the U.S. Embassy. That last piece of advice I didn't really need.

I rented a room on the Jirón Callao. I explained to the owner that I needed privacy and he left me alone. After settling in, I put together a plan of action. I would contact SIN as requested, but I would also try to see my ex-boss, Comandante Jiménez, now Cuban ambassador to Peru. He and I had always gotten on well, and even though I guessed learning that I had worked for the CIA must have upset him, I hoped he would at least hear me out for old time's sake and maybe help me get my family out of Cuba.

Captain Ramírez turned up at my new digs after a few days and suggested I write a letter to the new president explaining my dilemma. He advised me that such a move would give me an unfiltered voice in the Presidential Palace.

Don Francisco Morales-Bermúdez y Cerruti, a general in the Peruvian Army, had deposed the left-leaning Juan Velasco Alvarado, supposedly to improve relations with the U.S., when the Army and the Peruvian power brokers decided they'd had enough of the leftist government. Public trust in the Velasco government had plummeted when the people learned that he entertained a different prostitute in the palace every night and that the resulting case of syphilis had cost him first his leg and later his life. The country had made a huge swing from left to right with the coup, and I couldn't immediately determine how that would affect me. The new president had tried to calm public fears about abrupt changes in the so-called "Peruvian Revolution" by adopting the slogan "same revolution, different leaders." He had promised Peru a pluralistic government, so the minor crisis he might face if my presence became known publicly could help demonstrate his independence from the U.S. On the other hand, if he defied any U.S. request to detain and deport me, he might risk U.S. sanctions. Faced with this dilemma after he received my letter, he dispatched General Antonio Chávarri Urello to call on me.

A ranking member of SIN, General Chávarri gave me the definite feeling at our first meeting that he suspected me of working for the Cubans and this explained why the U.S. wanted me so badly. He knew of my efforts to stay in Canada and he had read my letter to President Bermúdez. He sounded me out about my plans if allowed to stay in Peru, as well as what I might do if they rejected my request. I told him I intended to abide by the rules delivered earlier by Captain Ramirez and that I wanted to talk to the Cubans about letting my family go. As I analyzed his questions, I realized that the Peruvians would not make any snap decisions. They didn't want to get their fingers burned by bowing to U.S. demands, nor did they seem to want me to stay.

The general told me that SIN had already detected U.S. agents searching for me. While they now knew I had entered Peru, they didn't know my exact location or plans. He suggested that I move to a new address nearby at 410 Moquegua, close to the Hotel Crillón. This made me nervous, because I knew that TIO maintained a suite on the upper floor of the Crillón for interrogation and recruitment purposes. I told him of my fears and he assured me that SIN would watch out for me. This raised a red flag immediately. I knew that TIO had put many SIN officers on its payroll either openly or covertly and that they might report my every move to TIO at the U.S. Embassy. I asked the general why he couldn't put me up in a safe house. He said that the government wanted to show, if necessary, that they controlled security in the country and that a grab similar to the one in Canada would not and could not happen in Peru. I didn't believe him, but I also knew that if they put me in a safe house, TIO could easily gain their cooperation and spirit me out of the country. I didn't know whom to trust, but I decided to let everyone know that I had landed in Peru as a precaution against another attempted kidnapping.

General Chávarri informed me that he had assigned my case to Lt. Col. Domingo Campos Montoya, a senior SIN case officer. While Chávarri had climbed up the ladder of promotion because of his loyalty to General Bermúdez, Montoya, a polished career case officer, had worked his way up through the years under various governments. Having my case transferred to a professional eased some of my paranoia.

Once on my case, Col. Montoya moved me to a private apartment/office complex at 132 Pasaje Tello in the affluent Lima suburb of Miraflores, just a few steps away from the famous traffic circle called the Óvalo, a tourist area filled with trendy restaurants and souvenir shops. A civil engineer and confidant of Col. Montoya, German Galvez Brandon, partly owned the building and operated several civil engineering fronts from this address. One of them, Tubolit, dispersed payoffs from Peruvian intelligence to street informants. Brandon fancied himself a part-time psychologist and offered his services to Col. Montoya to determine if I was crazy or something else. His efforts to analyze me seemed simplistic, but I played along as he appeared well connected to the intelligence services.

I soon realized that Montoya had tasked him with trying to ferret out information under the guise of building my case for asylum. At times his questions focused on Cuban espionage efforts in Peru, and other times on the Peruvian leftist movement, MIR, that showed a violent side from time to time. He tried to convince me that cooperating with SIN would help them decide whether or not to let me stay. I told him on more than one occasion that a government grants asylum and does not sell it.

In subsequent meetings I realized that Montoya planned to prepare an official report by SIN to President Bermúdez to assist him in making his final decision in my case. I hoped to convince Col. Montoya that I would cooperate with SIN, exhibited no mental illness, and did not pose a threat to Peru. Apparently the counterintelligence branch of the Peruvian Investigative Police (PIP) had done a very cursory study of my case and had recommended my deportation to avoid adversely affecting diplomatic relations with several other Latin American nations as well as the U.S. Aware of this, Montoya promised me that he would try to override it with an in-depth study.

José Jorge ran PIP-CI out of the PIP building on Argentina Avenue in downtown Lima. This fortress sits only a block or so away from the U.S. Embassy, at the intersection of Wilson and Argentina. His department kept foreigners suspected of left-wing activities, drug dealing and any other activities likely to lead to deportation under surveillance. Jorge also worked very closely with the chief of national security, Miguel Amable, who spent many hours every week in the U.S. Embassy. In light of all of this, Col. Montoya seemed to think that I stood a chance. To enhance that chance, according to him, he contemplated moving me to an army base for security. I refused. He also contacted

This shows the SIN headquarters building next to the Presidential Palace in Lima, Peru. It is the building with all the antennas. This intelligence building was the equivalent to the CIA buildings in Langley, Virginia.

the Ministry of Foreign Relations to extend my visa, and they assured him that my visa was in order and no other governmental entity would interfere.

This growing division within the Peruvian security forces represented a real problem. The faction wanting to cozy up to the U.S. wielded great influence, while Montoya led a small and more isolated faction. The SIN offices occupied the upper floors of the building located just across the street from the National Palace in La Plaza de las Armas. The Office of National Information (ONI) also shared this building, and to gain access to the upper floors required a special pass which Montoya gave me. On several occasions he asked that I come by the office to help provide him with material to write his report. On one occasion he spread several photographs of U.S. Embassy employees on his desk and asked me if I knew any of them. I didn't.

During this sojourn in Lima I tried several times to see my old boss, Antonio Nuñez-Jiménez, but the Cubans must have told him not to talk to me. The embassy always told me that he was busy or traveling out of the country. I didn't believe them, but I understood that since his government deported me, he knew his superiors would not want him seeing me.

Col. Montoya told me that his report would go to General Charon, the chief of Peruvian Intelligence. He, in turn, would add his recommendation and then turn the whole file over to the Ministry of Foreign Relations for a final decision. President Bermúdez would also weigh in on the final outcome, but I knew he didn't want to upset the U.S. They also involved a Señor Marchand, a sort of freelance problem solver for the Ministry of Foreign Relations and the president. As a civilian, he could take a different view than the military and the intelligence services. Marchand asked me to make a formal request for political asylum, so I spent several days writing it all out in longhand as they wouldn't provide me a typewriter. When I finished, I turned it over to him and asked him to make a copy for my own files. He said he would but he never did.

After some weeks had passed, Col. Montoya told me that the counterintelligence branch of the Peruvian Ministry of the Interior had issued its recommendation, advising against asylum because it might endanger recently improved relations with both the U.S. and Cuba. The Ministry recommended that I be driven to the border with Ecuador and forced out of Peru at gunpoint. Let the Ecuadorians worry about me after that. This solution didn't suit either the president or General Charon. They didn't want the U.S. to think that they had let me go after denying me asylum, and they didn't want to provoke the Ecuadorians either. They needed to find another solution that would let them save face, since they had told me in Canada that they would grant me asylum.

One day a Lieutenant Mendieta from SIN showed up and asked me to accompany him. He didn't say where, but when we arrived I recognized the place, the downtown police station where they held foreigners accused of drug-related crimes and other criminals before or during trial. He told me that I would remain there until a decision came down on what to do with me. I panicked! Surely somebody had made a mistake. I needed to get in touch with Col. Montoya. I noticed a phone in a nearby office, and while Mendieta left to talk to other officers, I quickly grabbed the phone and called him. When I told him what happened he said he would come right down. I replaced the phone in its cradle just as Mendieta returned. Before much else happened, Col. Montoya arrived and demanded information. Mendieta called him aside and apparently tried to explain his orders and who they came from. Col. Montoya explained to him that the Ministry of Foreign Relations had extended my stay in Peru by another 90 days, legally, and therefore they should not interfere. With that, they let me go. As I left, I noticed that from this downtown police fortress I could see my nemesis, the U.S. Embassy, a couple of blocks away.

I now expected another kidnapping at any moment. The U.S. knew my whereabouts and must have made a formal request for my extradition. I needed to change my plans. I guessed that most of Peru's intelligence officers probably also slept in the U.S. Embassy at night and collected money on the side. I faced real danger. I ducked out and spent the night in the apartment of Michael Mullen, an American friend unknown to Peruvian intelligence. The next day I fumbled to formulate a plan, or at least the best prospect I could devise.

I couldn't go to Chile because Pinochet owed his job to the U.S. Each and every other South American country had pledged allegiance to the U.S. Where could I go? The next day I returned to my place in Miraflores. I decided to go to the Swedish Embassy and ask them to contact my old friend Kai Groote, the former Swedish ambassador in Havana. He had promised his help if I ever needed it, and boy, did I ever.

I waited until the embassy was readying to close for the day before I entered and asked to see the chargé d'affaires. He escorted me to his office. I spent the next hour or more telling him how I had gotten here and why. He sat there with his mouth hanging open, not knowing how to respond or what to do. I told him to locate Kai on his embassy personnel register. He did, and told me that Kai now served in India. I asked him to send an urgent communication to him, telling him that I wanted to take him up on his offer of assistance. The chargé d'affaires told me that he could send the cable, but due to the huge time difference I might not get a response for a day or two. I told him that I would wait, and sat down in a big chair in his office. I saw that this made him uneasy. He told me that I couldn't stay any later than midnight, as he would close the embassy. I agreed. He brought out some vodka and put on some coffee and we made small talk. He disappeared a few times, supposedly to send the cable and then to check for an answer. The hours ticked by. Midnight arrived with apparently no answer. He told me that I should return first thing in the morning and we would send a new request and once again wait for a response. I really didn't want to leave, but he might call the police and have me removed and I didn't want that to happen. I left, telling him that I would return in the morning. He locked the door behind me and I headed out into the night.

I walked a few blocks to Arequipa Avenue, a major road running north and south through Lima and its suburbs. I had traveled no more than two blocks when an old American-made station wagon screeched to a stop next to me. Three guys who looked like they could play professional football in the States jumped out and grabbed me. In an instant they forced me face down on the rear floorboards, got in the car and placed their feet on my back. The car took off. They returned me once again to that downtown prison and hustled me up the stairs into the main office under the watch of Mendieta and a couple of other heavily armed guards. They refused to allow me a phone call.

Early the next morning, they put me back in the station wagon, drove me to the airport and turned me over to some U.S. officials, including Marshal

Weyn Sallada, who escorted me onto a waiting Braniff non-stop flight to Miami. As the plane taxied to the runway for takeoff, the marshal placed me under arrest. I asked him what the charge was, and he responded, "Destruction of property, Verne." He asked the stewardess to seat us in the rear of the plane away from the other passengers. Moments later we took off.

16. Framed

More U.S. agents met us on arrival in Miami, one from the State Department and another who didn't identify himself. Telling me I'd be spending the next day or two at a federal detention center before being flown back to St. Louis to appear in court, they turned me over to the detention center guards, who issued me an orange jumpsuit and a pair of plastic slippers. They placed me in a two-level housing unit and assigned me a room. Most of the people held there seemed young; over half were Hispanic, and by listening to the different dialects I identified Colombians, Cubans, Venezuelans, and Mexicans, mostly held for drug-related offenses and awaiting trial or transfer to a federal prison elsewhere to serve their sentences. They told me I could use a public phone on the lower level between 2:00 and 4:00 p.m., but could only call collect. I waited anxiously until 2:00 p.m., picked up the phone and gave the operator the number of my family back in Iowa. When they answered, I quickly filled them in. They told me they would contact an old friend and lawyer, and would accompany him to St. Louis to meet with me. I hung up feeling much better now that someone I trusted knew my situation.

Two days later, another U.S. marshal flew with me to St. Louis, where more marshals waited for us along with a reporter from a local TV station. They hustled me away from the reporter and into a waiting car, and then drove to the St. Claire County Jail located in Belleville, Illinois, about 30 miles from St. Louis. There they allowed me a phone call, so I again placed a call to my family. They informed me that the attorney would arrive the next day.

Three long days later the attorney finally showed up. He explained that he had been delayed a day at the federal courthouse in St. Louis talking to prosecutors and ascertaining the charges against me, whether bail was allowed, and so on. They gave him the information even though he did not practice in Missouri and could not practice law in federal court. He told me that he would contact one or two attorneys in the St. Louis area who met these requirements and put them in touch with me. He told me that everyone in my family would soon come to the jail for a visit. I told him to discourage that trip for the time being.

He informed me that I faced two federal charges: destruction of property at the St. Louis airport in 1966, and failing to appear for a court hearing later that same year. He said that he had read the articles printed years before in both the Winnipeg newspaper and the Des Moines *Register,* so he knew something of my case. "Listen," I told him, "I face issues well beyond your experience. I'll need a lawyer with a national security background." He just looked at me blankly. I thanked him for his efforts and he left.

A few days later the marshals returned to transport me to the courthouse in St. Louis for an initial appearance before the same judge from many years earlier, John Regan. He asked me if I had an attorney of record. I did not. I went on to tell him that I didn't have any money either and that they'd literally kidnapped me off the streets of Lima while I was still legally there under safe conduct. He evinced no interest in any of that. In fact, he said that the court couldn't concern itself with how I now appeared before it, only that I did. He would appoint an attorney to represent me, and after that he would accept any plea I wanted to make. He set bail at something like $1 million. This took all of 30 minutes, and then they drove me back to the jail in Illinois.

The jailor asked me if I faced any danger from the other prisoners being held in my wing. I asked, "Do you have any federal agents imbedded in with them? If you do, I'd like to be moved." He looked at me kind of flummoxed and told the guards to take me away.

The judge appointed Leonard Frankel to represent me, and he showed up a few days later. Judge Regan would oversee the first charge concerning the destruction of property, and Judge Wanglen would handle the failure to appear. Frankel told me that the first charge carried a maximum prison sentence of 20 years and the second a maximum of 5, so the sentences could well total 25 years. I just gasped. I couldn't comprehend losing 25 years of my life. Frankel told me that I faced a judge who was angry for having let me go so many years before. He added that given this personal animosity I should expect no leniency whatsoever. He asked me what I could suggest for a defense strategy. This told me he knew absolutely nothing about the history of my case. "How much time have you got?" I asked him. "All the time you need," he said, so I began at the beginning and ran through the events of the last ten years in rapid fashion. I could see he didn't know whether to believe me or not. "What do you think, Leonard?" He said he just didn't know what to say at the moment, but that he would have to break down my story and try to prove each step. He asked what I could offer as proof. I reminded him that they had kidnapped me with just the clothes on my back. The Peruvian Intelligence Services had retained all my personal papers and possessions, and I doubted they would send any of them to me. I also told him that the Cubans had put me on the plane to Jamaica without any of the notes I had saved. He shook his head at the difficulty and suggested we subpoena my CIA records. I think at that point we both realized that we faced an uphill battle. He left, saying that he would return after doing some checking.

They made life in the St. Clair County Jail very difficult. When called out of the cell block to another area of the jail, one walked a narrow space between the wall and a painted yellow line on the floor. Straying beyond the line meant that the nearest guard would club one with a wooden mallet. The food stunk. One day they served sandwiches made with green baloney. Nobody ate it, and most threw the stuff through the bars onto the floor. This so upset the jail captain that, to prove to us we should eat it, he grabbed a few pieces of the green meat from the floor and ate it. He didn't return to work for several days. They never served baloney sandwiches again in this dirty, poorly run lockup. Complaints to the federal marshals went without action. Federal rules require that a jail meet minimum standards, and the St. Clair County Jail certainly didn't, but nobody seemed to care.

Frankel returned after a week or so. He told me that the judge wanted a swift trial, as did the prosecutor. He had told them both that we needed to collect information and that doing so would take time. He had told the judge that we wanted to subpoena my CIA files, FBI records, State Department files, and so on. Apparently the judge got really angry at this and accused us of delaying the whole process. Frankel also told me that his research showed that, when federal and state agents searched my residence while I worked at McDonnell, they did so without a search warrant. The elderly landlady, overwhelmed by people presenting all kinds of badges, didn't even ask to see a warrant, something they didn't have anyway. He told me he would file pre-trial motions to suppress any evidence they might have seized during the warrantless search. He also told me that the judge might quash his motion now, but it might be overturned on appeal. Judges often employ this tactic knowing that, even if reversed, a jury never really forgets information illegally obtained and presented. It helps insure a new conviction if the case ever reaches that stage.

Frankel added that, because he served as a public defender, he couldn't use federal money to hire an independent investigator, so we might find it difficult to run to ground anybody able to back up my story. He said that the prosecution had no witnesses and no proof of any sort that I had been anywhere near the airport that night. There was no one who could say they had heard or seen me plan an attack. The prosecution would use the fact that I had purchased dynamite and blasting caps several days before the incident, but the agents who went into my apartment in my absence and without a search warrant had handled these items. They could have done anything they wanted while in my apartment illegally. That would make it my word against theirs in a court of law, and in 99 percent of such cases, the judge and jury believe the cops. I just looked at Frankel and told him, "I'm screwed unless the subpoenas get the information I need."

I asked him about the second charge, failure to appear, and how to answer it. He claimed that if we got the information we subpoenaed they'd have to drop that. Everything rested in the hands of the government, and they, a federal judge, a prosecutor, and the federal agents poised to testify against me would decide my fate. The government even paid my own attorney. How in the hell could I defend myself on a playing field tilted against me? Frankel just told me again that he felt certain we could get any conviction overturned on appeal because of the illegal search and seizure. That didn't mean much to me. I stood alone against the entire government. I didn't stand a chance in hell. On my side I counted only a few family members, while everyone else seemed to fade away for one reason or another.

They had kidnapped me out of Peru in February 1977 and Judge Regan scheduled the trial two months later. He did not grant us time to gather evidence. The subpoena duces tecum for my CIA files was discussed in chambers in the presence of Judge Regan, my attorney, the prosecutor, and agents of the CIA. The judge barred me from attending, even though the whole hearing concerned me. The CIA refused to produce my files. Instead, they summarized to the court the documents they would not present. They would not allow Judge Regan, a former Navy officer and now a federal judge, to see my records. He should have shut down the trial then and there, as 5 U.S. Code 522, the Freedom of Information Act, requires that a defendant receive any evidence that would tend to exonerate him. They left me with no defense to present. The court forced my attorney to sign a stipulation of facts accepting that my CIA file would never be examined, now or in the future. The trial amounted to a kangaroo court. TIO's threats had become real, and now they led me to the slaughter. The government that I swore to defend against all enemies, domestic or foreign, now planned to sacrifice me, and I was powerless to stop it.

Under Rule 16 of the Rules of Criminal Procedure for the United States District Courts, I had the right to seek discovery and inspection of all evidence against me, as well as documents and tangible evidence the prosecution might have access to that I didn't. However, under Section 2 of that same rule, some information, including reports, memoranda, or other internal government documents related to the national security interests of the United States, remained exempt to discovery.

I would have no access to exculpatory evidence. How convenient for the government. The Freedom of Information Act (FOIA) provides any person access to and copies of any document, file, or record in the possession of any federal agency or department. Under the same act, an individual has the right to gain access to his own record or to any information pertaining to him. There are nine specific exemptions to this rule, and Exemption Number 7(a) allows denial of FOIA documents related to the national defense, foreign policy, or material classified by the government. Also, under 7(g), if non-disclosure would tend to deprive a person of a fair trial, information can be still withheld if it would violate confidential national security intelligence operations that would cause to become known, through due diligence, the identity of intelligence officers, operations, sources, and/or methods. So the government can prosecute while denying exculpatory evidence for the defendant. How can one respond to this situation? Frankel and I faced an uphill and, finally, unwinnable battle.

The trial lasted all of three days. The government prosecutor did not present any motive for me to bomb the airport. Government psychiatrists ruled me sane. I had done well in my position at McDonnell Aircraft, so no motive there. I had no enemies at work, no beefs with the aircraft manufacturer or the government in general. To believe the government account, I somehow went from being a methodical and logical engineer just starting my career to a cold calculating nut for a moment, and then just as quickly returned to sanity. Things like that just don't happen.

The government presented the agents who had searched my apartment without a warrant. They testified that they had found some sticks of dynamite and some blasting caps as well as wrapping material for Christmas presents. They also called a few McDonnell employees who had worked with me in Building 211, who confirmed that I had gone to the Playboy Club in downtown St. Louis on the evening of the explosion and that I had appeared normal in every sense. They described me as a good employee and expressed their surprise when they learned of the charges against me. The local newspapers went crazy with sensational reporting before and during the trial. The judge refused to sequester the jury, so they faced a deluge of negative reporting each evening. When the judge quashed the subpoena, he also ruled out all testimony involving the CIA. I could call no witnesses to testify to my Agency employment. My attorney tried to raise the question of motive, or lack thereof, to no avail. He also tried to enter questions about why the judge suddenly decided to lower my bail to only $500 way back in 1966, also to no avail. He asked why the State of Missouri did not file charges and got no answer. He asked why the U.S. didn't try to extradite me from Canada during my year and a half there. No answer. He asked why the judge hadn't thrown out the results of the illegal search and seizure in my apartment. No answer.

The prosecution stated that they never looked at another suspect in the

CENTRAL INTELLIGENCE AGENCY
WASHINGTON, D.C. 20505

March 21, 1971

Mrs. Alice Lyon
RR 1 Moingona
Boone, Iowa 50036

Dear Mrs. Lyon:

This is to acknowledge recipt of your 11 March 1971 letter concerning your son Verne Allen Lyon.

This Agency is unable to provide advice on your request as Mr. Lyon is no longer connected with the Agency. However, I would appreciate your advising me of any future developments.

Yours truly,

Carl Dill
Carl Dill
for the Director
of Central Intelligence

This unique letter came to my family in 1971 after they had inquired about me. The original letter has long been lost, but this copy shows the CIA's response and clearly indicates that I was once connected with them. The date of 1971 is very odd because I didn't officially resign until 1973. I have never known quite how to interpret this.

case, in spite of all the anomalies. They loaded the dice against me from the outset, and nothing I or my attorney might do could affect the outcome. In such a lopsided presentation in a kangaroo court, it didn't take long to render a verdict: guilty. Given all that had transpired, I still stood absolutely stunned as the jury foreman read the verdict. How could this happen in the U.S., where we expect open and fair trials with all of the evidence fairly presented and considered? They had not permitted me a defense. Even alluding to exculpatory evidence would cause the judge to come down hard on me and my attorney. Everything I believed about the system of law and judgment in the U.S. came crashing down. In that courtroom I saw not justice, but revenge. This would certainly teach any intelligence officers deployed in hard targets not to resign as I had. My only hope now rested in winning the appeal, but that wouldn't stop me from going to prison.

Judge Regan, as required by law, ordered a pre-sentencing investigation. No one asked me even one question, and as far as I know, they contacted no one who would vouch for me either. With this "investigation" soon complete, Regan sentenced me to 15 years in the custody of the Attorney General of the United States. What had happened here? Why had he not given me the maximum? I believe to this day that he gave me a shorter sentence because he knew, as did my lawyer and I and all the rest of the federal agents involved in the case, that this represented a miscarriage of justice. Soon afterward I appeared before Judge Wanglen, who found me guilty of failure to appear in the original case and handed down a sentence of two years instead of the maximum of five, once again surprising my lawyer and me. This added up to 17 years, but it allowed for parole at the end of one third of the sentence, 68 months, if I remained alive and behaved myself as a prisoner.

I sensed my lawyer's disappointment. During the trial I could see the pain and resentment on his face as the judge tied his hands and restricted evidence. He told me that he would quickly file appeals on both convictions and felt certain he could win on the first one, but that an appeal could take up to a year. My heart sank. I asked him to contact my family in Cuba and give them the news. I could sink no lower than I was at that moment.

Or could I? Could I survive in prison known as a former federal agent? Would someone try to make a name for himself by attacking me? I really didn't expect any of the prison guards or administrative staff to care one way or the other.

U.S. marshals escorted me back and forth from the county jail to the federal courthouse and told me that even they, who had apparently seen every type of judicial misconduct imaginable over the years, were shocked at my treatment. Now I waited to hear where I would serve my sentence as a virtual slave of the Attorney General of the United States. I awaited my doom.

17. In Hell

The marshals who delivered me to Leavenworth that summer day in 1977 left without a word of farewell. An Assessment and Orientation (A&O) guard appeared from the dark depths, and only then did the Receiving and Discharge (R&D) guard open the door, allowing us to enter. Once again, they passed me along like a piece of property.

"We don't lose nobody here," said the A&O guard. He instructed me to follow him toward the far end of the cell house basement. To my left, barred windows allowed some light into this belowground dungeon. On my right I passed a series of small cells without doors, measuring about five feet wide by nine feet deep and maybe seven feet high. Between each of these cave-like cells, single metal frame beds stuck out into the open space. At the end of each bed stood a small metal cabinet. I saw approximately 125 beds in this underground crypt, most of them occupied. Nearing the far end of the row, the guard pointed toward one of the beds and said, "This one is yours for now."

"Put your shit in the locker and follow me back to my desk." I complied. There he handed me several sheets of paper that consisted of a personality quiz (multiple choice), a skills test (multiple choice), a health questionnaire, and a sheet of paper where I could name the persons I wanted on my visiting list (limit eight), as well as a booklet explaining my "rights and responsibilities" as a federal prisoner. I quickly went through the quizzes, randomly filling in the response areas, making no attempt to match answers with questions.

He handed me a flat piece of wood with several pegs of differing diameters protruding and a small bag that contained flat metal washers of different diameters. "This is to test your dexterity in case you want to work in the prison industries," he explained. "Place the washers on the corresponding pegs. You have three minutes." I took my time, barely completing the task in the three minutes. I handed the board back to him and he dutifully recorded the elapsed time and number of washers correctly placed.

"The number you got in R&D is your identity here," he said. "Each federal prison or correctional institution has its own three-number designation," he continued. "Leavenworth is 132, Atlanta is 131, and so on. Your number 89,649,132 means that 89,648 prisoners preceded you here."

If I needed additional soap, toothpowder, combs, writing paper or envelopes, I would tell him or the guard on duty. All outgoing mail was to be placed, unsealed, in a wooden box attached to his desk. Postage was free. Any mail going to my attorney could be sealed, but I needed to give it directly to the guard on duty. If any mail arrived for me I would receive it after the 4:00 p.m. headcount.

There were lots of rules to learn. A loud buzzer announced mealtime three times a day. I could not enter any other cell house, borrow anything from another prisoner, or attempt to bribe a guard. I could attend religious services on Sunday, but if I wanted to see the chaplain, I had to send him a "kite," a written request on a special form available from the guard on duty. The guard showed me a mimeographed sheet listing prisoners' numbers in one column and destinations and time in adjacent ones. "This is called the snitch sheet," he explained. "One will be posted on this desk each morning, and you should consult it every day to see if you are being called out somewhere. If you are called out, you need to get a signed pass from the guard on duty and remember to get a signed pass from the person who called you out so you can return here."

He then consulted a second list and assigned me yet another number, E68. "This is your laundry number. It will be on all of your clothing items except for socks and towels, which you can exchange on Tuesdays and Thursdays. You'll be in A&O for about two weeks while you adapt to prison life, have your emotional and educational levels determined, undergo any medical and dental exams necessary, be assigned a caseworker, listen to a lecture or two about prison life and await a cell and job assignment." I tried to absorb it all. I could go to the movies on Saturdays, go into the recreation yards, and mingle in with the general prison population. Additionally, they would open a commissary account for me with whatever funds I had brought in, so I could go to the "store" one night a week to purchase everything from tennis shoes to instant coffee.

The guard dismissed me and I returned to my bunk to lie down and try to think through this new life. Several prisoners sitting on their bunks or in their cavelike cells watched me as I lay down. I kept my eyes open and found I could not relax. I remained tense, remembering the admonition from the marshals to watch my back. At some point, due to sheer exhaustion, I fell asleep.

A piercing buzzer pulled me back to reality. I fearfully surveyed my surroundings. The other prisoners got up and headed toward the door, and one of them, a longhaired sharp-featured man with a dark complexion, motioned for me to join them. "It's supper," he said. "Probably the best meal of the day."

I got off the bunk, already completely dressed, and followed the line of men up the stairway. The top of the stairs intersected a hallway that radiated out from the central rotunda. Yellow lines ran down the center of the hall. Most of the prisoners walked inside the two yellow lines, and I followed suit. We headed away from the rotunda, through a set of steel-barred gates, and then turned left into the huge dining room. I saw a long table with silverware, plates, bowls, and trays built and decorated like the Conestoga wagons used by the settlers over a century earlier. I collected my utensils and followed the man who had gestured to me. We followed several others as they made their way toward one of multiple serving lines equally spaced along one side of the dining hall.

Out of the corner of my eye, I caught glimpses of other prisoners giving me the once over. I was a new fish in the tank, and they were sizing me up. A guard dressed in a blue uniform stood behind prisoners who were ladling out dinner. I received a fair amount of food, grabbed some bread and looked out over the seating area. "Follow me," said the same prisoner. We selected an empty table and sat down. "This place is segregated. Just take a look around," he said.

Indeed, toward the entrance and to the left sat the Blacks. Hispanics kept to themselves in another area, and the whites sat near the serving lines in the center and far corners. I saw a few mixed tables, but not many. I noticed scattered throughout the dining room several beverage islands that contained coffee and milk as well as plastic glasses and cups. Unarmed guards leaned against the outer walls. "Be careful where you sit and who you sit with or you could get into trouble," admonished my new friend. "It's okay to socialize a bit here, but choose your words with care."

Later that day I got called to the A&O desk, where a prisoner from the clothing room brought a pair of new black leather loafers. They fit perfectly. I kept the plastic slippers I had been wearing.

The same routine filled the next two weeks. Occasionally I would see my name on the callout sheet that would tell me where to go and at what time. One particular callout took me to the education office, where the prison employee in charge confronted me. He told me that they knew I had deliberately fouled up the aptitude and profile tests and that they would disregard the results. He told me that others did the same thing for differing reasons. Some apparently wanted to pass as "psychotic" or disturbed or whatever to escape work assignments. He had read the pre-sentence report done for the federal court in St. Louis showing my educational level, and information from "other" federal agencies that contained opinions on my mental, financial, emotional, and physical state. They now had records containing the results of several previous IQ (I tested at 141 IQ) and aptitude exams and said that they had nothing to offer me in terms of educational opportunities.

He told me they'd move me into the general population and a different cell house in a few days. They'd assign me a job. If I desired, I could later seek a job in the prison industries, where I could make a few dollars and occupy my time.

Other callouts took me to the prison hospital for medical and dental exams, X-rays, blood tests, a visit with the prison chaplain, and a visit with a case manager. When I entered the case manager's office, he was reading from a file open in front of him. He glanced up and told me to sit down. I did, and he identified himself as Dale Anderson. He would look after my progress or lack thereof while I resided in 132. He explained that they had selected a maximum security Level 5 penitentiary for me because my knowledge, past employment and language abilities made me a serious escape risk. He explained that under current federal prison guidelines I could expect to see a parole board after serving one third of my 17-year sentence if I kept my nose clean. He admonished me to keep to myself, do my own time, and keep my eyes open. He repeated the litany of rules: guards would count prisoners five times a day, every day, at 10:00 p.m., midnight, 3:00 a.m., 5:30 a.m., and a standup count at 4:00 p.m. He warned me again not to accept anything from other prisoners and not to touch or try to bribe any guard.

He told me that the prison educational programs didn't apply to me, as I already had university degrees. He emphasized that, contrary to what everyone might believe, going to church and making oneself known to the prison chaplain really helped when it came time to see the parole board. He also explained that he would do an update on me every 90 days or so, and added that if I faced a problem getting a visitor approved for my visiting list, I should come to see him. He told me to avoid "shots," prison slang for getting written up by a guard for any infraction of regulations. He explained that I got one phone call a month for ten minutes and had to schedule it once they assigned me to a cell house. In parting, he told me, "These are the rules. Follow them for your own good." He signed my callout paper and told me I could leave. As I walked back to the A&O unit I remember thinking to myself, "Now that I've heard the official rules, I wonder what the real rules are?"

In prison one notes degrees of acceptance from other prisoners. A nickname constitutes one such milestone. This allows prisoners to talk about one in a coded manner and keeps the guards from identifying the subject of a conversation. Prisoners rarely use one's real name; they assign a nickname by a sort of popular consensus. The nickname attaches an identity to a prisoner who has been stripped of everything else; a nickname makes one identifiable, and while some are flattering, others contain graphic descriptions that leave little to the imagination.

I received two, a rare occurrence indeed. They called me both "The Spy" and "Boom-Boom," both self-explanatory. I responded to both.

As I settled into 132, I learned several quite apropos code names. A Puerto Rican prisoner who served as a cell house maintenance worker passed the day with a broom in his hand, humming the same tune to himself over and over again. We called him "Looney Tunes." A Black prisoner who worked in the kitchen with the breakfast crew would steal food and bread and spirit it back to the cell, where he spent the rest of the day making sandwiches to sell later that evening. He charged two packs of cigarettes for a sandwich, and hence we knew him as "Two Packs."

Another prisoner won his name after arriving in Leavenworth. He lived in Cell House A and trapped and killed a couple of rats and mice on his own initiative. He presented the dead rodents to the cell house staff, and instead of filing a formal complaint about the infestation, he offered to trap and kill more. Word got around, and soon he had a cart, traps, brooms, and a pass to go just about anywhere in the prison. We often saw him with his cart and a couple of dead rats conspicuously piled on top. The guards didn't want to paw through his cart with dead vermin, so most of the time they didn't search him. He served as a "transfer agent" for contraband between cell houses, and everyone called him "The Rat Man."

One much-talked-about event involved the Rat Man. On a Thanksgiving Day in the dining room, when all the serving lines featured a turkey or two with all the trimmings on display, the Rat Man, in the kitchen, waited until the guards looked the other way for just a fleeting moment and grabbed a whole turkey, placing it under his cart with a couple of dead rats on top. He calmly wheeled the cart out of the dining room, past the center hall guards and back to the cell house. We all ate turkey sandwiches that night.

"Misty," a flagrant homosexual, plied his flesh in the cell house. If he liked you, he sometimes charged nothing at all for his services. "Farrah Fawcett," another homosexual, wore his hair long and looked uncannily like the movie actress of the same name. A Black gang stood guard while Farrah showered. A good seamstress, Farrah would make wrist and head sweat bands from towels, but to place an order you needed to approach one of her protectors, who demanded payment upfront in the form of cigarettes.

"Three Packs" made and sold prison "hooch" by fermenting yeast and fruit stolen from the kitchen. Once a week, when the guard Potter oversaw the making of the day's supply of bread, one of the prisoners assigned to the kitchen staff would create an "incident" that required Potter's immediate attention. In these moments of distraction, one of the prisoners assigned to the bread detail would reach into the still-running mixing machine and snatch as much yeast as possible. This he later sold to Three Packs, who would then make a new batch of booze ready for sale a week later. We all knew when this had happened because the bread for that day's consumption fell flat. The booze would ferment in pots placed above the dining room's dishwasher areas, behind the drop-down ceiling panels.

These monikers truly represented their bearers. They provided identities to individuals in an attempt to undermine what the government had done to them. Each prisoner could now claim a unique identity and defeat the stigma of being just a numbered piece of federal property.

After several days in the A & O basement of Cell House A, they transferred me into the general population, after the staff had determined in a cursory sort of way that the other prisoners did not present an identifiable or immediate danger to me.

Normally they assign a new prisoner to a multi-man cell in the A cell house. These cells have three sets of bunk beds, six wall lockers, and six individual metal floor lockers. One toilet sits in the center of each cell. They kept

This was taken in Leavenworth Penitentiary in 1980 during a Mexican festival that was allowed. From left to right: a Cuban prisoner, a Puerto Rican prisoner, me, my youngest brother, and a Colombian prisoner.

six men in these cells, and from what I could see they made no discrimination in placement due to race, type of crime, or other considerations. The cell block consisted of a building inside a larger outer shell. The actual cell block housed five tiers of cells, all connected by stairwells. Those located in the front with windows facing the front of the prison we called the "light side," while those that faced the prison's interior we labeled the "dark side."

One's work assignment also influenced one's cell assignment. The third tier housed most of the prisoners assigned to work in the kitchen. I got cell A320, on the light side, third tier, the second White person in the six-man cell with four Blacks. As the newest arrival, they pointed me to a top bunk near the toilet. I knew better than to complain.

My "cellies" briefly introduced themselves and then waited for me to do the same. While they already knew my name and reputation through the extremely efficient prison grapevine, I introduced myself. No one asked if I was guilty or not, since once inside the prison's walls, none of that matters.

I placed my meager possessions in my two lockers and made my bed. I asked what time to report to the kitchen in the morning, and they told me I should just go along with them. Exhausted, I climbed onto my top bunk to try to sleep. My cellies began to play cards and I feigned sleep in order to hear any conversation about me. The lights went out with a bang at 10:00 p.m., along with all the others in the cell house. The group kept playing cards in the dim light provided by the naked bulbs mounted to the outer walls. I kept listening until I fell asleep, but heard nothing of interest.

I awoke the next morning to the sound of bells and the commotion of my cellies getting dressed. When three bells rang out in quick succession, all the cell doors on Tier 3 opened with metal clanking on metal. Everyone rushed out and down the stairs en route to the mess hall. I fell in line and reported to the guard standing by the hall's open door. He looked at his list and, once he found my number, told me never to arrive late and said that I would get no pay for this assignment while working four to five hours a day divided into three shifts. He assigned me to clean tables, collect abandoned dishes, and help out in the dishwashing rooms.

I completed the breakfast shift and went back to my cell. It surprised me to see all of the cells unlocked and a few prisoners lounging about the cell house with seemingly nothing to do. I took off my dirty work clothes and headed for the shower. Each tier of cells had a shower stall consisting of several shower heads located in a space with a narrow opening. I turned the valve and began to enjoy the warm water. It felt relaxing as I shampooed my hair. However, a sixth sense warned me I wasn't alone. As I rinsed the soap away from my eyes, I saw that four Black prisoners now blocked the only entry and exit to the shower room. The biggest one, standing closest to me, grinned and announced, "This one's mine." I stood there with my heart racing in fear, expecting to die.

They could all read the shock and fear on my face and exchanged grins and glances between themselves. In that moment, I noticed a metal bucket with its detachable mop wringer a couple of feet away. I grabbed the wringer by its wooden handle and swung it with all my might at the one nearest me.

With a thud I felt metal hit flesh and bone and then with a crack I felt the bone give way. I continued to swing the wringer in a round house fashion and on the second arc, I caught the same man on the side of his face. He fell to the floor like a poleaxed ox. The other three ran for the exit, but the narrow doorway hindered their departure. While I screamed at the top of my lungs at them, the injured man slowly rose to his feet and, clutching the side of his head with blood streaming down his face, joined in the exodus. He mumbled some departing words that I couldn't understand and then they were gone.

I stood there alone, shaking uncontrollably, with the wringer still in my hand. Looking down at the shower drain I saw the man's ear, severed by the sharp edge of the wringer bracket, lying on top of the drain with water and shampoo running past. Without rinsing the remaining shampoo from my hair, I replaced the wringer in the bucket, grabbed my towel and headed back down the tier toward my cell. Dripping wet and naked, I concentrated only on reaching the relative safety of my barred cell.

My mind raced uncontrollably. Had nobody noticed? I heard no sirens, no guards running through the cell house. The prisoners seemed oblivious. The whole episode had lasted but a minute and had passed unnoticed. I couldn't believe it. At six feet, one inch and 185 pounds I didn't look like a pushover, but the fact that someone had openly tried to attack me astounded me. The had been testing me, a prisoner for but a few weeks. As my nerves calmed, I realized that two very important things had transpired: I had made the instant decision to defend myself without thinking of the consequences, and I now had the reputation of being somebody not to fuck with. I had learned an unwritten rule prevalent in every prison throughout the world: survive each day however you must and tomorrow will come. For the very first time I thanked my CIA training, at least in self-defense.

A few weeks later I saw that individual again, wearing a bandage wrapped around his head and coming out of the prison hospital. He never even looked at me. I don't know what he told the prison staff about losing a big chunk of his ear, but it must have been convincing. They kept him in the general population and no guard ever said anything to me. Some time later several prisoners told me on different occasions that word had spread throughout the prison that you shouldn't screw with the Spy. I noticed that my cellies treated me a little differently after that day, but neither they nor I ever said anything about the incident.

I learned an important lesson: even if one prisoner nursed a grudge or issue with another prisoner, nobody went to the guards about it. Prison 132 contained only two kinds of people: prisoners and guards. Like acid and water, they didn't mix.

We also had two kinds of guards: the regular hacks, sometimes called "pigs" because they acted like it most of the time, and the super cops, the guards that went out of their way to harass prisoners in any way they could. Prisoners I could divide into several groups: the predators who took advantage of weaker prisoners and demanded sex or extorted money in exchange for protection, the scammers, the drug dealers, the drunks, the lifers, the gladiators, and those who just wanted to do their time and get out. Sometimes a twist of fate could instantly move a prisoner from one category to another. I also learned another lesson. If one has a problem with an individual in the outside world, usually one can walk away, cool down, and eventually forget about it. In prison, however, you never, ever, let the sun set on a problem. You take care of it on your terms as soon as possible, because you know that the other person is thinking the same thing. Sometimes you can negotiate a truce, but only rarely. If you let a problem linger without showing strength and resolve, you end up with a reputation that will haunt you for the rest of your incarceration. You might not enter the system as an animal, but believe me, you become one if you stay there long enough.

My first view of Leavenworth had impressed me. Escape seemed impossible, with the strategically placed guard towers that were manned 24 hours a day, the high brick walls, the concertina wire, and the patrolling guard unit. Escape could only come by air, coupled with a riot; by tunnel; or by outsmarting the system. And yet, a few weeks into my time, the unthinkable happened. Five prisoners escaped.

Scuttlebutt had it that four of the prisoners had worked in prison industries in one factory or another, and that the fifth had just happened upon the scene as it unfolded and spontaneously joined the others. They had observed a small delivery truck coming and going through the north gate for several weeks and had familiarized themselves with the search routine. The truck and its driver passed through two gates to either enter or leave the prison. Between the two guard-operated gates lay a no-man's land where the truck was inspected on entry and departure. The inspectors looked under the hood and in the back and ran a mirror under the chassis.

The prisoners painstakingly measured the inside dimensions of the cargo bay of the truck and built a false wall, which they placed in a pile of other wood

This is my rendition of an idea I got from an Italian artist that I used to show what the guards at Leavenworth looked like: mindless brutes bent on punishment. Rarely would they come for a prisoner as an individual; they would come in a group to insure their success, whatever form that might take. They were never hired to think, only to respond to orders. Most federal prison guards come from the ranks of ex-military or people who didn't make the cut to become police officers. I had to cover this up with a painting of birds while I was working on it so the guards wouldn't see it. The other prisoners loved it.

products at the loading area of the first floor of the prison industries building. When the opportunity presented itself one morning, the prisoners emptied the truck and immediately jumped inside, stood with their backs to the real wall, and held the false wall in place between themselves and the cargo bay. When the guard gave a cursory look and saw nothing, he waved the truck through the sally port. At the first stop outside, the prisoners commandeered the truck and took off, giving themselves several hours' head start.

They only had a short time to enjoy their freedom, however. The authorities caught two nearby, shot one dead as he stepped off a bus in his home town, and apprehended the other two within three weeks. The feds tried them for escape and added five years to their sentences, then charged them with kidnapping the truck driver and added another 20. Since they were already doing life sentences for previous crimes, it really didn't matter.

I heard of several prior escape attempts when the prisoners would hide inside the trash compactor trucks that entered the prison almost daily. They got caught when guards poked long thin steel rods down into the garbage. The trucks also ran their compactor units a few times before leaving the sally port to crush any prisoner hiding inside.

Old timers told me that some years before, a train used to pull loaded railway cars into and out of the prison through the sally port. At one point, several prisoners commandeered the train and used it to crash through the east gate. This led to a big shootout. Nobody escaped, and a locomotive was never allowed inside the prison again. Prisoners would also try to get called as witnesses to other crimes so they could spend time out of 132 in some small county jail where laxer security and friends or family could abet an escape.

Every prisoner thinks about escaping. How could they not, given the inhumane conditions inside those walls? I thought about escape every night, but once I saw I would only serve between five and six years, I never actually planned one.

I looked for ways to pass the time: work in prison industries, work on my appeal, correspond with my family in the U.S. and in Cuba. I also started painting, something I had never done before. Another prisoner showed me how to stretch the canvas over the frames, how to mix the paints with oil, and which brushes to use. I painted remembered scenes from home and from Cuba. One time I painted the Leavenworth guards as bloodthirsty Neanderthals. To keep them from seeing the work in progress I would cover it with a painting of birds, but I always worried about smearing the paint, as oils take a long time to dry. I showed it to other prisoners though, and they loved it.

18. Doing Time

En masse we called the guards hacks, super-cops, pigs, screws, or "the man," but they got individual nicknames just like the prisoners. Some of these nicknames fit perfectly and described the guard in only a word or two. We called a small, slim Hispanic guard of Colombian descent "Sleeves." He wore thick pop-bottle style glasses and stood about five feet three inches tall. The government-issued short sleeved shirts that the guards wore hung on him like a long sleeved shirt. He looked ridiculous and very non-threatening. Most of the time he worked in the indoor gym located between Cell Houses A and C.

"No-Neck," fat and sloppy, had an IQ of maybe 95 on a good day. His head and chin sank so far into his shoulders that he appeared to have no neck at all.

"Dickhead," a redneck, shaved his head and displayed a scar that ran from his forehead to the back of his skull. His head looked just like the head of a penis. He chewed tobacco and constantly spewed obscenities.

"Claymore," an ex-marine from the Vietnam War, had suffered such shell-shock that he constantly twitched and talked to himself. He was so easily spooked that he wouldn't allow anyone within ten feet of him.

As with everything else in 132, just getting a simple haircut tried one's patience and reminded one of the surrounding paranoia. Normally they would hire a few prisoners who either had the skills of a barber before entering the gulag or had picked them up once inside. They worked long hours for low pay to accommodate the comings and goings of all the prisoners. To make up for that, a decent haircut cost anywhere from two to three packs of cigarettes. The rules forbade giving anything to another prisoner, so you could not just take the cigarettes to the barbershop with you. You selected "your" barber and made a deal to pay in advance or after the haircut, out of the view of the guard on duty.

Now the prisoner cutting your hair might be having a bad day, or perhaps someone had paid him to commit an act of violence. You never knew. A prisoner just like you, he faced the same constant stresses as everyone else. Two or three times each day, the guard on duty stopped the haircutting and told the barbers to sweep up all of the hair on the floor. They collected all the hair in a bag and later burned it to make sure that prisoners didn't get their hands on any wig-making supplies.

They issued each barber a razor, a comb, shears and scissors at the beginning of each workday and he had to turn them in each night. Failure to do so would result in a trip to the hole and sometimes a search of the entire prison.

I quickly learned the difference between prisoners doing life without any possible release, "lifers," and the rest of us "short-timers," who nursed some hope of eventual release. Lifers had already died. They had suppressed that part of themselves that remembered what freedom felt like. They had long ago broken ties with family and friends and the outside world. They took no interest in newspapers or newscasts, because whatever those said or printed held no relevance for them. They kept to themselves and avoided establishing relationships with the short timers. They didn't even see the short timers, except as transients in "their" prison, where they would live until they eventually died.

The lifers recognized each other and hung out together in the mess hall or walked the exercise yard together talking about health issues. They avoided talking about a world that no longer existed for them. The lifer slowly developed a self induced trance over the years, having long ago exhausted all legal appeals and finding that no one cared any longer about their cases, which lived only as footnotes in dusty law books. Family and friends had once written letters and visited, but no longer. For the lifer, one day, one year, one decade, followed another without distinction. Time seemed to have stopped altogether. I believed they secretly wished themselves already dead.

They would never again have a woman, hold a child, walk in the moonlight, enjoy the comfort of an old easy chair, or enjoy a stroll down the street. They guarded their privacy. They knew several of the guards on a more personal level, since they had literally spent years together and come to trust each other. The guard knows that the lifer doesn't want any changes and has no desire to disrupt the prison's daily schedule. In fact, prison wardens have even consulted lifers about proposed changes and what reactions to expect from the general prison population, since they know the prison so well.

Lifers have a set routine and demand respect from all others. They will tolerate the antics of newcomers or short timers for only so long before they confront them. The lifer may approach a short timer with annoying habits and warn him to cease and desist, but only once. After that, the lifer may just kill the other prisoner. That could earn him another life sentence added to the one he already has, but so what?

The lifers have seen it all. Other prisoners respect them and often ask them for advice on prison policies or about certain guards or wardens. Lifers often serve as the middlemen in smuggling operations inside prisons. Over the years, the bond between a lifer and a guard may reach the point where the guard doesn't see anything really wrong in bringing in something that will make the lifer's time easier. The guard also knows that the lifer will vouch for the guard as okay and that other prisoners should take it easy on him. The lifer waits only for death itself. He knows that his only time beyond the walls will take place in a pine box for the short trip to the prison's pauper graveyard, where others like himself have ended up. Hollywood makes movies about zombies, but prisons produce the real thing.

Like the other short timers, I looked at time as something that passed and that one either didn't have enough of or had too much of. I recall reading somewhere that we humans act like we have all the time in the world, or we would nervously glance at the clock wishing we could slow its passing or even stop it. In prison, minutes, hours, weeks and months held little if any significance for me. I now measured time in years, and I viewed it as an enemy that slowly drained my life and energy. I looked at it as something to survive and defeat. It confused me and I found myself in limbo without it.

You probably look at time as a tool, as in, "It's time to go" (I'm not going anywhere), "time is money" (not for the prisoner), "time for a change" (nothing changes for me), or "a time to enjoy" (a prisoner doesn't find any joy in time). You use time and watch it pass, while a prisoner endures its slow ticking.

The judge who sentenced me gave me time, 17 years, even though I considered it as time taken from me, something I could never replace. Other prisoners ask the question, "How much time did you get?" as though time held weight that could be carried around in a pocket. When a prisoner appears before the parole board, they want to know how much time he has served, making him calculate how much time he has left and how much time he has already lost. However, since the monotony of life behind prison walls doesn't allow any of the normal markers delineating the passage of time, prisoners lose their pre-incarceration concepts. For a prisoner time can speed up, slow down, stop, or cease altogether. He can't remember what he did last week, yesterday or even this morning. I may not succeed in explaining this to someone who has never experienced years isolated from society, friends, family, and the hustle and bustle of everyday life on the streets. This disorientation doesn't normally occur to the really short timers, prisoners serving merely hours, days, weeks or months in lockup. It happens to those of us serving multiple years, indeterminate sentences, decades, or life.

This disorientation begins to eat away and erode other concepts as well. Once a prisoner loses the concept of time, along with the loss of his identity

Our prisoner tennis team at Leavenworth. I am second from the left. We played the prison staff, as well as teams from surrounding colleges from time to time. We normally won the matches. I have several trophies from those days.

and sense of self-worth, he enters a world of delusion, isolation and fantasy. He begins to modify events to remember them as he chooses and not as they actually happened. The unreal becomes real, life before imprisonment fades to a distant, faint memory, and only the now, today, this moment, exists. The future will not vary from today or last year. The past doesn't matter. Yesterday, today and tomorrow run together in a blur. Self-motivation, ambition, and hope all get put on the back burner, fade, and, in many cases, die. For many, an inner fire goes out and they enter survival mode. One exists but one no longer belongs to the here and now like the rest of humanity. One slips into a state of limbo, adrift without expectations, destiny or time of arrival.

A visit, a phone call, or a transfer can bring this self-induced limbo to an abrupt halt, and that can cause serious damage. The lives of a prisoner's family and friends go on without him. He misses birthdays, weddings, school graduations, deaths, and other milestones that mark one's passage through time. A visit from someone can mean big changes. A prisoner informed of the loss of a dear one or other calamities in the lives of those on the outside, feels helpless to do anything about it. The visitor leaves and goes on to deal with the situation, but the prisoner deals with it alone, without guidance, without recourse. Oftentimes it sends him over the edge. He acts out his frustrations, gets labeled a mental case, receives medication such as Haldol or Thorazine, and turns into a zombie lost in time and space. Prison 132 housed dozens of these cases. I doubted they would ever return to reality, even if released someday.

Another phenomenon I noticed was the constant mania of counting. Prisoners count days, months, years, and decades, while the guards count the prisoners every four hours and the number of hours left on their shifts. The counting, the counted, and the counters mark the daily reality in this warehouse of forgotten souls.

One of the most dreaded punishments handed out in the federal prison gulag is known as the grand tour. A variety of avenues lead a prisoner to the tour: too many run-ins with the guards, filing lawsuits, letting the public know about prison conditions, frequent contact with the press, or secret Bureau of Prisons decisions. Regardless of how one got there, the tour looks the same. It starts with an unannounced transfer begun at any time day or night, but usually after 10:00 p.m. so that any contingency plans a prisoner might have in place cannot serve. A group of guards suddenly appears at the cell door and orders the prisoner to follow them to the catacombs beneath the prison. Other guards make quick work of placing his belongings into a duffel bag and carting them off, all accomplished in a matter of minutes.

The following day a fellow prisoner can try to let the prisoner's family and friends know about the transfer, but by then the prisoner has already left 132 for destinations unknown. Now his friends, family, and any legal representation can only guess at his whereabouts. It might take weeks or months before they finally find him again within the gulag. First the guards drive the prisoner a few miles to a local county jail for a few days or even weeks. The local jailer makes good money from housing federal prisoners and, under instructions, he does not let them send or receive any mail, visits, or phone calls. Each jail differs in the quality and quantity of food, personal space, exercise facilities, and so on. They keep the federal prisoners separated from the local lock ups. The federal prisoner has no funds on him. They've packaged up all his personal items in boxes that are stored somewhere, so he goes without basic necessities. Sometimes the marshals forget his medications, so the prisoner winds up with serious medical issues because of this "oversight." With no money or stamps, he can't send mail, and since nobody knows his location, he doesn't receive any from family, friends or his lawyer either. Normally the county jails have no law books, so a prisoner in transit has no redress to the justice system. The prisoner sits in limbo. He doesn't know his destination or when he might arrive.

A prisoner moved from county jail to county jail can actually disappear for months on end. Several times prisoners have spent over a year on the grand tour. If at some future point they actually had the opportunity to complain to the courts, the Bureau of Prisons would argue that security needs had forced them to treat the prisoner in this fashion, and the court would always find in the BoP's favor.

The prisoner becomes disheartened, disoriented, frustrated, and physically weak from the constant disruption of his daily routine. Federal prosecutors know this works well, and they employ the tactic often. Prisoners who renounce their pending lawsuits usually find that their tour ends earlier than others who remain steadfast in their goals. This tour system brings an economic benefit not only to the local jails, but also to the marshals. They receive a per diem for each prisoner in transit, and if the local jails provide meals at a lesser cost, as they usually do, the marshals pocket the difference. This adds up to quite a sum at the end of the year and makes a nice bonus for corrupt marshals. The jailers also take advantage of the system by accepting a prisoner around midnight one day and then letting the marshals remove him early the next morning. This way they can charge for two days for a stay of few hours. Punishing the prisoner, frustrating his appeals and making money fuel the Grand Tour.

UNICOR, a trade name for Federal Prison Industries, resulted from a marketing effort in the late 1970s to put a more modern look on the decades-old Federal Prison Industries (FPI), which was originally created in 1934 within the federal Bureau of Prisons and which mandated minimal job training for prisoners. FPI aimed to occupy prisoners' time and to supply all agencies and departments of the government with a steady supply of things like brushes, furniture and shoes. Legally they couldn't sell these things privately, since FPI employed prisoner (slave) labor at ridiculous rates and their prices would undercut civilian manufactured products of a similar nature.

The FPI board of directors included representatives from the Attorney General's office and experts from the private sector. Normally a representative from a major labor union also sat on the board and would approve the prisoner pay rate of pennies an hour. He felt good doing this because, by law, federal prisoners are actually slaves according to the Thirteenth Amendment to the Constitution. That amendment states in Section 1 that "Neither slavery nor involuntary servitude, except as a punishment for crime whereof the party shall have been duly convicted, shall exist within the United States, or any place subject to their jurisdiction."

The FPI program grew rapidly as the prison gulag expanded and the prison population rose at an ever increasing rate. Not only did the program keep prisoners occupied several hours a day, but even at substandard wages of pennies an hour it provided prisoners a source of income that offered them independence from family and friends outside. The government's deep pockets purchased modern machinery to boost production and hired qualified civilians to oversee the prisoner work force. Though these civilian workers made more than the average guard, they also were trained, in a cursory way, to fulfill the duties of a guard when the need arose. However, because these civilians worked hand in hand with prisoners who had access to tools that could also manufacture contraband and weapons, they looked out for themselves and adopted a friendlier attitude towards the prisoners they worked with. A "live and let live" atmosphere flourished within FPI. A distinct level of distrust developed between the run-of-the-mill guard and the FPI civilian employee. I believe that division still exists today.

An FPI staff member, the prisoner's case manager and the associate warden would all screen any prisoner who wanted to work in FPI in order to weed out those who posed a threat to the institution. If a prisoner maintained a clean record while locked up, he would get a job that matched his perceived abilities. Somewhere between 15 and 20 percent of all federal prisoners worked in FPI.

Prisoners coveted these jobs because, even though they paid almost nothing, they still paid better than jobs for cell house orderlies, grounds keepers, kitchen staff and the like that paid only a few dollars a month. Some prisoners, however, opted for the alternative jobs because they offered less work.

Bernie Phillips, who was a civilian resident of Leavenworth and director of the furniture factory, not a prisoner, offered me the position of head clerk. Dale Noll and Joe Montana served as his two assistants. I got along well with all three, as they never hovered over my shoulder. Apparently they'd read my "jacket" (prison file) and followed my case in the newspapers, and had decided they didn't know if I belonged in prison or not, but they could use my skills to their advantage. I also got along well with one of the floor supervisors, John Patterson, who told me on several occasions that he didn't believe I belonged in 132. In fact, he would tell me that if we ever met on the street he'd buy the beers. The supervisor of the FPI maintenance shop, Mr. Richter, told me the same.

Prisoners do not lack ingenuity. What I witnessed one day restored my faith in these captive masses and their ability to wage an ongoing war with their keepers. Everyone knows that in federal prisons, as in 132, folks can get drugs and other contraband. Much of the prison population consists of drug dealers and pushers, and these people find a way to satisfy their habits: marijuana, heroin, cocaine, speed, LSD, crack, or alcohol can all be obtained for a price. Even with all the security measures that the prison administration imposes on guards and prisoners alike, greed and need rule the game.

I painted this while incarcerated at Leavenworth. It is my version of the four horsemen of the apocalypse. I painted a second copy of this scene, but it was sold at an auction that the Salvation Army held at Leavenworth once a year. They kept 15 percent for "handling." Because it was against the rules for guards to give anything of value to prisoners, many would give a prisoner a photograph of their family members to paint and then purchase the paintings at the auction.

Illegal drugs and other contraband enter and leave prisons in a myriad of ways. Contact visits make it easy: a visitor loads a small quantity of drugs in a latex balloon, seals it, and then secretes it in his mouth just prior to entrance. Once in the visiting room, a hug and kiss transfer the balloon from the mouth of the visitor to the mouth of the prisoner, who instantly swallows it. Both cut the visit short, since they know the balloon could burst due to stomach acid activity. The guards strip-search the prisoner before he enters the visiting room as well as on departure, so trying to hide a package on the body doesn't work. But once the prisoner is released from the visiting room, he heads back to his cell, where he regurgitates the balloon. However, the balloon might be flawed and burst in the prisoner's stomach, releasing the drug and causing seizures and, in some cases, death from overdose.

Another option is to bribe a guard or other civilian employee to bring in contraband, a surprisingly common practice. Prison guards come from the ranks of former soldiers, police officers, and others who enjoy having authority over other human beings but find that the job doesn't pay well. Many of the guards cannot enjoy the lifestyle of the wardens and prison officials above them on the totem pole, so they find other ways to supplement their income. Some guards actually approach a prisoner with the offer of bringing in contraband in exchange for cash.

A guard with time in the system will identify a prisoner doing life with no possibility of parole or release and establish an understanding over time that the guard looks the other way when he sees the prisoner in question doing something prohibited. After a while, the prisoner feels comfortable talking to the guard. Conversations between a prisoner and a guard fall under the ever-watchful eyes of other prisoners, and one wants to avoid the label "snitch," which can, and often does, bring a death sentence.

The guard deals only with the selected prisoner to minimize risk. The prisoner takes merchandise orders from others and passes them along to the guard. The money for the purchases gets passed to the guard in the mail or by person or by dead drop. Then the guard brings the contraband inside the walls in a lunch bucket or on his person and hides it in a preselected spot, where the prisoner accesses it. Having retrieved the contraband, this prisoner sells it to others. The guard makes money, the prisoner go-between makes money, and the prisoner who ordered the merchandise makes money. Everyone wins.

Prison authorities know that this happens on a daily basis, but they can do little about it. If they catch the guard, they fire him but do little else to avoid bad publicity. They punish the prisoner, of course, but not too severely, as he may seek legal aid and publicize the incident.

However the contraband finds its way into the prison doesn't matter; it's available. I would order a small flask of Scotch at the end of each year. The process required friends or family to mail $50 to a post office box in Leavenworth with my request and prison number. On New Year's Eve, all locked down for the night, I would find, under my pillow, the bottle of Scotch. I would carefully drink it slowly over the next day or two and then dispose of the bottle in the kitchen trash that no one ever searched before they hauled it away.

One day, however, I witnessed an event remarkable for its ingenuity and planning. As normal after breakfast on the weekends, I went outside to the large exercise yard and sat with my back to the rail on the highest tier of the baseball stadium. I could see everything down in the activity yard and could readily observe anyone approaching me.

I remember a cloudless day with no wind. As I enjoyed the sunshine, I heard a familiar sound in the distance; the sound of a small model airplane engine straining under a load. I scanned the sky for the sound and saw the plane come in low over the prison wall. It had a good sized wing span and I recognized the Fox 35 engine. I could see a pouch slung low between its landing wheels, and by the long thin wire trailing behind I knew it was radio-controlled model. I couldn't tell where the controller might be or even if he could see the plane, but it came steadily on, crossing both the large and the small yards. All at once, it released the pouch, which arched toward the ground. The aircraft, free from its burden, immediately gained altitude and soon disappeared beyond the prison wall. The pouch hit the ground and all hell broke loose. Prisoners waiting for the delivery sprinted toward it, while others who realized what had just transpired ran in all directions. This created a dizzying spectacle, while the guards in the towers high above the walls futilely yelled warnings over loud speakers. When squads of guards arrived in the yards and closed the access gates, the prisoners had long since dispersed, hidden, or consumed the air-freighted contraband.

They searched us all before they sent us back to our cells, but to no avail. All the prisoners felt a sense of accomplishment. The prisoners won for a day, and did it openly and in the face of their oppressors. I could only imagine that in the near future the guards would need to install anti-aircraft guns. Though detached and removed from the action, I reveled in this victory.

The prison population, divided by race, city of origin, and degree of security, also divided itself into several gangs that vied for membership and control of illicit operations both inside and outside the walls: the Detroit Niggers, a group of Blacks from the Detroit area; another group of Blacks called the KC Mob, which originated in Kansas City; and the Aryan Brotherhood, a group of Whites with identifying bandanas, mustaches and tattoos. There was also a group of Blacks from the Washington area known as the DC Blacks and a Hispanic group called La Raza, as well as an Italian group with Mafia connections known as The Wise Ones. One small contingent contained former members of the Black Panther Party and other radical groups. They kept to themselves in the mess hall, did military exercises together and studied the Koran. A group of foreigners, a couple of Canadians, a Frenchman, Yugoslavians, Greeks, Puerto Ricans, Mexicans, and Colombians, just didn't belong to any group. Because I had traveled the world, I guess, I spent more time with this group than with any other. It included two of the Puerto Ricans who had shot up Congress decades before and three Yugoslavians convicted of hijacking a commercial airliner. They could discuss politics and other subjects at levels the average prisoner could not.

These groups looked after their own and vied for control of the drug trade, homosexual services, contraband, violence, retribution, group defense and finances. They also would hold parleys from time to time to settle differences between the gangs. They would decide discipline within their own groups, and they aimed to keep things as peaceful as possible to avoid getting the guards involved. If no one rioted or got killed, no one got transferred and business continued as usual.

Sometimes, however, rival groups within the same gang went to war over something or other. The cause might seem quite trivial if viewed from the outside, but in prison any feud between prisoners became serious; people died because of jealousy or just for talking to the wrong person at the wrong time.

I've repeatedly used the word "prisoners" here to describe my colleagues and myself within the walls. On the outside they use words like "inmate" and "convict," but I never heard someone on the inside use those terms. "Prisoner" leaves no doubt as to our status.

In 1978 the Eighth Circuit Court of Appeals overturned my conviction based on a faulty search warrant. Could I get out? My victory celebration didn't last long. The second trial took place almost exactly one year after the first, in the same courtroom with the same judge. He didn't order the jury sequestered, and once again the newspapers filled with pre-trial hype. Judge Regan ignored several rules of procedure in preparing for the second trial. He ignored the time limitation of 90 days for a retrial and went well past 120 days. Additionally, he had read the pre-sentence report after the first trial and should have recused himself from presiding for the second one. Since federal judges with lifetime appointments act like God on earth, they don't feel bound by laws, rules, or higher court decisions. Again, Regan allowed no testimony about my CIA ties. The prosecution again offered almost no evidence, but the press quickly tried and convicted me. Still, my lawyer and I were shocked that the jury convicted me yet again. The judge couldn't add to the sentence previously given, so he just reinstated it and I returned to Leavenworth as if nothing had happened.

19. Survival

With my family still in Cuba, I continued to monitor the news. In the spring of 1980, the Peruvian government announced that it would not force a few Cubans who had managed to get inside its embassy compound in Havana to leave. The Cubans removed their guards from the embassy, and hundreds of people left everything behind and rushed to the embassy. Within hours they occupied every square inch of the property, including tree limbs.

An ugly diplomatic standoff between Cuba and Peru ensued. After lots of posturing on both sides, the Cubans announced that they would allow anyone wanting to leave the island to do so, but set a time limit. Each person wanting to leave needed to register with the government in order to recover any subsidies, ration cards, or property. Also, those leaving could exit solely through Mariel, a sleepy port city west of Havana. They opened a registration station called El Mosquito there and the mass exodus began. Hundreds of boats from Florida plied the 90 miles between Cuba and Key West for the next several weeks in April, bringing about 125,000 Cubans into exile. My family sent thousands of dollars to contacts in Miami to pay for passage for my wife and son, but they never got the chance to get out.

Castro decided that, because the elite of Cuban society (doctors, lawyers, industrialists) had abandoned Cuba when he took over in 1959, he would now export the other end of the spectrum as well. He slipped in convicted criminals, homosexuals, the mentally infirm, and the rest of the "social lumpen" and placed them on the boats headed for Florida. Many of the other Cuban passengers recognized what was happening, and upon arrival in the U.S. they notified customs and immigration officials.

In many cases, U.S. immigration paroled these people into the country and gave them a clean slate to start a new life. Some took advantage of this, while many others did not. Immigration detained the most violent immigrants they could identify and sent them to two of the most secure federal prisons: Leavenworth and Atlanta.

Several dozen of the worst arrived at 132, locked up in Cell House D and

189

on the top floor of the prison hospital, isolated from the general prison population. Life in 132 changed dramatically. The Cubans yelled and screamed all
day and all night. They threw their feces and urine at prison guards, tore their
cell bedding into shreds, broke the plumbing fixtures, smeared food everywhere, and destroyed everything they could. The windows of the second floor
of the hospital looked out over the small recreation yard, and after the Cubans
broke out all of the window panes, they began to yell at the prisoners in the
recreation yard asking for cigarettes, matches, anything we could throw to them
over the wire fence.

One of the prison dentists, a Bolivian national and naturalized U.S. citizen,
Miguel Rico, knew that I spoke Spanish, so he asked the prison authorities if
I could help out as an interpreter. They agreed, and soon I was interpreting for
not only the medical staff but also the custody staff as well. I got to know several
of the Cubans, and they spelled out their histories to me and asked me to let
their family members in the U.S. know their location. I told them I would do
what I could.

After the initial period of interpreting for the prison, U.S. Immigration
and Bureau of Prisons personnel replaced me as an interpreter and I no longer
interacted with the Cubans personally. However, as I walked the small yard's
oval pathway, several of them pressed to the still broken windows would recognize me and we would talk the best we could. Through these communications I learned more of their plight and mistreatment by the system. Their
stories upset even the Mexican and Mexican-American prisoners, who normally
didn't get along with the Cubans. Members of La Raza approached me and
asked me to write an article about what was happening inside 132.

I hesitated at first, because I knew that the Bureau of Prisons would retali-
ate against anyone who focused the spotlight of public attention on it. The
high and thick walls surrounding 132 were designed not only to keep the prisoners in, but also to keep the prying eye of society out. My hesitation ended
one day when I overheard a conversation among three guards about how they
had beaten several of the handcuffed and shackled Cubans into unconscious-
ness and left them without medical assistance for a couple of days. These people
had not come to the U.S. of their own free will. Hustled out of institutions in
Cuba and placed on boats, they had not had the time or opportunity to inform
family or friends of their departure. Since their imprisonment in the U.S., they
had had little or no opportunity to contact family. I didn't condone their crimes
in Cuba, but I couldn't ignore their current fate. I decided to write the article
regardless of the cost.

I followed the prison rules and spent many a night in the prisoner law
library using one of the very old and dilapidated mechanical typewriters that

This is my version of Genesis. I used a model from a copy of *Playboy* for Eve and a model from a body-building magazine for Adam. The painting depicts the earth and moon in the background, indicating that perhaps life didn't begin on Earth. Additionally, Adam and Eve are looking at and pointing to different deities in the universe, indicating that maybe our current form is a result of alien influence in our DNA. This painting hangs in my home and causes a lot of controversy.

prisoners could use to write legal briefs, letters to their lawyers, or articles for the media. When I finished in early 1981, I sent the article to *WIN Magazine*, a quarterly published by the War Resisters League that often exposed government waste, abuse and fraud. They informed me that they planned to publish my article in the May 1981 edition. I awaited the arrival of my copy with some trepidation.

Every prison has one. It goes by different names, such as the Special Holding Unit, Administrative Detention, or Solitary. It exists as a prison within a prison to punish a variety of offenses that prison officials decide go against their ideas of security and order. We knew it as "The Hole." Conditions include bread and water diets, a cold concrete or steel bed with no bedding, no hot water, and total isolation from everyone and everything. It is not a place you want to go, but guards can send you there on a whim at any time, as I found out.

After breakfast I reported to my desk in the furniture factory office in the prison industries building, just like I did every other weekday. I performed all of the clerical duties for the factory that made wood furniture for use by federal judges, the IRS, and other federal offices. I earned a few dollars to buy my art supplies in the prison commissary, pay for postage, and actually send a few dollars home to my wife and son. The job also gave me something to do all day, and if careful, I could make copies on the only copier, located on the top floor in the business office.

Around noon Bernie, the furniture factory superintendent, told me to report to the captain's office immediately. He wrote out the pass, shook his head to let me know no one had told him what had happened, and wished me luck. We both knew the order represented the potential for real trouble.

I reported to the captain's lair in the basement of the D cell house. As I waited there for the next several minutes, my anxiety increased. When they called me into the office, I found the captain, the lieutenant, a sergeant, and the mail room officer all glaring at me. The captain got on the phone and called the associate warden of custody (AWC) to join them. I didn't like this one bit. Something big was going down, and somehow it revolved around me. Before the AWC arrived, the rest of them started in. The captain lifted a copy of the current *WIN Magazine* from his desk and asked me why I had written to a "commie" magazine and spread lies about the internal workings of 132. They asked me what typewriter I had used to write the manuscript, when I used it, and how I "smuggled" the article out of the prison. I had just begun to respond when the AWC came in and repeated the same questions. I asked to see the magazine. The captain threw it at me. I picked it up and searched the index for my article, which bore the title "Slave Labor in America's Prisons." The editors had added graphics, and I thought it looked pretty good. I had started to read the article when the captain yelled at me, "Hey, fucker, answer me!"

I knew anything I might say wouldn't matter before this kangaroo court, and I saw no way to avoid the inevitable. The AWC said I had endangered the security of his prison and he had ordered the mailroom guard to confiscate every copy of the magazine mailed to prisoners. He then ordered me to administrative detention in building 63 AD, the Hole. And with that, two guards in the room grabbed my arms, twisted them behind my back, placed me in handcuffs and dragged me from the room.

We went up the stairs and down the hallway leading toward the dining room, where several prisoners were performing their daily cleaning chores. In a matter of minutes the word would spread that they had thrown the Spy in the Hole.

The guards took me directly to Building 63, a two story brick building, a prison within a prison, so secure that the guards on duty inside 63 AD don't have the keys to get out. They relied on the guards patrolling the building's perimeter to open and close the only access door. They jerked me inside and then into a room to the right of the entryway, empty except for a metal table. They told me to strip and lie spread eagle on the table. Once I had complied I watched the guards rip my clothing to shreds. They never said what they hoped to find, but they certainly showed me who held the power.

One of the most hated lieutenants in 132, Blevins, entered the room and then moved to a spot out of sight behind me. Guards grabbed my arms and pinned me to the table. "You're a worthless piece of shit, Verne," said Blevins. "Prison time proves it. Society doesn't want you, and I'll make sure no woman ever wants you again." With that he kicked me in the balls as hard as he could. The red hot pain seared through my groin and my knees buckled. The guards released my arms and I fell to the floor in a fetal position. Then the lieutenant and the two guards went at it, kicking me and yelling obscenities. Another well-placed kick to my balls put me over the edge and I passed out.

They dragged me from the room, up a flight of stairs and down the corridor, passing several cells. Stopping in front of one, they opened it and pushed me inside. A guard threw in a pair of underwear and a t-shirt and locked the door. I reached the steel bunk on my own and collapsed. I don't know how long I lay there before the cell door opened and the medical officer, Dr. Jarvis, entered along with two guards. As he examined my swollen testicles, the guards offered their explanation. According to them, I had slipped on the stairs and fallen, and of course they had summoned the doctor right away. I didn't say anything, as it would do no good. They'd record the guards' version as the official record, even though everyone knew they had lied. Dr. Jarvis completed his cursory exam, asked if I needed anything and, getting no reply, left. They locked the cell once again and left me alone with my thoughts and the pain.

I awoke to the noise of the breakfast cart creaking down the tier. I could only guess at the early hour. I tried to stand up straight, but the pain hit me again and I slumped to the floor on my knees. Later the guard found me in that position. He placed a biscuit and gravy on a Styrofoam plate, folded it in half and pushed it through the bars. He also pushed through a Styrofoam cup and told me to hold it. As I complied, he deliberately poured my one cup of coffee for the day onto the cell's floor. "Oops, sorry, Verne," he said. I unfolded the plate and ate the mess. I found a plastic fork buried inside the goo.

I spent the next few hours talking to other prisoners on the tier. Some had done weeks and months there for a variety of reasons. They advised me that if I cooperated with the guards, things would eventually get better.

The second and third days passed like the first. I still got my food all mashed up in a folded plate, but now I did receive my lukewarm coffee each morning in my cup. I savored it. They also gave me a plastic toothbrush and a can of tooth powder, as well as a small towel. I could purchase some instant coffee from the prison commissary. Normally it came in a small jar that allowed you to spoon out what you needed and then seal it up to maintain freshness, but not in the Hole. They poured the instant coffee into a small brown paper bag, as the guards considered a glass jar a danger to them. In the heat and humidity of Kansas it didn't take long for the powdered coffee to turn into a brown gloppy mass. For a cup of coffee I had to pull off a piece of this melted mess, put it into a Styrofoam cup, add cold tap water and then spend the next half hour trying to dissolve it by stirring it with the handle of my toothbrush.

On the fourth day the guards came for me. Now I would stand trial before the same people who had dragged me here and beaten me. After informing me of their impartiality, they read the charges against me: abuse of the prisoners' mailbox; illegal use of a typewriter; lying to a guard; theft of government information (they considered the facts I had included in the magazine to be official secrets); inciting prisoners to riot; and several others. I don't remember them all. They asked how I pleaded. I mustered my courage and said "Not guilty!" The plea made absolutely no difference in this kangaroo court. They quickly found me guilty and decided my punishment should include loss of my job in prison industries, loss of my single cell in the B cell house, loss of ten days of "good time," restricted mail privileges, and another five days in the Hole. Additionally, they gave me a new job assignment: swinging a sledge hammer with construction crew #3 in a cell house remodeling project. With that they took me back upstairs to my cell. I spent the next several days going over the appeal that I would file as soon as I could.

The federal prison system has three levels of appeal for any disciplinary action against a prisoner. The first, commonly referred to as the BP-9 (Bureau of Prisons Form #9), involves a multi-copy form requiring times, dates, and offenses and then providing a very small area to describe the appeal. To get the form one must ask a guard and explain one's appeal. This guard then informs the guard against whom the appeal is aimed, usually insuring retaliation. One can't do anything about that but take one's chances. I filled out the BP-9 and sent it to the warden with no real expectations for any relief.

While I awaited the warden's decision, my time in the Hole ran its course and they transferred me to a six-man cell in the A cell house on the dark side. When I presented myself to the guards in A cell house, they told me to get a cart and return to the Hole to get my "shit." Guards have property and prisoners have "shit." I wheeled the cart back to building 63AD and got a large duffel bag. I returned to A cell house and lugged it up to the second tier. Inside I found a mess: torn photographs, ripped books, mixed up letters, smeared paintings, and shampoo poured over everything. What could I do or say? I had signed a receipt before I got the duffel bag, unopened, and the receipt stated that I had received my property in good condition. I couldn't even officially complain. The anger swelled up inside me. I decided that in the future I would drastically reduce the quantity of things I kept in my cell, just in case they did this again. I spent the rest of the day unpacking and salvaging what I could clean. Several prisoners passed by my cell and offered condolences. One of them even slipped a copy of *WIN Magazine* into my hands. All 2,000+ prisoners in 132 knew what had happened, and for a moment I was their hero.

After a few days I received the reply to my appeal: denied. I then asked for the BP-10 form, the next level of appeal, and after filling it out and attaching a copy of the denied BP-9 form, sent it to the Bureau of Prisons regional office in Kansas City. Weeks later the answer came back: denied. I filed the final appeal, a BP-11, with Norman Carlson, director of the BOP in Washington, DC. Several weeks later I received a reply: denied. Any further action would require that I file a complaint with the federal court in Kansas City, which handled all actions filed by prisoners from 132, including complaints about overcrowding, contaminated food, lack of medical care, beatings, confiscation and destruction of prisoner property, violation of privileged mail services, visiting room restrictions, lack of educational facilities, and habeas corpus petitions. The courts usually delay all responses for as long as possible in hopes that the prisoner will get transferred, die, or just give up in abject frustration. Not one federal judge in that area would rule in favor of any prisoner petition. I'd reached the end of the line.

While working as chief clerk in the prison furniture factory, I had done a lot of favors for other prisoners. I would use my typewriter accessibility to type up their legal writs and petitions, and I would steal pens, paper, and a host of other items they needed. I also used the only copier in prison industries to make copies of documents, letters and photographs, all for free. Sometimes I would be "paid" with items from the commissary or receive items stolen from other areas in the prison. I had a wooden easel custom made to fit in my cell so I could practice my oil painting, a couple of hefty wooden storage lockers to keep my painting supplies in, and just about anything else I needed to make life a little more comfortable.

I had noticed while working in the factory office that some prisoners thought that we had cushy jobs, with chairs to sit on, air-conditioned offices, and so on. A few thought that we had cooperated with the guards in one way or another to receive such jobs. A few prisoners clung to these misconceptions as fact, including an Eskimo from Alaska with a Russian last name of Ivanoff. He worked in the furniture factory and fell into that category. He and I had not exchanged more than ten words during my time in 132.

He spent his days in a booth spraying lacquer on wooden furniture and often took off his breathing mask while working. The constant breathing in and out of these toxic fumes had turned him into a drug addict. He actually looked forward to going to work to get his daily high. On the weekends we saw him leaving the prison hospital with his daily dose of Thorazine, a potent drug used to control behavior.

A couple of months before I got out, while walking the track in the small exercise yard with a couple of other prisoners from Iowa, I heard someone behind me scream "Lyon." I stopped in my tracks and turned to see Ivanoff stumbling towards me. He grasped a long homemade dagger in his hand, muttering my name. What to do! I saw the ballfield backstop fence, where a large plywood box held golf putters for use on the never completed mini-golf course. I opened the lid and grabbed one of the clubs and then turned to face the enraged drugged prisoner coming my way. Why he had it in for me I didn't know, but he looked determined. I started walking toward him to show my readiness for a fight. When only a few yards separated us, I felt a bullet whiz by and saw the ground swell and explode a few feet in front of me. I knew it had come from the guard tower over my right shoulder, and then I heard the sound of the shot. Ivanoff stopped in his tracks, as did I. I realized that the guard in the tower was shouting at us to lay down our weapons. I heard the siren go off and noticed all the other prisoners in the yard frozen in their places. A group of guards came running. I held onto the golf club until a few of the guards reached Ivanoff and disarmed him. Then I dropped the putter and put up my hands.

The guards forced my hands behind my back and cuffed me. Other guards dragged Ivanoff away. I knew our destination: the Hole.

They took Ivanoff, clearly high and now incoherent, to the prison hospital. They took me, in turn, to the Hole and into the same holding cell they had beaten me in some time before. Soon Lt. Seever entered and ordered two chairs brought in. He told me to sit in one and then told the guards to remove the cuffs. He asked me what had happened. I told him that the attack came without provocation, without notice, and that I could not explain why Ivanoff would want to kill me. The phone rang and he answered it. He listened for several minutes and, after replacing the receiver, he told me that several prisoners in the yard corroborated my story. The phone rang again, and after listening for a few minutes he replaced it and told me that the hospital staff confirmed that Ivanoff had told them that someone promised him two cartons of cigarettes to kill me. Seever didn't tell me if he knew who had ordered the hit.

He knew that I had just a few weeks until my release and that, though not a model prisoner, I wasn't a troublemaker either. He told me he believed this was an isolated incident and that he would allow me to go back to my normal routine. This shocked me. How could he know so quickly that this incident didn't involve anyone else? How did he know that I could safely re-enter the general population? Those questions haunted me as I walked back to my cell. Who had ordered this, and why? Should I worry about another attempt? What should I do?

That night several prisoners came by and offered advice. Some thought the government had ordered the hit and that explained why Seever could say it wouldn't happen again. Others thought someone with a grudge against me had paid for it. I couldn't think of anyone who fell into that category except the guy whose ear I had cut off several years before. They had transferred him to another prison, but that didn't mean anything. In the gulag, prisoner communications often outpaced official ones. I spent the next few days and nights straining my memory, trying to identify who and why, to no avail. I had openly stated many times that upon release I would ensure that the truth came out about what the government had done to me. I knew several individuals and groups that were poised and ready to help me with interviews, publications, and news conferences. Maybe the government had finally decided to silence me, after bungling the job in both Peru and Canada. They could succeed more easily inside Leavenworth. They could buy my life cheaply here: two cartons of cigarettes. Make it look like just another senseless murder where one prisoner kills another over some petty quarrel. Because it had failed, and in public, they would need time to regroup. They had lost the element of surprise and put me on my guard. The eyes in the back of my head that I had developed over the years grew ever more acute.

I took precautions to finish all the legal work for my fellow prisoners, as I didn't want to leave them in the lurch after I left. I didn't want to make any new enemies. I carefully avoided any incidents that could possibly affect my release. I disposed of any contraband by giving it to others. I avoided watching TV on the bottom floor of the cell house, a scene of frequent fights. With only three or four channels available, you took your life in your hands if you changed the channel without first asking permission of everyone else. The prison staff tried to alleviate this source of contention by placing two additional TV sets on the floor, each set to a different channel. That move did little to change the situation, as many prisoners wanted their accustomed seats and didn't want to move.

I got sent to the "Dressing Out" office a couple of weeks before my actual release, where they measured and weighed me and issued me a set of civilian clothing, consisting of a pair of polyester trousers, a cotton shirt, new underwear, a cheap leather belt, a pair of black shoes made in Leavenworth's own shoe factory, and a small vinyl hand-held duffel bag. Everything else, including my paintings and paints, legal papers, photographs, and other personal items, they boxed up and mailed to my mother's home. My cell looked much like it did the day I moved in, bare bones. Every day someone I knew among the prisoners came by to wish me luck and tell me not to come back. Even a few guards, when they saw nobody watching, stopped me briefly to say goodbye and wish me luck.

The captain called me to his office one day and told me he had no state warrants seeking my detention on any other charges, and if that didn't change in the next few days, I would walk out of the front door a free man. The assistant warden for custody (AWC) took me into his office and told me that the Bureau of Prisons had carefully monitored my time in Leavenworth and from time to time had sent a summary of their observations to an office in Washington, D.C. He told me they had received a few such requests and refused to identify the office or the exact nature of the information requested. Clearly the CIA wanted to know about my impending release and my intentions. They knew I had contacted several people and agencies that were critical of covert operations and government misconduct and that wanted to meet with me, and the CIA worried that I might join forces with them. The AWC told me to report to my federal parole officer within five days of arrival in the Des Moines area. After that, they reviewed my prisoner account at the prison and told me that I would receive the sum of $82. Ironically the number of dollars matched the year of my release, 1982.

Oddly, prisoners that I had known for years, some lifers and some short timers, now walked right by me without acknowledging my presence. This happened after they had said their goodbyes and served as a self defense mechanism. I would soon leave, and they would not. They needed to keep their minds enclosed within the 40-foot-high walls. To dwell on someone on his way out would disrupt their coping mechanisms. Just like the day I arrived at 132, I felt alone once again. I couldn't sleep and lost my appetite.

The director of the furniture factory, Dale Noll, stopped me one day walking the small yard. He wanted to thank me for all I had done for the factory, and he told me that he wished me well and that he and the other supervisors in the factory believed that I should never have been in prison. Another factory supervisor, John Patterson, stopped me a few days later to say the same thing. He added that he would be proud to be seen with me in public and that he would buy me a beer anytime. The main dentist, J. J. Jones, and his assistant, Miguel Rico (from Bolivia), also called me into the dental office on the pretext

This is one of my paintings that sold at auction. I painted it from a small black and white photograph of Ernest Hemingway's home in Key West, Florida. I added color and some trees to enhance the scene. I was told that a doctor of Cuban descent purchased it. Over the time I was incarcerated, I probably sold at auction at least 20 different paintings. Some I wish I had back.

of giving me a dental exam before my release. Then they closed the door and broke out some civilian food, and we consumed a small feast. They also believed that I should never have served time. They wanted to thank me for the interpretive services I provided when they treated the Marielitos. After my release, Doctor Jones invited me to the wedding of his daughter and Miguel gave me free dental service in Kansas City for a year or two after my release. Just goes to show that not all prison guards will treat you badly.

A couple of days before my release, I noticed that a prisoner I knew by the name of Long had returned after his recent parole. I knew him as a fellow pilot who received the *Aircraft Owners and Pilots Association Magazine* every month. We had spent many an hour talking about aviation. It surprised me to see him again. When we got the chance to talk, he told me what had transpired. Upon his release, he had no family left and no real friends on the outside. The Bureau of Prisons could no longer hold him, as he had maxed out by reaching his mandatory release/parole date. He had stayed in the Kansas City area in a cheap hotel and burned through his meager cash on prostitutes. When he'd spent it all and had no place to stay, he went to the nearest post office, threw a brick through the window, and sat down to wait for the police. They contacted his parole officer to have him sent back to Leavenworth. In the prison system, he would enjoy having his janitorial job as well as "three hots and a cot" in prison slang: three meals a day, a private cell, free medical care, and friends, none of which he had found on the outside. Institutionalized by a lengthy sentence and with no support base on the outside, these folks usually return. This guarantees the prison system, state or federal, a steady supply of both new and old prisoners in a revolving door that provides job security for prison staff while costing the American taxpayer billions of dollars a year.

On the verge of release, I spent time sitting by myself on a bleacher seat in the small exercise yard. I took time to reflect on five years and eight months locked away from society, how and why it had happened, the things I had seen while in prison, and what I could expect on release. The flood of memories washed over me like a wave. To this day, I find it hard to comprehend.

I replayed the month of December 1966 over and over in my mind. I was preparing for Christmas, had purchased presents to take home, and was feeling a bit sad about the breakup with my girlfriend. I remember the night of the explosion at the airport, the same night I went to the Playboy Club in St. Louis at the invitation of fellow engineers at McDonnell. I heard about the incident later when I drove one of the engineers back to his car. We were listening to the radio when we heard the newscast. My life went downhill from there.

Sometime over that same weekend, a secret grand jury indicted me for destruction of property at the airport. I have no idea what evidence they saw, if any. Grand juries, meeting in closed session, amount to a prosecutor presenting an argument for indictment. They don't need any evidence to get the "true bill." I was arrested, charged, and then released on a ridiculous bond of $500. During the whirlwind, my old employers at the CIA contacted me and assured me not to worry and to meet with them. I did and ended up in the Directorate of Operations headed to Canada and then to Cuba, kidnapped from Peru, tried in St. Louis twice and sentenced to 17 years in the care and custody of the Attorney General of the United States. Now I prepared to end a sorry chapter of my life and return to the free world. I didn't know what awaited me. I had no friends left, nowhere to live, no job prospects, no money, and a minimum of two to a maximum of five years of federal parole to complete, under which I would have to make a monthly report to a parole officer and hope for the best. I didn't know what the CIA had in store for me, if anything. I did know that they, through the federal Department of Justice, held a sword of Damocles over my head. I might seem free, but I felt a leash around my neck. I had learned that if the government wants to destroy you, you do not stand a chance. They had made me an example to others in the CIA working without cover overseas in hard targets: do not buck the Agency or you will end up like Verne.

The day I entered Leavenworth I traded my name and identity for a number, changing from a person to a piece of property belonging to the U.S. Attorney General. Time had stood still for almost six years, and now I had no future. Every day that ended with my cell door sliding locked behind me meant that I had survived one more day and the scratches on the wall contained one more mark. The walls of Leavenworth not only kept me in, they kept the outside world and life itself out. The words from Dante's *Inferno*, "Abandon hope all ye who enter here," had taken on a solid reality in Leavenworth. I had seen despair beyond any I could imagine. I had seen murders, prisoners framed for crimes they did not commit, prisoners raped while the guards did nothing. I had seen prisoners' personal property, never much to begin with, destroyed by vicious guards. I had seen prisoners deemed "unruly" by prison staff put on the "Grand Tour" for years at a time. I had seen prisoners who were so demeaned by the system that removed from them all vestiges of life that they came back to prison just to survive. I had seen prisoners who started their lengthy sentences with frequent visits from family and friends later reduced to having nobody come to visit for years on end. The system, whether state or federal, breaks the prisoner and makes him totally dependent on the authorities for his survival. Prisoners became "inmates," like patients in a mental or medical ward.

Authorities want the public to believe that prisons don't just deprive a prisoner of his or her freedom, but help rehabilitate him as well. Nothing could be further from the truth. Persons serving life sentences or sentences of decades in length need no rehabilitation. They will never survive on the streets after such long absences. They lose family, friends, motivation, and, last of all, hope.

Even after prisoners serve their sentences and pay their debt, society demands more punishment. Released prisoners find it almost impossible to find meaningful work. In most states they lose the right to vote, and in many states they have to start paying back money to pay for their incarceration. They lie on job applications to avoid the stigma of prison and hope they don't get found out, an impossibility in today's world of the internet and instant communications.

God forbid that a crime occurs where you live, as society will look for the weakest person to blame it on and the police will plant, invent, or enhance evidence to assure conviction. In a corrupt system, politicians just tell us we must get tougher on prisoners. In today's world of instant news and analysis, commentators and pundits convict someone in the press in just hours. People in the U.S. naively believe a person is "innocent until proven guilty," and so say our laws and courts, but this seems far removed from reality.

Like all prisoners, I thought about how we could change the system for the better. The quality and variety of food, mostly starches, needs changing. Private cells should replace the current crowded, dirty, and noisy living quarters. Work assignments based on favoritism assure that even the meager pay goes to a select few. All prisoners should have jobs available so they don't have to rely on family or friends on the outside to make a phone call or buy stamps. Prison industries operate for profit and provide few skills usable outside the walls. These industries also operate old machinery that is unsafe for prisoners and guards alike. Prison law libraries need law books, typewriters, and copiers, more space, and longer hours of availability. Contact with family members and friends will determine if a prisoner has any chance of succeeding once released, and we need larger, less crowded visiting rooms that are open longer hours. Lawyers and prisoners need to know prison staff will not read their legal correspondence. Almost every state and federal prison violates this right of confidentiality.

Prisoners usually get sent to prisons far from their homes, more so in the federal system than the states. We should try to place a prisoner as close to his home as possible. The courts usually assign a level of security to a prisoner much higher than necessary to keep the old walled prisons full and in use, which requires more guards and higher maintenance costs. My list of complaints goes on and on. I didn't think about or care about prisons before I found myself in one. Now I know first hand the financial and ethical costs of this American gulag.

My return trip to Leavenworth in 2016. I went on a motorcycle trip with a friend, also retired, from Vermeer. We went to the prison to see the "dark side."

My last day in the exercise yard found me contemplating what to do after release. How would I ever tell family, friends, and the public what had really happened and why? Who would listen to an ex-convict, and who would believe me? What path could I choose to correct the wrongs I had suffered? Could I do it alone? I had no resources and no contacts, except for a few people in Washington, D.C., and back home that believed in me. The task that lay before me was daunting, to say the least.

I determined to give it my best effort, as well as to try to reunite my family in Cuba. These two issues occupied my mind, but I had no idea how to accomplish either. I walked back into my cell for the last time and tried to sleep, but I lay there wide awake until they came for me early in the morning to finally "dress out" and leave. I nervously awaited my future.

20. Rebirth

At 8:01 a.m. on the morning of May 24, 1982, the electric gate of 132 slid open and I walked out into bright sunshine, free! I looked in vain for my brother's van. I wondered about the delay. The guard known as No-Neck leaned out from the front tower and yelled, "Lyon, your family had an accident!" and shut the window. I sat down on the top step, clutched my broken guitar and small duffel bag, and wondered what to do.

After 30 minutes my brother's van turned into the U-shaped driveway. He saw me and flashed his lights. I ran down the steps as fast as I could and met him as he came to a stop. We exchanged embraces and congratulations.

We drove east out of Kansas and then turned north in Missouri headed for Iowa. My brother handed me a beer. "I haven't had a real beer for almost six years and you give me a light beer!" I complained. The miles home passed quickly.

I spent the next several days in shock trying to get used to freedom: walking out the door without a key, walking at night under the stars, stopping to see children laughing and playing. I breathed it all in. Then reality set in; I had no job and no place of my own to stay.

I received a phone call from a Methodist minister, the Rev. Chet Guinn, who had visited me in 132. He asked me to come to Des Moines and discuss plans. I met him at a building housing several non-profit agencies: a shelter for battered women, a clothing pantry, a food pantry, a ministry dedicated to working migrants, and a ministry dedicated to helping recent arrivals from El Salvador and Guatemala. The building director offered me a room and handed me a key. Only a week ago I had had to ask permission to exit and enter a doorway, and now I could come and go as I pleased.

The Reverend Guinn had formed a support group of clergy of different denominations to assist me. I set about immediately to acclimate myself to civilian life. I obtained my driver's license and applied to the governor for restoration of citizenship. I also met with my parole officer, Ed Ailts, at the federal building in Des Moines. Ailts told me he had reviewed my file and had determined, on his own, that I didn't present any danger to the public or myself.

I assured him that he had reached the right conclusion. He also showed me newspaper clippings covering different aspects of my saga over the years that his staff had collected. He told me that I would have to provide monthly financial reports to his office and that I would need his permission for any travel. He informed me that he or his staff would call on me unannounced and that I should avoid any type of arrest. After saying all that, he paused and added that he didn't think the monthly visits were necessary, but he offered no explanation for that reprieve. He would determine how long I would remain under his supervision. I asked him about possible travel to Cuba to see my family. He laughed. That couldn't happen without his permission, and I couldn't even obtain a passport without the okay of the Attorney General of the U.S.

With my immediate needs met I faced the daunting tasks of trying to communicate with my family in Cuba and planning how to counter the CIA's fabricated case against me. I contacted my wife in Havana by phone and explained the restrictions the government had placed on me and the unlikelihood that I could travel to Cuba. This devastated both of us. I would continue to try to send some money whenever I could.

On the CIA front, my alma mater, Iowa State University, under its visiting lecturer's program, invited me to speak. On the day of my presentation at the Memorial Union building on campus, 400 people filled the lecture hall. The administration brought in extra chairs, but it was still standing room only. I talked about my recruitment at ISU and how then University President Parks and Dean of Male Students Millard Kratovil both knew about the CIA's recruitment efforts. I spoke for almost three hours, answered questions, and basked in the prolonged applause.

Not long after that, the well-known former CIA officer John Stockwell also spoke at Iowa State. He asked me to introduce him. John had quit the Agency after a career in Africa, Vietnam, and Angola and had written a book entitled *In Search of Enemies*. He planned on forming a group to speak out against covert actions and asked me to join him. I accepted his offer and joined ARDIS (The Association for Responsible Dissent). The group included Daniel Ellsberg (the Pentagon Papers), Margaret Brenman-Gibson (professor of psychology at Harvard Medical School), Louis Wolf (co-editor of Covert Action Quarterly), John (Jack) Ryan (former FBI special agent assigned to counterterrorism operations), Peter Dale Scott (professor at UC Berkeley), David McMichael (former CIA analyst), Philip Roettinger (former CIA officer assigned to the coup in Guatemala in 1954), and Jim Wilcox (former CIA officer assigned to Japan); all dedicated to exposing the role of covert operations in American democracy. A young University of Texas student in Austin, James Otis, did the legwork and set up all the speaking gigs for ARDIS.

The CIA had launched an Officer in Residence program in which they sent senior case officers to campuses where they taught classes related to national security issues. Each of these CIA officers had full access to student files and the final say as to which students could enroll in the secret classes. The CIA paid the CIA officer's salary and incidental expenditures, and the university got a free instructor while the CIA sniffed out future recruits. Since the class contained classified material, the CIA studied student records to clear them before the lectures.

When the students at the universities learned the true intent of the program, protests erupted across the country. The universities called in police to protect the CIA officers as well as property. In response, students called in members of ARDIS to come and speak to packed auditoriums about the conflict raised between academic freedom and the national security state. We spoke on radio stations and to civic groups. My presentation zeroed in on my own campus recruitment. We invited the CIA to debate us in open sessions; they refused, citing national security and secret classifications. The ensuing uproar forced them to close the program at several schools. My two year minimum parole period approached and I wondered what effect my open defiance of the CIA as a member of ARDIS might have.

In late 1984, Ed Ailts called me in for a meeting. I hadn't seen him for a while, and the last time I did see him I had shown him a U.S. passport that had arrived unexpectedly about a year into my parole. The passport showed up in the mail complete with a recent photograph, but I had no idea where the photo, clearly taken after my release from prison, came from or who had taken it. The passport flabbergasted Ailts as well, since it required the approval of the Department of Justice. He suggested I turn it over to him, but I refused. So when I once again arrived at Ailt's office I had no idea what to expect. All the staff greeted me with stern faces. Ed called me into his office, looking grim, and announced he had some news for me. Steeling myself for bad news, I saw one of the other parole officers enter the room carrying donuts. At that point Ed smiled and offered his congratulations on completion of my parole. Now I was truly a free man!

ARDIS morphed into ANSA (the Association of National Security Alumni). With little funding compared to the deep pockets of the CIA, we set the stage for a battle between David and Goliath. We began publication of a news magazine titled *Unclassified* and expanded our base. In the magazine, we suggested that the Pentagon and Congress should oversee U.S. covert operations. We stated: "Covert actions are counterproductive and damaging to the national interests of the United States. They are inimical to the operation of a national intelligence system, corruptive of civil liberties, including the judiciary

20. Rebirth 207

and a free press. Most importantly, they contradict the principles of democracy, national self-determination and international law to which the United States is publicly committed." Among ourselves we referred to the CIA as the "Committee to Intervene Anywhere."

Our readers and donors increased. The CIA subscribed, as did the Association of Former Intelligence Officers (AFIO), the "official" organization of retired U.S. intelligence officers. Mostly funded by the government, AFIO presented itself as the official voice on intelligence-related issues and did everything possible to undermine our activities and discredit us in the eyes of the public.

We crisscrossed the country speaking to eager college audiences. I remember one significant presentation I gave to the students and faculty at the Rochester Institute of Technology (RIT) in New York. Faculty members there had noticed the CIA's Officer in Residence program operating on campus and some of the secretive goings on in conjunction with a classified Kodak Corporation program. Rumors had it that the institute's president and some of its board members had direct contacts with the CIA.

I arrived on the campus a day before President Carter would visit for a speech. As I entered the largest lecture hall on campus, I noticed among the overflow crowd several men wearing the lapel pins of the Secret Service. During my presentation I revealed that the CIA directly paid the president of the institute, Dr. Richard Rose, and discussed his work with Kodak to print counterfeit documents and money for use by the CIA in covert actions. These documents included false passports, press releases, official foreign government letterhead, and more. The CIA selected RIT students to fabricate these documents and swore them to secrecy. I also exposed the conflicts of RIT's board members who oversaw funding and operations while also connected, directly or indirectly, to the CIA. When I pointed out that Dr. Rose had taken a sabbatical from RIT to work for the CIA in Langley, the crowd went into an uproar.

Reacting almost immediately to my presentation, President Rose resigned, as did some other exposed board members. Kodak suspended its secret program for a while, but I assume they have since restarted it. I also spoke at Georgetown University (in the CIA's back yard and its main base of recruitment), at Northwestern University in the Chicago area, at the Rayburn Office Building in Washington, D.C., and at the University of California–Santa Barbara, the University of Colorado in Boulder, the University of Iowa, and Grinnell College, to mention a few. I joined the Campaign for Political Rights in D.C., the Bill of Rights Foundation in Chicago, the National Committee Against Repressive Legislation (NCARL), the Chicago Committee to Defend the Bill of Rights, the CIA Off Campus movement, and many others. The IRS audited me three years in a row. Since I never made enough money to precipitate an audit, they probably acted on behalf of the CIA.

In 1994, ANSA pulled off another coup. When the AFIO turned down an offer from the KGB to hold a joint meeting using current and former spies from both the CIA and the KGB to address covert action issues before the American public, the Russians contacted ANSA. We immediately went to work obtaining visas for four KGB officers to come to the U.S. for joint presentations at major university campuses to talk about the foolishness of covert actions undertaken by both the CIA and the KGB. When our government dragged its heels in issuing the visas, we contacted several members of Congress seeking their help and soon the visas arrived.

We arranged nine forums on campuses from D.C. to California, all well attended. While in Des Moines, the group stayed at my home. My stepdaughter (from my second marriage), in middle school at the time, told her history teacher about our guests. That prompted a call from the school asking if I and one of the KGB officers could give a short presentation to her history class. We agreed and spoke to a packed audience of students and teachers.

I also participated in a documentary by Turner Original Productions titled "Secrets of the CIA" in 1994. Several major TV channels in the U.S. and in Europe aired it to critical acclaim. The film illustrated the extremes to which CIA officers, motivated by patriotism, would go, discovering only later how their work had adversely affected not only their own lives but those of their families and friends.

I sought a pardon from then President Clinton, and my friend Tom Harkin, then U.S. Senator from Iowa, sponsored the petition. In the end I had over 30 supporting letters attached from former CIA, FBI, DEA, MIA and State Department people. Senator Harkin wrote:

> In my judgment, Verne clearly deserves a full presidential pardon. His original "conviction" has all the earmarks of a CIA covert action to provide a cover for Verne infiltrating into Cuba. And his actions since release from prison are reflected in several dozen letters of support from ministers, church workers, a member of the Iowa House of Representatives, several ex–intelligence officers, ex military officers and others he has touched in his work at the Hispanic Ministry on hunger and advocacy issues. I have 47 letters in my file calling on President Clinton to grant a pardon. And Governor Branstad has already granted Verne a pardon to restore his Iowa citizen rights.

The pardon attorney, probably after consultations with the CIA, denied the petition but offered no explanation.

Meanwhile, with my new passport which had arrived in late 1984 or early 1985 in hand, I contacted the Cuban Interests Section in D.C. and asked for a humanitarian visa to visit Cuba. The Cubans asked me to come in for an inter-

ANSA board members in the U.S. Senate office of Senator Tom Harkin of Iowa. We gave the Senator an award for trying to get me a presidential pardon from President Clinton. *Left to right:* **Lou Wolf, Mike Springmann, Diane Kuntz, Senator Tom Harkin, Dave MacMichael, Verne Lyon and Allen Orton.**

view. Soon after, I met with their consul, who called me into his office and offered me a drink of Havana Club, Cuba's renowned rum. He told me that the Cubans still resented my CIA work there, but that "El Caballo" (the Horse, as people informally called Fidel Castro) had decided that I could obtain a visa if I traveled to Nicaragua to get it. Cuba and the Sandinistas had recently established close diplomatic relations.

So I flew to Nicaragua and immediately called at the Cuban Embassy in Managua, but found it closed. A guard posted out front asked me my business and I told him I needed to collect my visa because I had a reserved seat on the next day's Cubana flight to Havana. He informed me the embassy would reopen in three days, so I left a note with him explaining myself and leaving my local address. Later that night I received a phone call from an embassy employee. He would pick me up at the Intercontinental Hotel the next morning. That morning I walked past empty lots, now cleared of the rubble of the 1972 earthquake, to the hotel and waited outside. Soon a VW bug drove past, went down the street a block or so, turned around and then stopped in front of me. From

Yuri Totorov, left, a former KGB official assigned to Japan and the U.S., and me. We were at the National Press Club in Washington, D.C., that day to announce the Russians' 30-day tour of the U.S. with members of ANSA. Yuri and I remain great friends.

inside two men called out my name and motioned me into the car. We drove for about 30 minutes and turned off the road and headed down a dusty lane into an orchard. We continued for about half a mile and came to a stop in front of a seemingly abandoned shack. Inside, however, I found it well furnished. The men introduced themselves as members of Cuba's G2 intelligence service.

They offered me a cold beer and told me they had the power to grant or refuse the visa after asking me a few questions. I reminded them that the government had already promised me the visa and that I had now missed my flight to Havana and didn't have the money to buy another.

Brushing aside these issues, the agents spent the next two hours asking about my CIA activities in Cuba. They wanted names, contacts, communication methods, and so on. I refused to answer. I would not betray my country. I reminded them that I had asked for and received a humanitarian visa. Besides, they had blown their chance to interrogate me when they deported me from Cuba in 1975. They agreed that Cuba had erred back then in not offering me a better solution to my problems, which they understood. I repeated over and over that I only wanted to see my family. They finally relented and told me to meet them in the airport waiting room at 7:00 a.m. the next morning. With that they drove me back into Managua.

At break of dawn the next day I grabbed a taxi to the airport. As instructed, I went to the waiting room, but found no one. Air Cubana had no scheduled flights out of Managua that morning. I felt hoodwinked until the agents emerged from a side room and motioned for me to follow. We boarded a Cubana airliner waiting on the tarmac as the only passengers, a flight arranged, they said, at the highest levels. "Pick a seat, any seat you like," they laughed.

In Havana, we exited the plane into a small building near the main terminal. We went through a few doors and out to a waiting car. As we drove into Havana they told me I had a room at the Hotel Capri, one block from my former home at the Hotel Nacional. They had paid for the room and all services and arranged for my wife and son to join me there. They told me that in four or five days they would return to pick us up and take us to a secluded beach house east of Havana, where I would have use of a fishing boat along with its crew. I couldn't believe all of this. If they were trying to impress me, they had succeeded.

My wife and I hadn't seen each other in almost ten years, and the reunion overwhelmed us both. My mother had gone to Cuba twice during my incarceration to take clothing and money to my family, assuring them that I had not forgotten any of them. Now questions arose. "Why didn't you tell me what you were really doing in Cuba? Why didn't the U.S. Government do anything to help us out of Cuba?" my wife wanted to know. "Can you get us out now?" I tried, in vain, to explain my dilemma of trying to avoid using her or any member of her family for political gain, and I reminded her that because of my discretion, she had not faced charges in Cuba. I held a finger to my lips and pointed at the walls. I suggested a walk outside to avoid any "bugs" and to converse in private.

A few days later, the G2 boys showed up and drove us out to a fully stocked beach house they'd probably bugged as well. We spent the next few weeks taking long walks on the sand and discussing everything that had happened to both of us. I told her I would make a desperate pitch to G2 to let her and my son leave, but that I had no control over their decision. A couple of times during our stay at the beach, a fishing boat showed up with a crew of two and a security guard to take us out to fish, reminding me of the fun I had had while I worked at the Academy of Sciences. During the Hemingway Fishing Tournament held each April I had managed to catch a swordfish. As our days now flew by and my departure approached, we went through the same emotions we had faced when the Cubans had deported me some ten years before.

The Cubans refused my wife permission to leave with me, so I made plans to return again as soon as possible. I left all the money I had and promised to send more when I could. As I waited in the lounge at Jose Martí International Airport for my flight to Mexico City, the G2 boys took me aside, offered me a Scotch on the rocks, and made a proposal. They told me they knew about my anti–CIA activities in the U.S. and my work with ANSA. They wanted me to convince the ANSA board to open a small office in Havana to show solidarity with the Cuban Revolution. The Cubans would provide the office space free of charge, place no roadblocks in the way of our coming and going from the island, and subsidize our stay as well. If I agreed to this deal they'd consider my request to get my family out of Cuba.

On the flight home I considered their proposition. I knew they had previously offered my old friend and ARDIS member, John Stockwell, a small office in Havana. He had turned it down, probably because his Vietnamese wife didn't wish to return to a communist country. Phil Agee, on the other hand, tired of moving around the world one step ahead of the CIA, had accepted the offer. He had already helped the Cubans and others, identify CIA officers and, as I later found out directly from him, had advised the G2 people to watch me closely while I worked undercover in Cuba. Phil eventually moved to Cuba and opened a travel agency.

At home, I spoke with several members of ANSA privately about the Cuban offer. None of them favored linking the organization to a U.S. enemy. I returned to Cuba the following year without any problems and repeated the scene of the year before: a family reunion and more talks with G2. The Cubans didn't take well to the negative response from ANSA. They did pay my expenses again during this trip, but I noticed a definite cooling of relations. Then one day the G2 boys showed up at the hotel and asked me to accompany them to meet the head of Cuban Intelligence and Counterintelligence at his home. We drove to the western edge of the city and entered a walled home. Inside the well furnished home they introduced me to General José Abrantes, interior minister and head of the intelligence apparatus DGI, also known as G2, and Manuel Pineiro Losada, director of the Americas Department of Cultural Affairs and the former number two in counterintelligence. I noticed that they had three different color TV's turned on, all tuned to different U.S. stations. The average Cuban had neither color TV's nor access to these U.S. channels. Abrantes also had one of the best stocked bars I had ever seen. He offered me a Scotch on the rocks (how they knew my preferred drink always surprised me) and told me to relax. I found that hard to do under the circumstances.

For the next several hours General Abrantes talked about my previous stay in Cuba, acknowledging my contributions to the Cuban Academy of Sciences and the Atmospheric Physics Institute and adding that most of my former coworkers spoke highly of me. He also told me that my CIA work had presented some major headaches to the Cuban government. He brought out a surveillance photo of me using a dead drop near my house, and another in Old Havana. He also mentioned several names of Cubans and foreigners who had provided information to me on various occasions, and he told me that the Cubans had monitored my contacts with the Mexican CIA agent caught some years earlier, Humberto Carillo Colón. Clearly they had had enough evidence to prosecute me back in 1975. I asked him why they had chosen to deport me instead. He said they had known when I resigned from the CIA while still working in Cuba, and that my dedication to my Cuban family had impressed them. They also knew I had done a lot for most of the average Cubans I had interacted with. Having weighed all this, they had decided to deport me. That seemed like a thin excuse, but I had no better explanation.

He asked me about my activities against the CIA's covert actions, which they had followed with interest. I explained that I meant to work out my own quite personal revenge against the Agency for what it had done to me. Once again he circled back to the Cubans' interest in hosting ANSA in Havana. I told him that we had to avoid the label of "traitors," and that an office in Cuba would undermine that battle. I also told him that some members had opposed Phil Agee's actions in exposing CIA officers and putting their lives in danger.

He told me that Phil knew I had kept him under surveillance as he rode his motorcycle around Havana. Apparently Phil couldn't finger me as a CIA officer because I didn't appear in any State Department register, but he did warn the Cubans that they should watch me. Years later, when Phil joined ARDIS and then ANSA, he confided to me that the Cubans had asked about me and that he indeed had suggested that they keep an eye on me. I appreciated his truthfulness.

Finally, General Abrantes told me that he would issue instructions granting me a lifetime visa to come and go from Cuba, but the government would not yet allow my family to leave. Any future determination on that issue depended, he assured me, on my attitude and future actions. I knew exactly what that meant: if I refused or failed to convince my colleagues back home to accede to the Cubans' demands, they might never let my family go. I told him that I would continue trying but I could not guarantee anything. He understood that and invited me to come back to Cuba anytime I desired. On that note we shook hands and I left with the driver, who took me back to my hotel.

I explained General Abrantes' offer to my wife and my response. She got angry and I couldn't really blame her. We had no guarantee that we could ever resume a normal relationship. I knew that I couldn't remain in Cuba without a job or steady income, so we would have to bide our time once again. My entire Cuban family held a goodbye dinner for me the next day, and I returned to the U.S. and renewed my efforts to get the U.S. government to assist me in extracting my family. Clearly, however, they had no real desire to help me, an outcast and minor irritant who refused to go away.

The Association of National Security Alumni greatly impacted the public's knowledge about the CIA's covert actions, but we didn't have deep pockets and our funding ran out. Interest in intelligence issues waned, some of our influential board members died, and magazine subscriptions fell. After several years of dedicated efforts, the Association withered on the vine. Several of us remain in touch, and some have written books about their experiences, including Mike Springmann and James Everett. I think the CIA decided that it had defeated us, and the harassment that all of us had experienced from time to time petered out.

Meanwhile, nothing happened on the Cuban issues, and both my wife and I lost hope that we would ever get back together. The U.S. refused to help me and the Cuban government continued its unacceptable offer. Eventually, politics and distance led to divorce. I did manage to get my stepson out of Cuba later via Spain with the help of friends. He lives in South Florida with his family and we visit often.

I continued to run the two non-profits until 2000, when I could no longer afford it. I decided to go back to work in the engineering field and accepted a position with Vermeer Corporation, a medium sized manufacturing company in Iowa. The company built a line of specialty construction equipment in one division and agricultural equipment in another. As their Latin American field engineer, I spent a lot of time traveling to Central and South America as well as the Caribbean teaching our buyers how to use the equipment and training their operational crews. My hard-won facility with Spanish finally paid off. I also took advantage of my frequent travels to Latin American to look up old contacts and get caught up on their lives. I eventually remarried; my second wife is a beautiful lady from Chile.

As I put the finishing touches on this book, I realized that my 51-year saga had come to partial fruition. In presenting the disastrous relationship I had had with the CIA and our government, I had sought no compensation, no imprisonment for those who had lied to and manipulated me, nor do I today even seek the full pardon I deserve. After all these years I only want to present my story and let the readers decide what they believe. I recall that when I went into the CIA completely in 1969, they required me to swear an oath that read, in part, "I do solemnly swear (or affirm) that I will support and defend the Constitution of the United States against all enemies, foreign and domestic; that I will bear true faith and allegiance to the same." I never faltered in that oath. I did all they asked and expected of me, from those days at ISU to this very day. I did not fail in spirit or commitment; the people who recruited me, who put together the plan to insert me into Cuba with a fabricated legend, the people responsible for the St. Louis bombing, the people in the Directorate of Operations who perpetuated the cover-up that continues to this day, and the

This is me, my wife Mayo (left) and our daughter, Valeria, taken a couple of years ago at a private cabin. Valeria looks just like her mother.

Department of Justice and the court system that exacted a heavy and never-ending price for doing my country's bidding, all failed. I am no longer a first class citizen in my own country, and many people still believe the Agency, which lied, deceived, manipulated, and fabricated stories about me. Those who know me know that I have never wavered from my version of events over all of these decades. Those who still believe the CIA and government version must still believe all their other lies: the weapons of mass destruction never found in Iraq, the Gulf of Tonkin incident that never occurred but drew us deeper into the Vietnam War, the bombing of the USS *Maine* in Havana Harbor, an accidental explosion that led directly to the Spanish-American War, and so on through history.

The director of the CIA at the time of my recruitment, Richard M. Helms, himself convicted of lying to Congress, banked his pension and averred that he wore his conviction as a badge of honor. My story may seem insignificant in the overall scheme of things both past and present pertaining to the CIA and its abuses, but its lesson lingers: we cannot trust a government committed to manipulating us, the people, through lies and deception. Ironically, the CIA displays these words from the Gospel of John, chapter 8, verse 32 at its headquarters: "And ye shall know the truth and the truth shall make you free." In my case, at least, it has.

Index

Numbers in **bold italics** indicate pages with illustrations

Abrantes, Jose 213
Agee, Philip 212–213
Ailts, Ed 204, 206
airplane hijackers 90–91, 101, 103, 106, 135, 139
Africa 134–135
Allende, Salvador 107, 118, 122, 124, 129, 133
Alvarado, Juan Velasco 118
Amable, Miguel 155
Amateur Rocketeers 19
American Club 89, 94, 105, 138
AMLOVE 56, 72
Anderson, Dale 170
Andros Island 74
The Association for Responsible Dissent (ARDIS) 205–206, 212–213
The Association of Former Intelligence Officers (AFIO) 207
The Association of National Security Alumni (ANSA) 206, 208, **210**, 212–214

Baird, Vaughn 148–150, 152
Balaguer, Joaquin 109
Bank of Montreal 72
Batista, Fulgencio 77, 81
Bay of Pigs invasion 119
Bjarnson, Dan 146–147
black market 104, 120–122, 135
Black Panthers 74, 92, 96
Boone, Iowa 14 **15, 18**, 19, **20**, 23, 46
Bosch, Juan 109
Brandon, German Galvaz 155
Brenman-Gibson, Margaret 205
Broe, Bill 122
Bryant, Gary 30, 34, 67, 70
Bucher, Lloyd 102

Caamano, Francisco 107, 109
Camp Peary (The Farm) 55–57, 65, 146

Canada 66–67
Canadian Broadcasting Company (CBC) 146
Canadian National Railway 73
El Capitolino 81
Castle Bank and Trust, Ltd. 118
Castro, Fidel 76, 79–80, 84, 93, 99–103, 107, 113–114, 118–124, 130, 13, 209
Castro, Ramon 103
Castro, Raul 103, 133
Central Planning Board (JUCEPLAN) 106
Chavarri Urello, Antonio 154
Cienfuegos, Cuba 105
Collier, Cecil 145
Colon, Humberto Carillo (code name Jose Maria Zaloo) 95–96, 98, 100–101, 107, 138, 213
Comba, Howard 150
Committees for the Defense of the Revolution (CDR) 106, 115, 133, 144
contraband 185–187
Converse, Jerry 30
Cuatro Caminos 79, 116
Cuba 50, 52–53, 56, 58, 60, 62–63, 65, 68–69, 71, 75, 80–81, **82**, 132, 136, 146, 153, 166, 189, 204, 208
Cuba al Servicio al Extranjero (CUBALSE) 121
Cuban Academy of Sciences 78, 81, 84, 125, 139, 213
Cuban Institute for Friendship Among Peoples (ICAP) 71, 79
Cuban Ministry of Foreign Affairs (MINREX) 79–80

Davenport, Iowa 14
Devine, Ana 97
Devine, Bill 97
Dill, Carl **165**
Dominican Republic 107, 109

Dorticos, Osvaldo 136
Dostlik 94

East Germany 125
Echeverria, Luis 134
Elbrick, Charles 93
Elizabeth (Liz) 23, **39**, 42, 50
Ellsberg, Daniel 205

Federal Bureau of Investigation (FBI) 30,
    35, 78, 92, 96, 122, 129–130, 148, 150
Federation of University Students (*FEU*) 100
Fernandez, Amado 78
Fernandez, Pedro 75, 77
Four Horsemen of the Apocalypse (paint-
    ing) **185**
Frankel, Leonard 161–164

Genesis (painting) **191**
Gonzales, Eliseo 78
(the) grand tour 182–183, 201
Granma 75, 102, 124
Groote, Kai 158
Guantanamo, Cuba 94
Guevara, Ernesto "Che" 80, 95, 123, 133
Guinn, Chet 204
Gus 27–28
Gutierrez, Felix 119

Habana Viejo (Old Havana) 81, 135, 137, 213
Harkin, Tom 208–**209**
Harris, William 27–28, 33–34, 38, 40, 48–
    50, 52–54
Havana/La Habana 69, 71, 74–75, 81, 82,
    87–88, 116, 126, 132, 147, 211
Heine, Mr. 87
Helms, Richard 35, 132, 216
Hemingway's house (painting) **199**
High Altitude Research Vehicle **127**
La Higuera 95
The Hole 191–194, 196
Hoover, J. Edgar 35
Hotel Capri 211
Hotel Deville 100
Hotel *Havana Libre* 102
Hotel *Jagua* 105
Hotel *Nacional* **76**, 84, 88, 94, 96, 111, 211
Hotel *Nueva Isla* 90, 101, 135
Hotel Savarin 70

Iowa State University 19–21, 23, 25, **26–27**,
    28–30, 33–34, 37, **39**, 48, 52, 205, 215

Jarulin, Kamile 84, **89**
Jiménez, G. 93

Johnny Express 119
Johnson, Lyndon B. 35, 133
Jones, J.J. 198, 200
Jorge, Jose 155

Katzenbach, Nicholas 46, **47**
Kennedy, John Fitzgerald 76
Kingston, Jamaica 145
Kissinger, Henry 105, 123, 130
Kosygin, Alexi 135–136
Kratovil, Millard 30, 205
Kuntz, Diane **209**

Lake Riviera Resort 148
Lambert Field 41–43
Langley, VA. (CIA headquarters) 69–70, 87,
    92, 96, 111, 156
Lansdale, Edward 53
Leavenworth Penitentiary (#132) 10, 167,
    171, 175–**176**, 184–**185**, 188–190, 201, **203**
Lenin, Vladimir Ilyich 86
USS *Liberty* 30
Losada, Manuel Pineiro 213
Lyla Express 119

MI6 95
USS *Maine* 87, 216
the *Malecon* 75, 78, 106
Malone, New York 71
The Mambesi Shipping Line 74
Mariel, Cuba 189
Marsden, Harry 149
Martin, Lionel 102
McDonnell Aircraft 38–41, 47–48, 162, 164
McLean, G. Campbell 148
McMichael, David 205, **209**
MHCHAOS 35, 132
military draft 22, 25, 38
Montalbano, William 119
Montana, Joe 184
Montoya, Domingo Campos 154, 156–157
Montreal 71, 73, 76
Morales-Bermudez y Cerruti, Francisco
    153–154, 157
Moscow 86–87, 125
Mullen, Michael 158

National Center for Scientific Investigation
    (CNIC) 104
National Security Headquarters 136
Nelson, Merle 150
Nicaragua 209
Nixon, Richard 132
NOC (No Official Cover) 56, 61, 72–73
Noland, Jim 107

Noll, Dale 184, 198
Nunez-Jimenez, Antonio 79, 84, 88, 103, 114–115, 148, 153, 156

Ober, Richard 35
Office of National Information 156
Operation 40 54, 119
Operation Mongoose 53
Organization of American States 133
Orton, Allen **209**
Otis, James 205
USS *Oxford* 75, 116, 118

Parks, William Robert 30, 205
Pastors for Peace 139
Patterson, John 184, 198
Pauly, Michael 149
Peru 113–114, 147, 152–154, 163, 189
Peruvian Investigative Police 155
Phillips, Bernie 184, 192
Pinochet, Augusto 130
presidential pardon 208
Pringle, James 96
prison gangs 187–188
USS *Pueblo* 102

Radio Americas 120
Radio Swan 120
Ramirez, Armando Socarras 94
ration book 120
Red Square 86
Reed, Harry 102
Regan, John K. 46, 161, 163, 166, 188
Regla, Cuba 81
Reserve Officer Training Corps (ROTC) 21
Richards, George 69
Richardson, James 152
Rico, Miguel 190, 198, 200
Roa, Raul 92, 101
Rochester Institute of Technology 207
Rodriguez, Carlos Rafael 134
Rodriguez, Felix 95
Rodriguez, Rogelio 66–68
Rose, Richard 207
Royal Canadian Mounted Police (RCMP) 68–69, 73, 146–147, 149–150
Ryan, John 205
RYBAT 65, 72

safe conduct 152–153
safe house 66, 68, 71
St. Clair County Jail 162
St. Louis 41–43, 45–46, 48, 50–52, 54, 60, 67, 68, 72, 81, 96, 112, 130, 140, 160–161
Sallada, Weyn 159

Salamon, Jose Felipe 56, 72
San Roman, Rafael Castro 78–79, 81, 84, 88, 100, 102–103, 107, 111
Sanjenis, Joaquin 119
Schneider, Rene 124
Scott, Peter Dale 205
SDS 34
"Secrets of the CIA," Turner Original Productions 208
Servicio de Inteligencia Nacional (SIN) 153, **156**
"Slave Labor in America's Prisons" 192
Springmann, Mike **209**, 214
the Stasi 125–126
Stockwell, John 205, 212
Swan Islands 119
swine flu 104

TIO 72, 79, 81, 85, 87, 91–96, 98–107, 111–112, 114, 118–120, 122, 124–125, 128–130, 132, 135–136, 139–140, 142, 146–147, 150, 153–154, 163
Toronto 66–67, 70, 153
Totorov, Yuri **210**

Unclassified magazine 206
UNICOR (Federal Prison Industries) 183–184
Union of Soviet Socialist Republics (USSR) 85, 90
U.S. State Department 151
Universidad Tecnica del Estado 128
University of Havana 81, 88, 100, **114**, 133

Velasco Alvarado, Juan 153
Venceremos Brigade 93, 139
Vermeer Corporation 214
Vietnam 22–23, 25, 28, 34, 36–38, 43, 66, 72, 93, 96
Villa, Jose 119
Vlahovich, Dareslav 149

Walnuchuck, Paul 147, 149–150
The Weather Underground 74
Welles, Sumner 77
Werner, Louis, II 41, 49, 51
Wheeler, John 96
The White House **61**
Wilcox, Jim 205
WIN Magazine 191–192, 195
Winnipeg, Canada 146, 150
Wolf, Louis 205, 209

Zaharov, Vladimir **85**
la zona congelada 76